THE BEDSIDE BOOK OF
WATERCOLOR WISDOM

500 Practical Hints, Tips, and Solutions for All Artists

Trudy Friend

DAVID & CHARLES
— PUBLISHING —

www.davidandcharles.com

CONTENTS

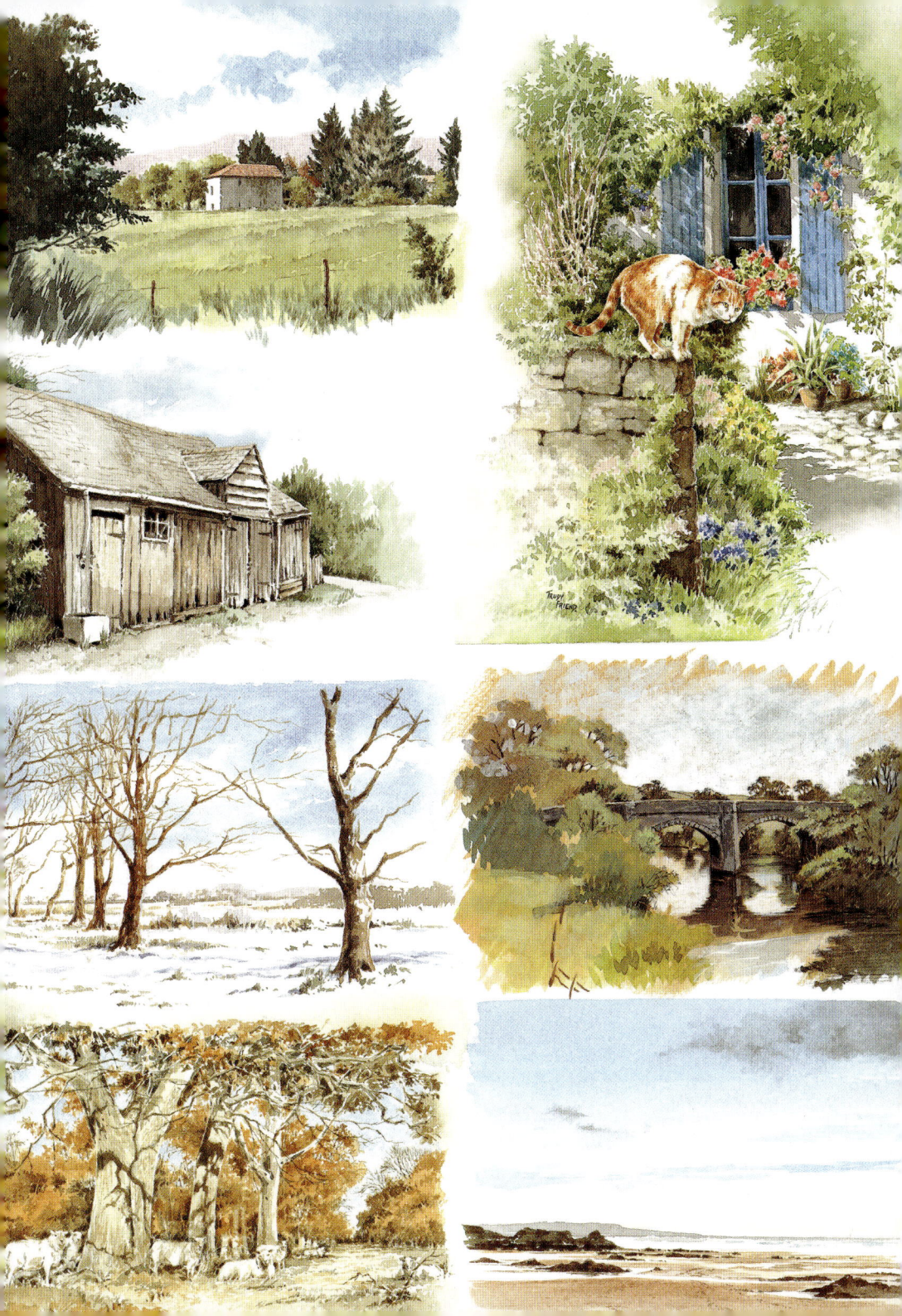

INTRODUCTION

The aim of this book is to provide a learning experience that will help to guide you along an exciting path of self-discovery. If you have already embarked upon your own artistic journey, you may discover within these pages new ideas or variations to add to those you already use – enhancing and enriching your own ideas and methods. If you are a beginner or 'improver' in watercolor, this section is designed to show you the importance of understanding the basics and knowing how to use them as a firm foundation upon which to build both your drawings and paintings.

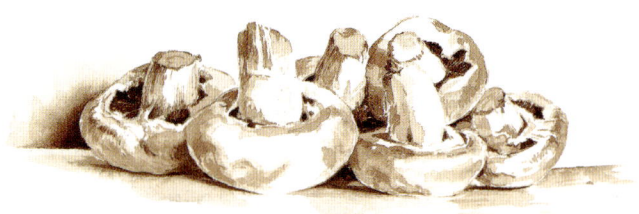

Sketching and drawing

In addition to being valuable in its own right, drawing is the most important basis for good paintings, and for this reason, each painting demonstration throughout the themed chapters of this book is accompanied by a detailed drawing. Preliminary sketches enable you to look closely into your subject matter and familiarize yourself with all the intricate components before you embark upon any brushwork.

Try to think your way into all of your drawings and paintings – I call this 'putting your thoughts on paper'. The 'wandering line' is an approach to drawing where the pencil is allowed to wander lightly over the paper surface, following the form of objects freely as you observe and depict the contours. Onions, with their many surface veins, are ideal subjects for observing contour lines (see Fruit and Vegetables: Three Dimensions).

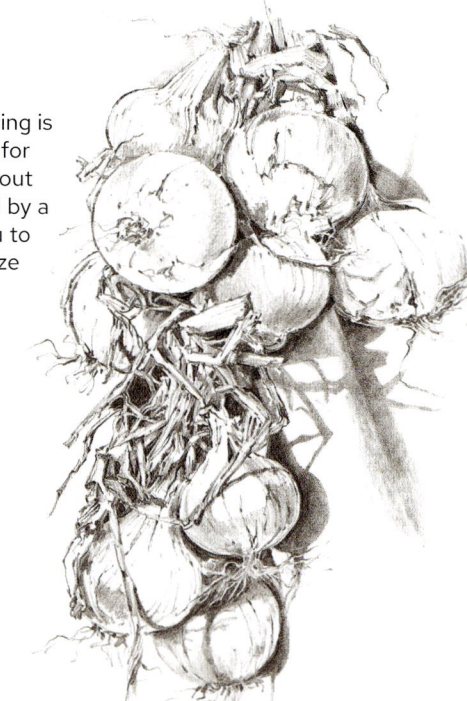

There is also a diagrammatic approach, where you can put your thoughts on paper by using pencil guidelines and observing the 'shapes between' in your preliminary drawings, as demonstrated in Guidelines (see also Flowers: More Complex Shapes). By drawing in a linear way and accentuating the parts where you want to reinforce your knowledge prior to painting, you can develop a deeper understanding of the subject and produce a convincing interpretation.

You can draw in a 'painterly' way; this is illustrated in Flowers: Garden Scenes, where simple marks with a pencil, similar to brushmarks, are used to represent the background areas. And yet another way to put your thoughts on paper is to actually draw directional arrows on your sketches. In this way you are stating what you feel about what you see, and the arrows act as a reminder for brushstroke directions when you paint.

Brushstrokes

You should try to become involved with your subject and media in order to gain as much knowledge of them as possible. The best way is to start with brushstroke exercises, and for this reason each themed chapter begins with a 'Brushstrokes' spread – on one page you can see the basic strokes, and on the facing page how each of these can be used within the specific theme. Practicing in this way will also help you to discover which papers and brushes suit your own personal style. From these basic strokes you will discover many more of your own to incorporate within your watercolor paintings.

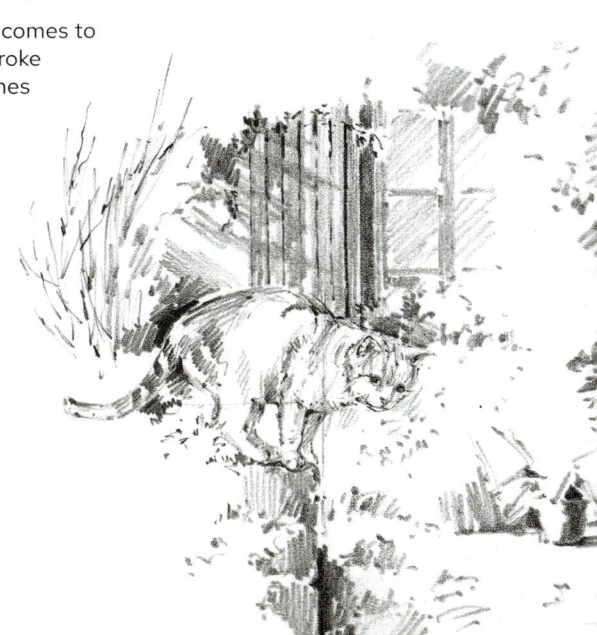

Once again, the importance of drawing comes to the fore here – even the simple brushstroke exercises in Getting to Know Your Brushes (see Materials and Techniques) require some basic knowledge of shape and form, best obtained initially from close observation and drawing exercises.

You do not need to be 'tight' in your general approach to painting, but I do believe that discipline leads to freedom – should you choose to eventually paint with freely applied brushstrokes in a loose style, you can experience nothing but benefit from going back to basics in your approach every now and then.

Learning from your mistakes

As with so many aspects of watercolor painting, it is practice that can help you steadily improve – providing, of course, that you learn from your mistakes. It is by trial and error that we learn our most lasting lessons, and only by facing problems head-on can we resolve them.

Mishaps do occur from time to time, and even when you feel you have mastered a particular technique things will occasionally go wrong. Alternatively, sometimes there can be 'happy accidents', when an unintentional effect actually enhances the painting – though it is not a good idea to expect these to happen.

I feel it is unwise to discard any paintings with mistakes – even when things do go disastrously wrong – until we have learned all we can from them and repaired them wherever possible, as shown in Rescuing Mistakes (see Materials and Techniques). This may involve a simple solution like redrawing, using another medium over the watercolor, or cutting out and mounting the idea that has been successful. Slight corrections can be made by scraping away the offending marks with the point of a sharp craft knife. Should a large part of the picture prove to be disappointing, you can redraw and paint gouache over the entire painting. Using plenty of water with the pigments is one way of removing mistakes quickly, as described opposite (see Working with water).

Choosing and stretching paper

It is worth experimenting with papers of different weights and surface textures. Personally I prefer to work on paper that has been stretched beforehand – except when using a heavyweight paper. You may not wish to stretch a 300gsm (140lb) paper, nor may it always be necessary, but it is advisable to stretch anything below that weight.

To stretch paper you need a roll of gummed paper, scissors, a solid board that is slightly larger than the sheet of paper, a large container of water (a bath is ideal), a clean sponge and a clean paper kitchen towel. To start, cut the gummed paper into four strips slightly longer than the sides of the paper, and leave them where they are easily to hand.

Wet the paper thoroughly – immersing it in water is best – and allow the excess moisture to drip off it before placing it on the board, with a margin of board showing around the edges, and gently smoothing it flat with the sponge. Moisten the gummed strips and apply them with half the width on the paper and half on the board. Smooth out any air bubbles and blot gently with the paper kitchen towel.

Allow to dry flat at room temperature before using – if you tilt the board while the paper is drying, the excess moisture may accumulate along the lower edge, causing the gummed strip to lose adhesion and lift away when dry. Should the paper buckle or 'cockle' when drying, it may still dry flat eventually. If it is undulating when completely dry, simply remove it and repeat the process; you will soon learn with practice.

Working with water

It is wise to remember that watercolor painting means using plenty of water, and that when learning new techniques it is far safer to err on the side of too much water than too little. Without fluidity of your medium, the fluidity of your thoughts and ideas being interpreted in an exciting way is hampered.

To give you confidence in using a lot of water with pigments, mix a green or neutral brown in your palette to produce a rich hue, then add more water than you think may be necessary while still retaining the pigmentation. Paint a simple shape using freely applied strokes, then immediately blot off with a paper kitchen towel until the paper is dry. If you have used enough water, you will see that only a pale stain remains on the paper, which means that if an image painted in this way does not appear as anticipated, you can remove almost all traces of it by blotting off immediately.

Becoming involved with your work

We all learn from each other and from our surroundings each day of our lives – for learning is a continuous and expanding process. Be aware of everything and keep your 'artist's eye' open to all possibilities. The best artwork comes from the commitment and involvement of the artist. The more you give of yourself to the creation of your work, the more successful you will feel it to be.

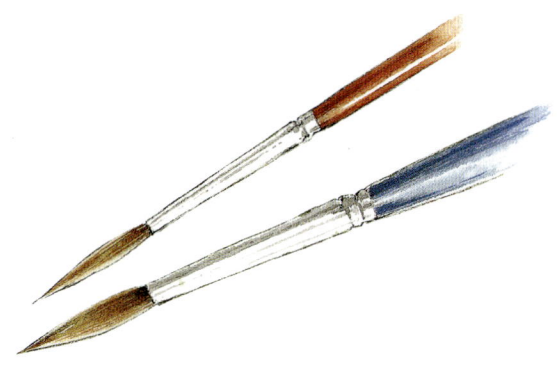

MATERIALS AND TECHNIQUES

When drawing for painting, it is important that you understand how to use your materials to best effect, which ones work together and which suit your style and capabilities. Choose the best you can afford and practice using them to develop your skills.

Choosing pencils

Graphite pencils for preliminary work for painting can be from the hard H range to F or, if a softer effect is required, from HB to the very soft 9B. As underdrawings for watercolors HB to 2B work well, as they are neither too hard to cause indentations nor too soft so marks smear when water is applied. Practice with a variety of pencil grades; press gently or heavily on your pencil to create thick and thin lines as you work.

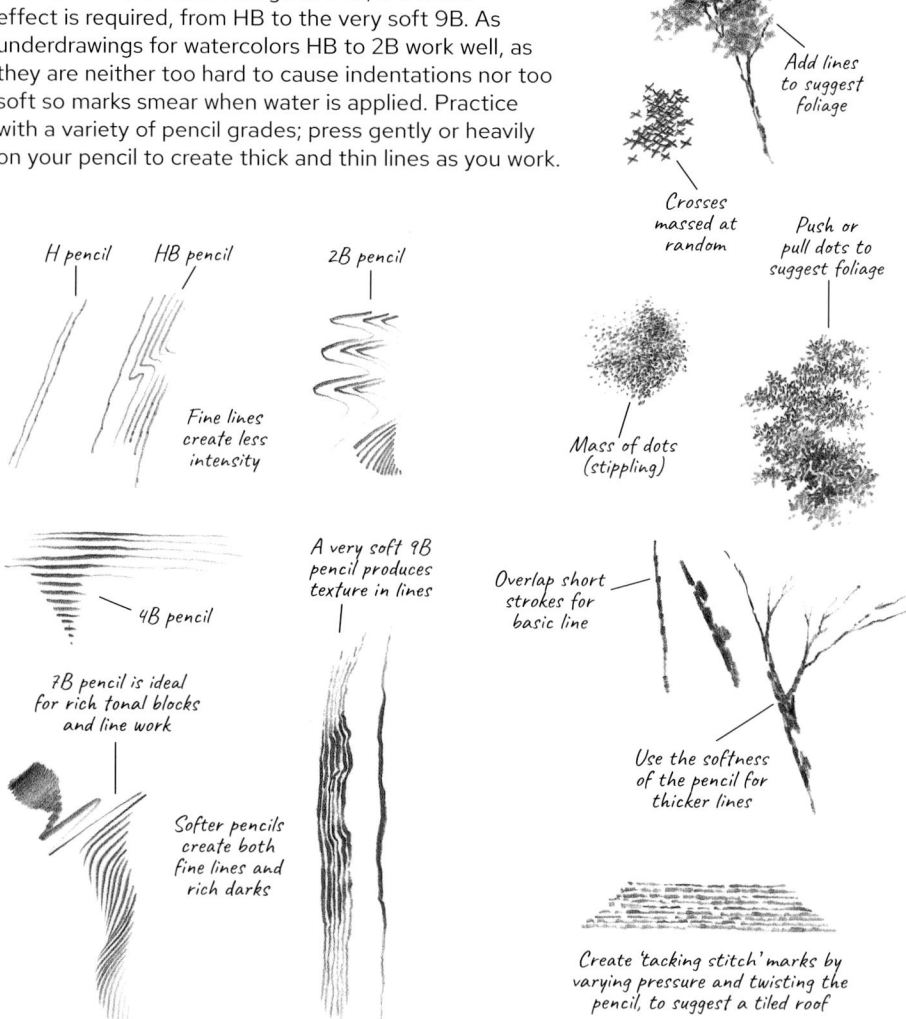

Add lines to suggest foliage

Crosses massed at random

Push or pull dots to suggest foliage

H pencil

HB pencil

2B pencil

Fine lines create less intensity

Mass of dots (stippling)

4B pencil

A very soft 9B pencil produces texture in lines

Overlap short strokes for basic line

7B pencil is ideal for rich tonal blocks and line work

Softer pencils create both fine lines and rich darks

Use the softness of the pencil for thicker lines

Create 'tacking stitch' marks by varying pressure and twisting the pencil, to suggest a tiled roof

Brushes and their marks

Although many brush movements are the same as pencil movements, the element of water mixed with pigment allows shapes to merge and blend. A larger surface area can also be used with a brush – from the tip 'on your toes' position through to the full extent of the hairs laid horizontally, as explored in more detail in Getting to Know Your Brushes. It is this variety, and the many angles and pressures that can be applied, that adds excitement to brushwork.

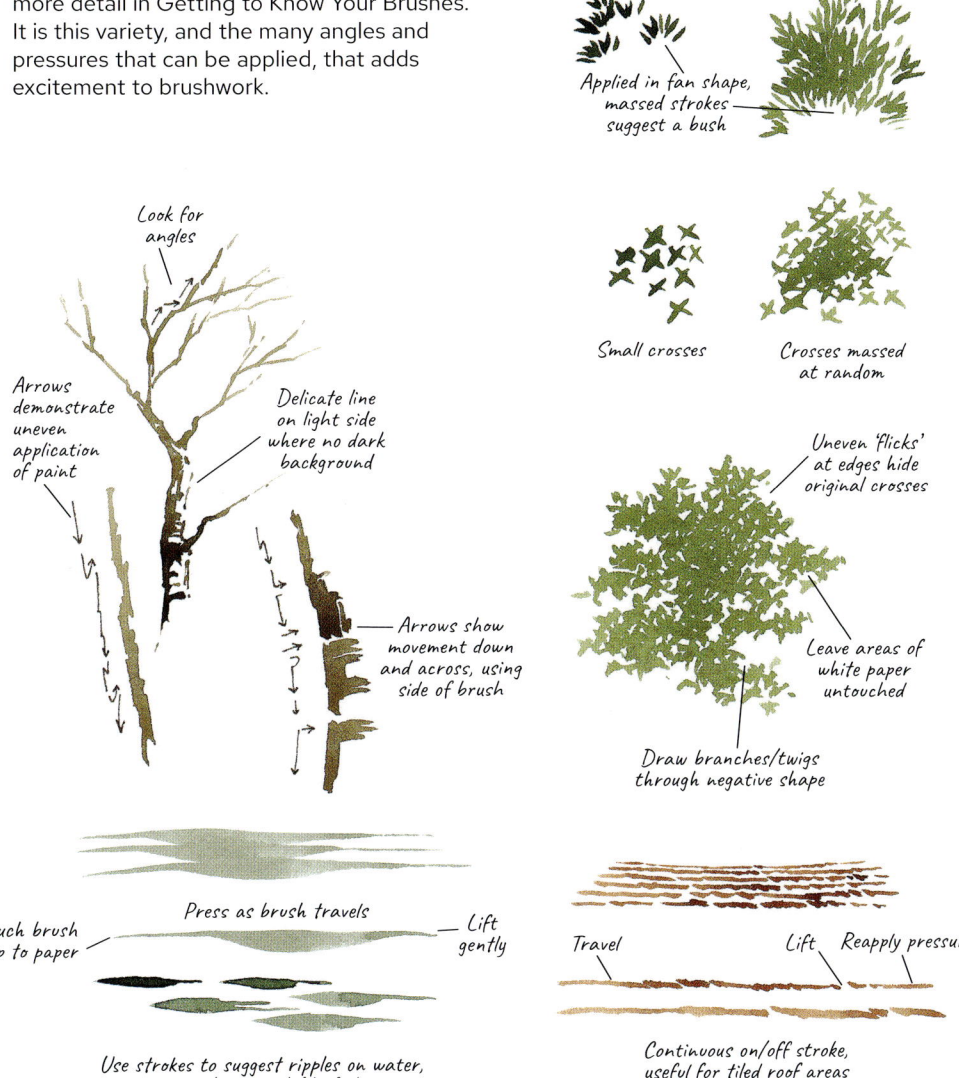

Single dots merge when repeated and placed close together

Diagonal strokes begin to suggest leaf shapes

Applied in fan shape, massed strokes suggest a bush

Small crosses

Crosses massed at random

Look for angles

Arrows demonstrate uneven application of paint

Delicate line on light side where no dark background

Arrows show movement down and across, using side of brush

Uneven 'flicks' at edges hide original crosses

Leave areas of white paper untouched

Draw branches/twigs through negative shape

Touch brush tip to paper

Press as brush travels

Lift gently

Use strokes to suggest ripples on water, similar to 'one-stroke' leaf shapes

Travel

Lift

Reapply pressure

Continuous on/off stroke, useful for tiled roof areas

Observation

Learning to look at your surroundings with an 'artist's eye' requires a special kind of observation. As well as observing the positive forms in a group, also note the negative shapes between and around them.

Personal grid method

Place a tracing paper overlay over a still-life photograph. Look closely; observe where one object touches or crosses another – the contact points. It is from these points that your grid lines may be drawn. From a contact point, draw horizontal and vertical lines on the tracing paper. Look along the lines; note where other parts of your subject(s) fall along them as in (A) and (B).

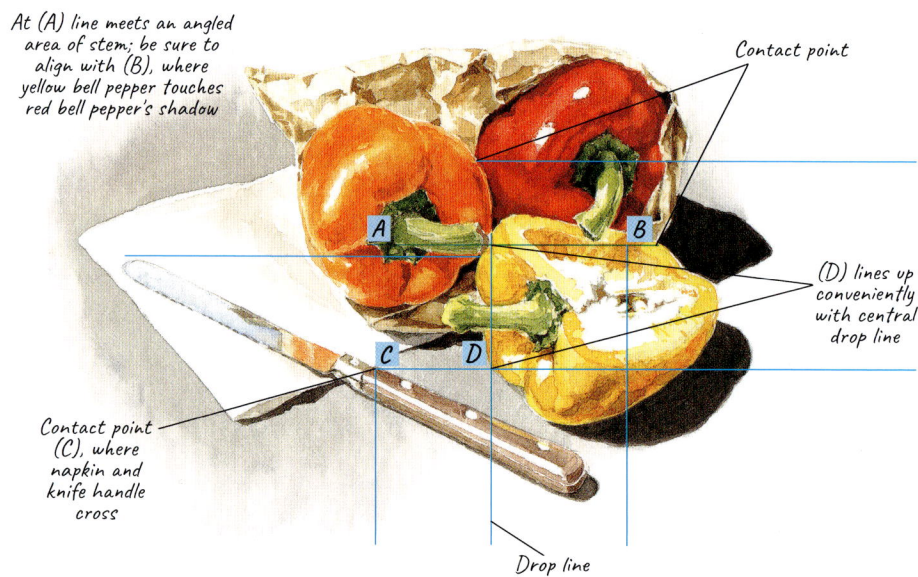

At (A) line meets an angled area of stem; be sure to align with (B), where yellow bell pepper touches red bell pepper's shadow

Contact point

(D) lines up conveniently with central drop line

Contact point (C), where napkin and knife handle cross

Drop line

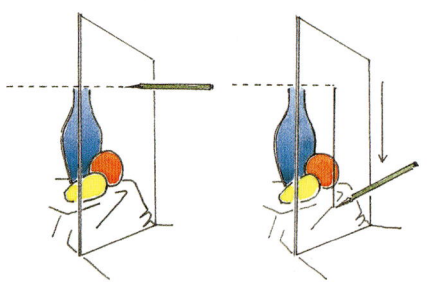

When working from life, imagine a sheet of glass in front of the subject. Hold the pencil tip in a position where you could place a mark on the image behind. Run the pencil down – your 'drop line' – and if the line meets any contact points, move the pencil horizontally, to try to meet another contact point.

Negative Shapes

Negative shapes are the shapes between the actual objects. They enable you to place your objects correctly in relation to each other when used in conjunction with your personal grid.

Choosing a starting negative shape

The bell peppers drawing shows examples of different sized negative shapes. Practice starting a study of still life with the most important negative shape – the shape that, when it is drawn, will help you place the most objects accurately, in relation to each other. Here, it's the medium shape, as it will lead naturally, with guidelines, to being able to complete all three peppers.

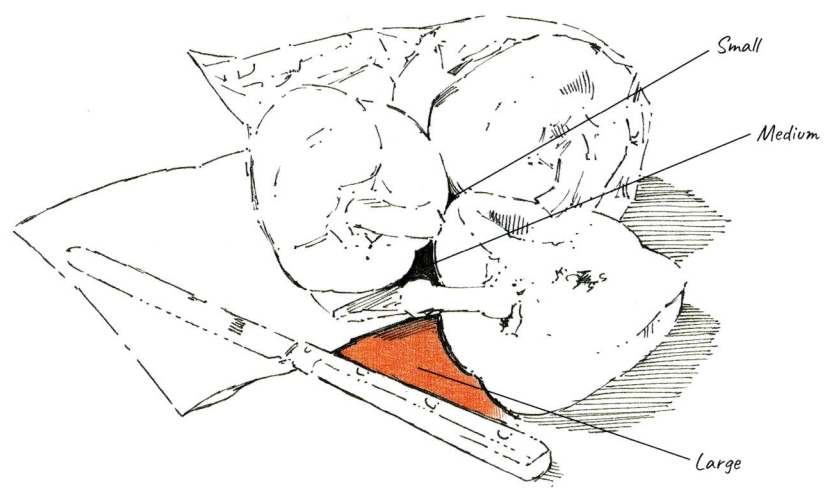

Small

Medium

Large

In this drawing of a sheep and its lamb, the negative shapes between the sheep and lamb's legs are quite simple and easy to draw, and help you fix the proportions of the animals accurately.

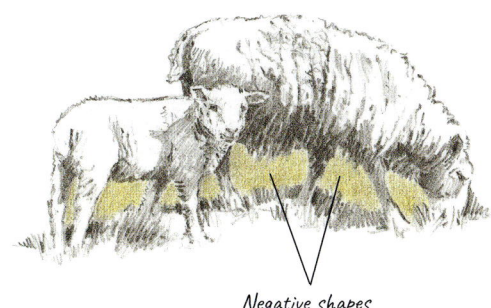

Negative shapes

Guidelines

Once you have established your personal grid of vertical and horizontal guidelines, and allied this to negative shapes, you have a scaffolding on which to build. Look for further 'shapes between' to help accurate placement.

Finding guidelines

The areas colored in green show how to use a guideline to complete a 'shape between', to create more shapes to relate to each other for greater accuracy. It's like a jigsaw puzzle, where the pieces fit together. To avoid getting lost with an intricate grid, include solid tonal negative shapes and shadow shapes.

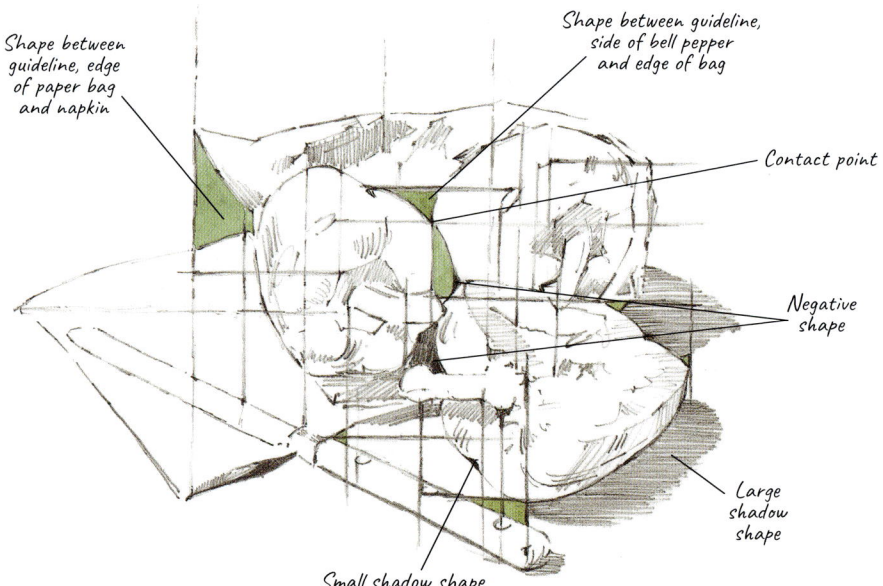

Shape between guideline, edge of paper bag and napkin

Shape between guideline, side of bell pepper and edge of bag

Contact point

Negative shape

Large shadow shape

Small shadow shape

Composing with guidelines

This rough sketch of a tractor (see Still Lifes in the Landscape: Vehicles with Rounded Shapes for the final drawing) shows how you can use guidelines to plot out your composition from the start.

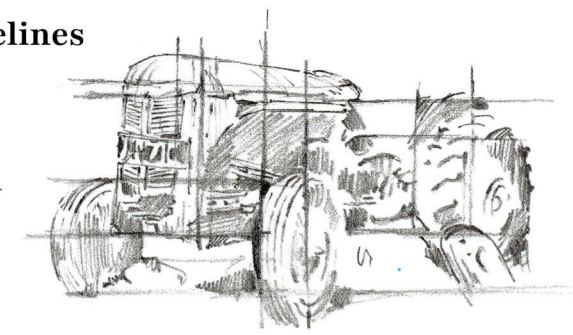

Tone

Before you start watercolor painting, think of your
subject in black and white – a black-and-white photo
will help you understand the range of tones.

Toning for tone or toning for color

Improving your awareness of tonal contrasts can help you establish tonal
blocks (masses of light against dark and vice versa) that create the design.
Practice tonal blocks with pencil, or one neutral watercolor. Some suggest
color (toning for color); others relate to shadow areas (toning for tone).

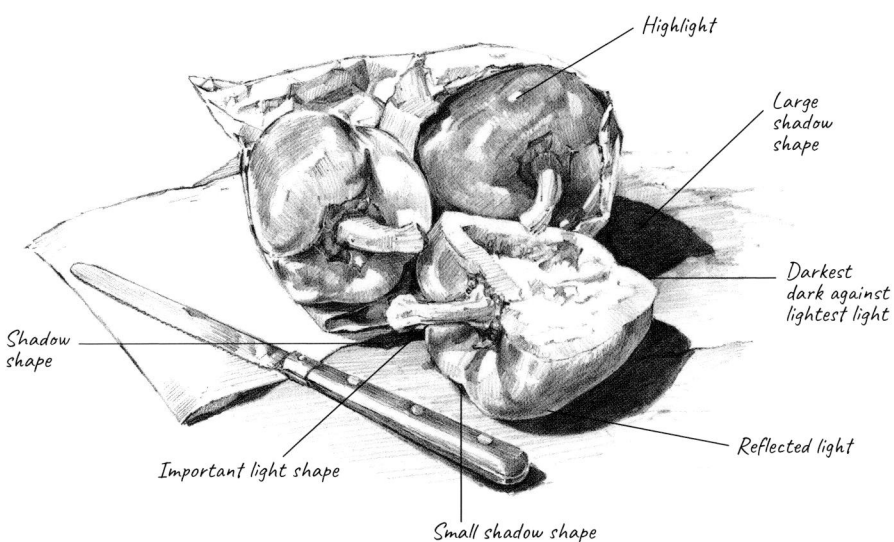

Highlight

Large
shadow
shape

Darkest
dark against
lightest light

Shadow
shape

Reflected light

Important light shape

Small shadow shape

Tonal blocks

Whether toning for tone or toning for color, it is the variety of tones and contrasts that
bring excitement to your pencil work. Make a series of eight tones to refer to as work
progresses: look for the tonal contrasts in your subject, and use as many as available.

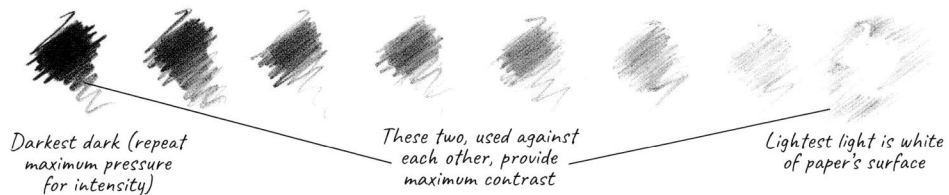

Darkest dark (repeat
maximum pressure
for intensity)

These two, used against
each other, provide
maximum contrast

Lightest light is white
of paper's surface

Drawing within Shadows

Strong sunlight, with its resulting cast shadows, allows you to use contrasts of light against dark. Look closely within shadow areas to see a further variety of tones, more closely related but at the same time still very clear.

Ways of adding shadows

Old buildings present a wealth of interest, and strong sunlight brings out exciting tonal contrasts. Using a smooth-surfaced white drawing paper, tone in an area to represent cast shadow and then draw within it, either in a linear way or with more tonal blocks. Alternatively, you can draw the objects prior to adding a tone that suggests a cast shadow over your drawing. This kind of drawing requires good pencil control.

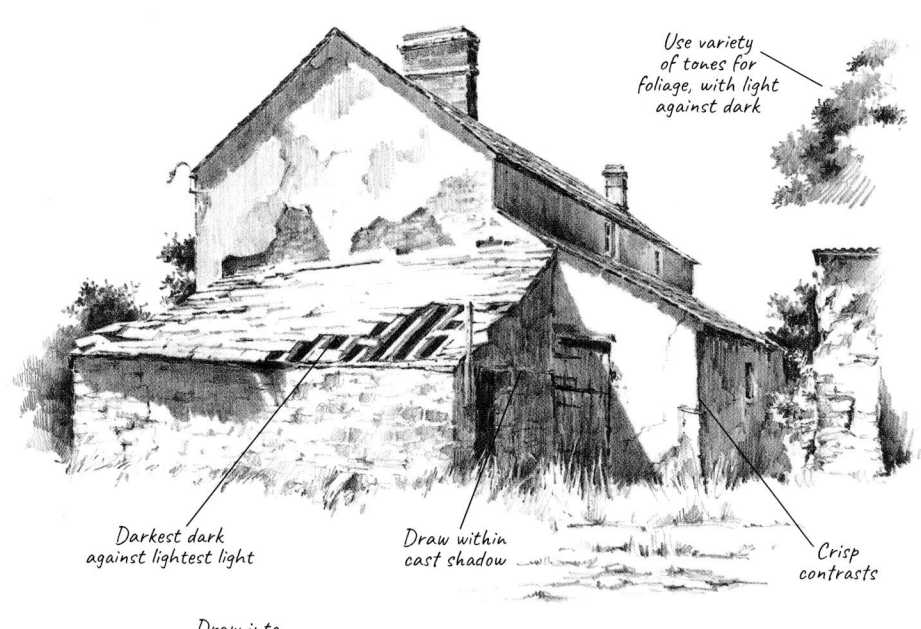

Use variety of tones for foliage, with light against dark

Darkest dark against lightest light

Draw within cast shadow

Crisp contrasts

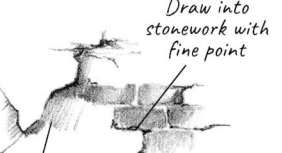

Draw into stonework with fine point

Start with crisp line and then tone away to represent shadow behind plaster

Toned bricks with light cement

Start the stroke with vertical movement then horizontal strokes

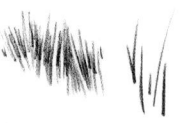

Mass grass in different directions

Use a variety of strokes

Following form within shadow shapes

Study shadows closely, especially the way in which cast shadows curve and disappear behind light forms that cut across. This will help you understand how to create a three-dimensional impression of the subject. A simple example is when a cast shadow over grass causes dark shapes to cut into light (behind) and light into dark (foreground).

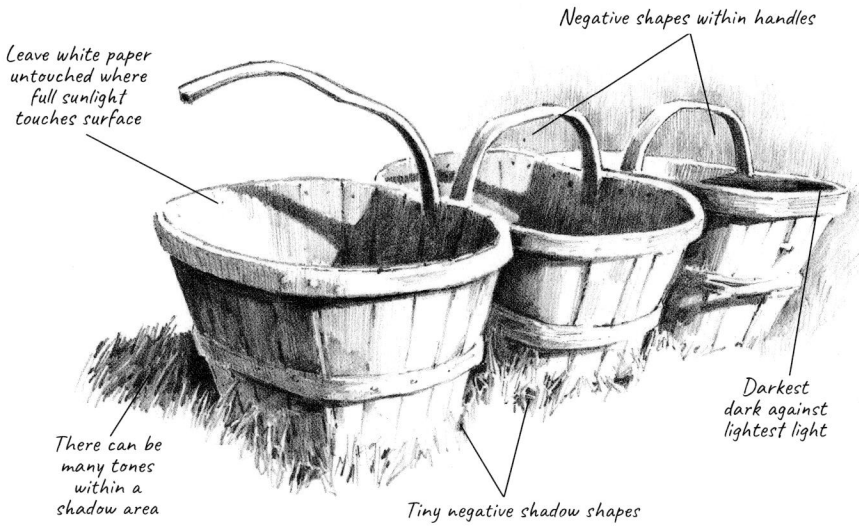

Negative shapes within handles

Leave white paper untouched where full sunlight touches surface

Darkest dark against lightest light

There can be many tones within a shadow area

Tiny negative shadow shapes

Practicing with tone

To render tone effectively in many situations you need to learn pencil control – use as many completely different subjects as you can to build this up.

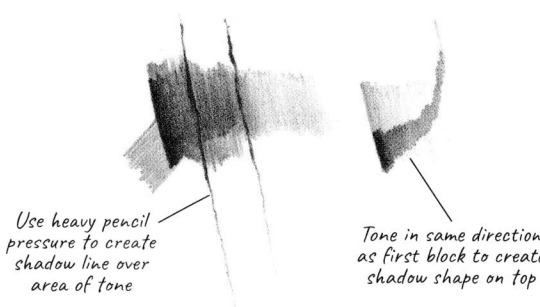

Use heavy pencil pressure to create shadow line over area of tone

Tone in same direction as first block to create shadow shape on top

Tonal watercolor exercise

Observe details within a shadowed area – pebbles on a beach within the shadow of a rock, for example – and paint them using one color, then mix a neutral shadow tone (not too much pigment) and sweep the shadow shape over the pebbles.

Tone in Watercolor

These exercises show the effects of varied pressure and angles of the brush. To achieve a diversity of tones you can either use a variety of diluted washes, building one upon the other, or blending the washes together.

Diluting paint

Lift a good reservoir of water into your palette – more than you might normally use – using a large brush. Wet a smaller brush and lift some pigment from the pan, adding it to the water until you have a pale tint. Brush this onto watercolor paper. Add more pigment and try the resulting mix again. Continue to do this until you have a range of tones. Even your darkest tones should be fluid.

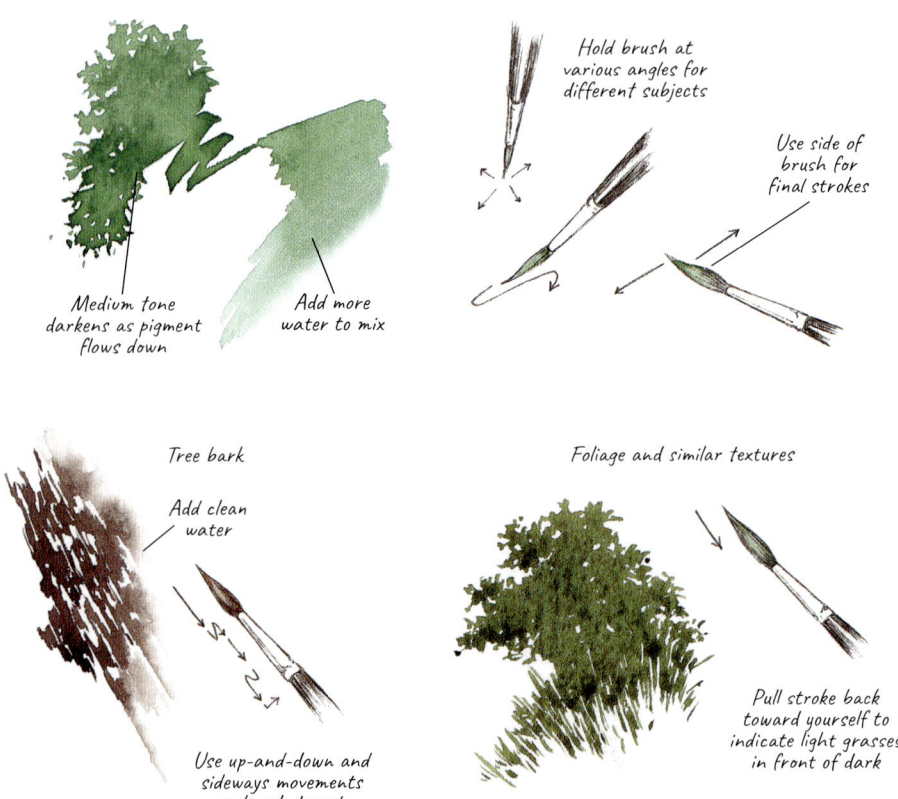

Medium tone darkens as pigment flows down

Add more water to mix

Hold brush at various angles for different subjects

Use side of brush for final strokes

Tree bark

Add clean water

Use up-and-down and sideways movements as brush travels

Foliage and similar textures

Pull stroke back toward yourself to indicate light grasses in front of dark

Blending to make curves

Not all tree bark has a rough texture, and the smoother surfaces of some tree trunks offer opportunities to blend from the dark side of the bark into the light.

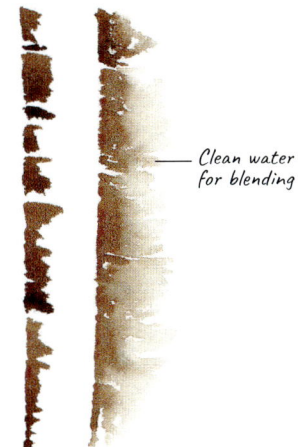

Clean water for blending

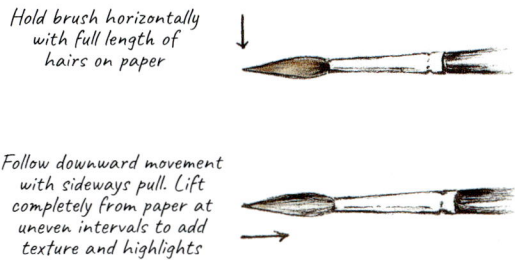

Hold brush horizontally with full length of hairs on paper

Follow downward movement with sideways pull. Lift completely from paper at uneven intervals to add texture and highlights

Repetitive images

This exercise helps to develop the ability to work at speed when reproducing flat areas of repeated pattern, such as bricks or stones.

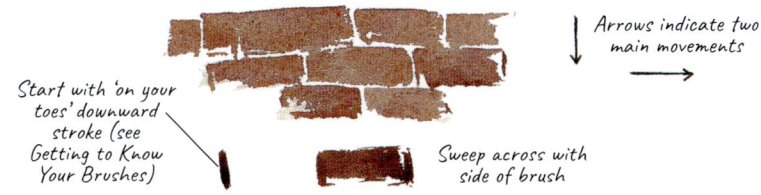

Arrows indicate two main movements

Start with 'on your toes' downward stroke (see Getting to Know Your Brushes)

Sweep across with side of brush

Moving images

These images are best achieved by swiftly applied strokes, so be prepared to practice painting at speed to achieve spontaneity.

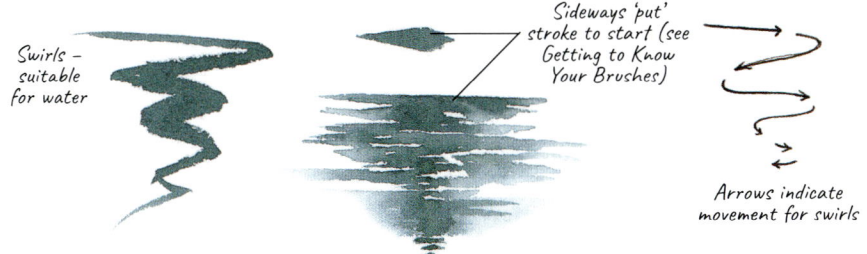

Sideways 'put' stroke to start (see Getting to Know Your Brushes)

Swirls – suitable for water

Arrows indicate movement for swirls

Getting to Know Your Brushes

These one-stroke brush exercises are designed to develop confidence.
Practice them regularly to gain more control over your brush and to be able
to vary the speed at which you work and the thickness of your strokes.

Directional strokes

One-stroke leaf shapes may be executed both
upward from the stem stroke, or starting away
from the stem and traveling toward a twiddle.

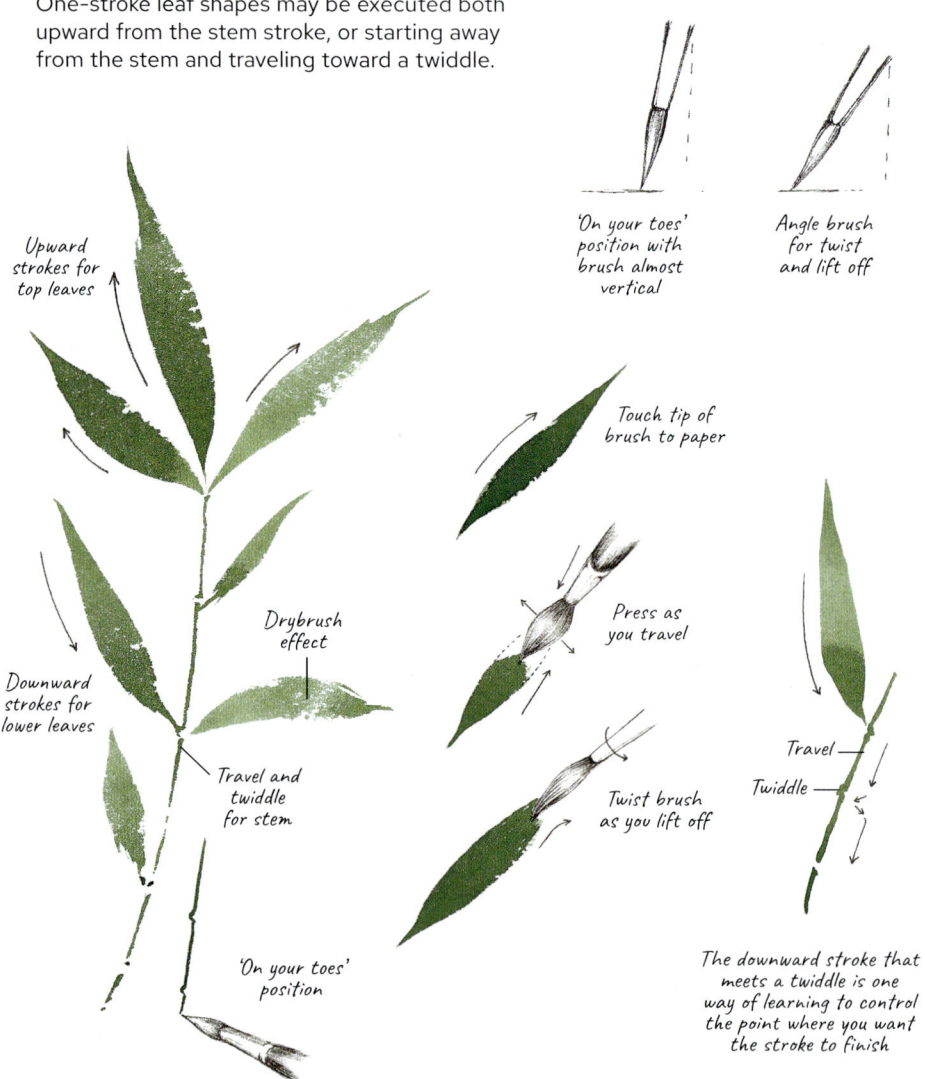

'On your toes'
position with
brush almost
vertical

Angle brush
for twist
and lift off

Upward
strokes for
top leaves

Touch tip of
brush to paper

Drybrush
effect

Press as
you travel

Downward
strokes for
lower leaves

Travel and
twiddle
for stem

Twist brush
as you lift off

Travel

Twiddle

'On your toes'
position

The downward stroke that
meets a twiddle is one
way of learning to control
the point where you want
the stroke to finish

Combining long and short strokes

This exercise is an extension of the one shown opposite and demonstrates how to place short strokes alongside sweeping, extended shapes. The slender stem and 'tails' on the ears encourage concentration and control.

Basic 'put' stroke

This stroke places the whole length of the brush once upon the paper, lifting off immediately. It can be extended by placing and pulling downward a little before lifting off.

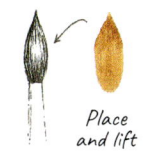

Place and lift

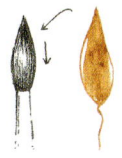

Longer shape. Pull down a little as you lift off

Directional 'put' strokes

A series of 'put' strokes in formation can be executed by placing the stroke at one angle, lifting off, turning the brush to a different angle and placing another stroke, and so on. The series of 'put' strokes can then be joined by a curved or angled (stem) line to represent a recognizable image. After having practiced the exercises below, you'll be able to combine them to produce a complete image in the form of an ear of corn with a stem and long, tapering leaves as seen to the right.

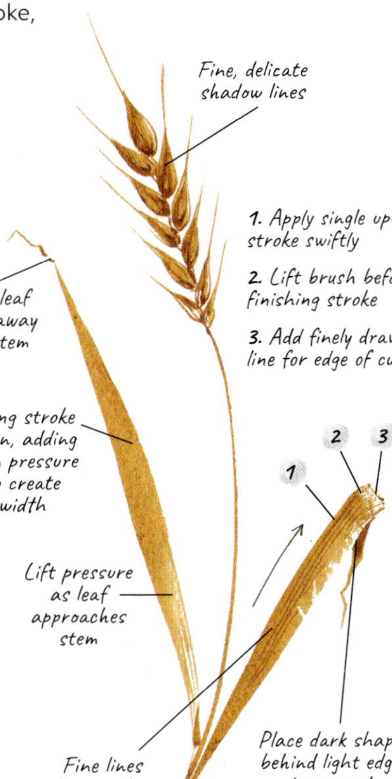

Fine, delicate shadow lines

1. Apply single upward stroke swiftly

2. Lift brush before finishing stroke

3. Add finely drawn line for edge of curve

Consider direction of strokes

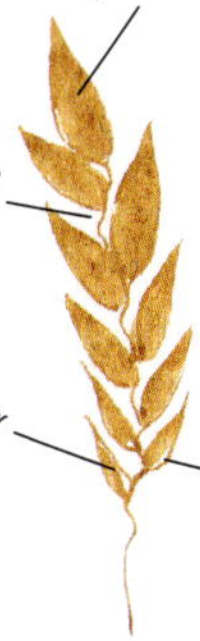

Full brush pressure

Start leaf stroke away from stem

Draw joining line with tip of brush

Bring stroke down, adding firm pressure to create width

Make smaller shape with tip only

Draw brush line away from shape for highlight

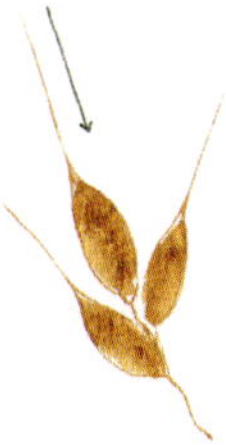

Lift pressure as leaf approaches stem

The downward stroke that meets the tip of an image is one way of learning to control the point where you want the stroke to finish

Fine lines drawn when leaf is dry suggest veins

Place dark shape behind light edge to suggest underside of leaf in shadow

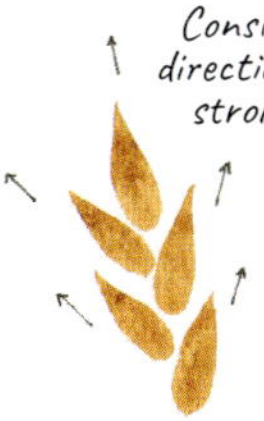

Combining tonal blocks and drawing

Here, we look at combining areas of tone and contrasting them with lines, drawn with the point of a brush, that follow the form of the object. Although the effects of colored and tonal shapes are important, it is also necessary to enhance images with the use of freely applied linear work at times. When applied in a curve that follows the form, these lines help us to give the impression of a 3D object.

Angles of application *(1)*

There are times, within a single brushstroke, where you may need to adjust the angle of your brush more than once.

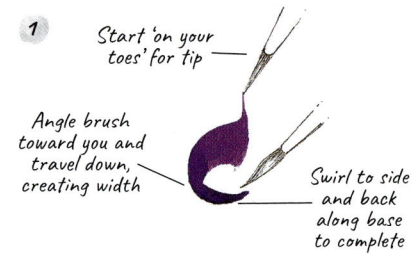

1 Start 'on your toes' for tip

Angle brush toward you and travel down, creating width

Swirl to side and back along base to complete

Combining tone with line *(2)*

In this complex image, based on a seed pod, it's not only brushstrokes that are considered but also relationships between tonal shapes and form-finding lines.

Flat tonal application *(3)*

Seed head, stem and leaves are brought together by working continuously from one into another to maintain even application. Use free-flowing pigment, diluted to achieve a pale hue as an undercoat over which, when dry, further tonal shapes and drawing can be applied.

Using background images *(4)*

When images are grouped en masse, the lighter areas can be enhanced by what is placed beside or behind them.

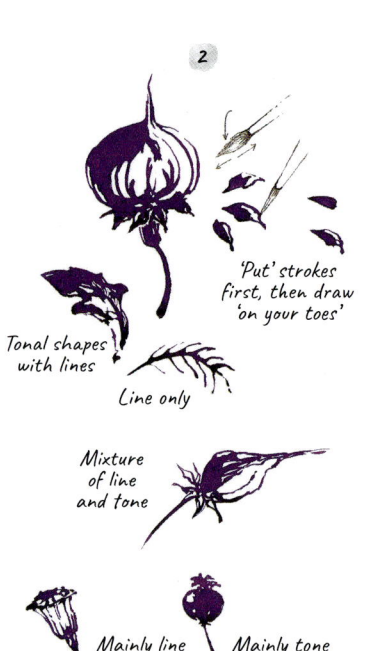

2

'Put' strokes first, then draw 'on your toes'

Tonal shapes with lines

Line only

Mixture of line and tone

Mainly line   Mainly tone

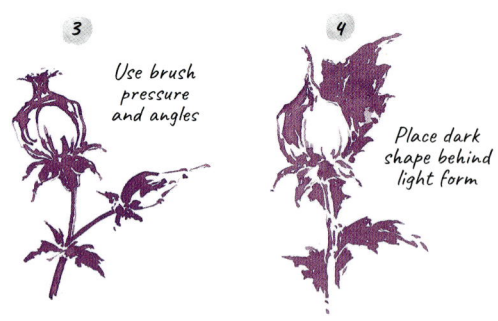

3 Use brush pressure and angles

4 Place dark shape behind light form

Blending

Blending, whether within the objects themselves or a background color blended away from the objects to disappear into other colors or the white paper, is an exciting effect to achieve. The secret is to avoid adding too much water to the pigment already on the paper's surface – if you do, the point at which they meet may produce effects that are not the ones anticipated.

You can apply this blending technique to many subjects, including skies, where it can suggest the soft edges of clouds against the blue of the sky behind.

Uses of blending

Blending can be used to great effect on both flat and curved surfaces. Consistency within a curve is important, and this is demonstrated in the subject of a tree trunk. The studies of foliage show the versatility of the misty and other effects that can be achieved by blending.

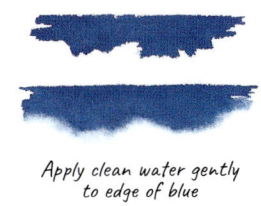

Apply clean water gently to edge of blue

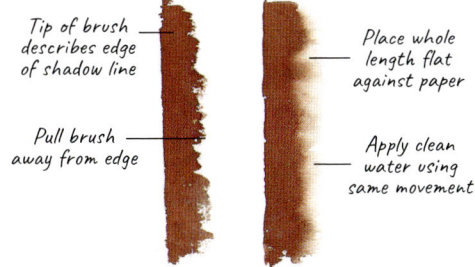

Tip of brush describes edge of shadow line

Pull brush away from edge

Place whole length flat against paper

Apply clean water using same movement

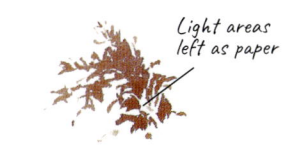

Light areas left as paper

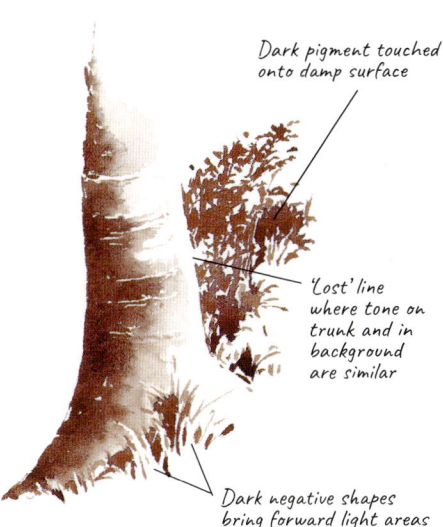

Dark pigment touched onto damp surface

'Lost' line where tone on trunk and in background are similar

Dark negative shapes bring forward light areas

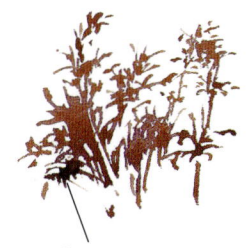

'Drop in' area

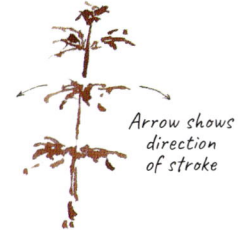

Arrow shows direction of stroke

Watercolor Techniques

*A common beginner's mistake is to add insufficient water to the pigment,
or to not mix together enough in the palette to cover the intended area
of paper – err on the side of too much, rather than too little, water.*

Wet into wet

This technique, in which paint placed
upon a damp surface spreads naturally,
producing a diffusion of forms that find
their own edges, helps to achieve a
loose, soft effect. Used in the form of a
muted background, it gives emphasis to
more detailed work.

The sky-painting exercise shows the
basic technique using one color. Wet
an area of paper evenly and hold the
paper, angled, up to the light in order
to observe the sheen and establish
evenness. Using a dilute mix of blue,
commence drawing into areas of the
damp surface with the tip of the brush
and watch the color spread on contact.

Drybrush

A drybrush effect is often created
accidentally at the end of a stroke when
paint on the brush is drying rapidly. You
can create this effect intentionally, to
give the impression of texture or muted
highlights. With less liquid than usual in
your brush, drag it across rough paper,
depositing pigment on the raised areas
but leaving the 'troughs' free of paint.
A flat brush was used here.

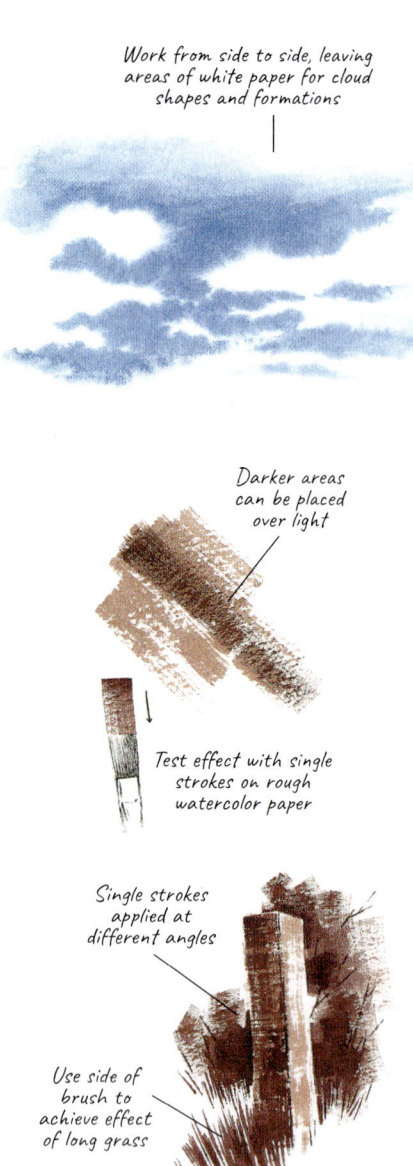

*Work from side to side, leaving
areas of white paper for cloud
shapes and formations*

*Darker areas
can be placed
over light*

*Test effect with single
strokes on rough
watercolor paper*

*Single strokes
applied at
different angles*

*Use side of
brush to
achieve effect
of long grass*

Washes

The secret of successful watercolor washes is to allow the first wash to dry thoroughly before the next is applied. You need to build only a few glazed washes to intensify tone.

Flat wash (1)

Load the brush with plenty of paint and, starting from the top, work down the paper from side to side using sweeping horizontal strokes, across one way and back in the opposite direction. Keep loading your brush as you work, to avoid an area becoming too dry to accommodate the following stroke.

Gradated wash (2)

To achieve a wash that progresses from a dark to light tone, add more clean water to the pigment for each successive stroke across the paper. To avoid creating a striped effect, experiment with the amount of water you add for each brushstroke line, and do not go back over a wash you have already laid.

Variegated wash (3)

Choose two or three colors and blend one into the other as you work down the paper. You can also create a wider band of the main color and reduce the width for the second or third bands. When painting a sky, you can add clean water to the final strokes to suggest a light horizon.

Board angle (4)

Support your paper – pinned or stretched upon a board – at an angle that will allow the brushstrokes to flow into each other without causing dribbles.

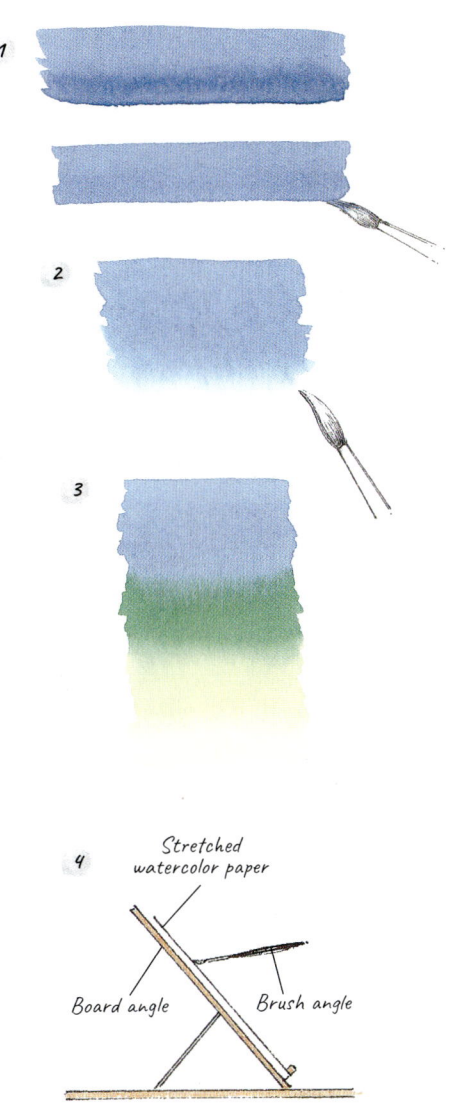

Stretched watercolor paper

Board angle

Brush angle

Table top

Highlights

Highlights are best depicted by the use of untouched white paper. Decide which areas are to remain white before you start to paint, and make preliminary sketches.

Painting around highlights

Sometimes pure white paper is not required for a painting, but a paler tone is. In this case, lifting off excess moisture and pigment is the answer, and the two techniques work well when used together.

This unfinished study of a prawn shows the underlying washes before subsequent layers of color build up the intensity. Start by painting around the white area, as demonstrated in the study of peppers (as seen in Observation).

With no dark background, use a delicate line to bring the shape forward

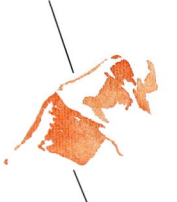

Pull the paint away from the highlight and across the form

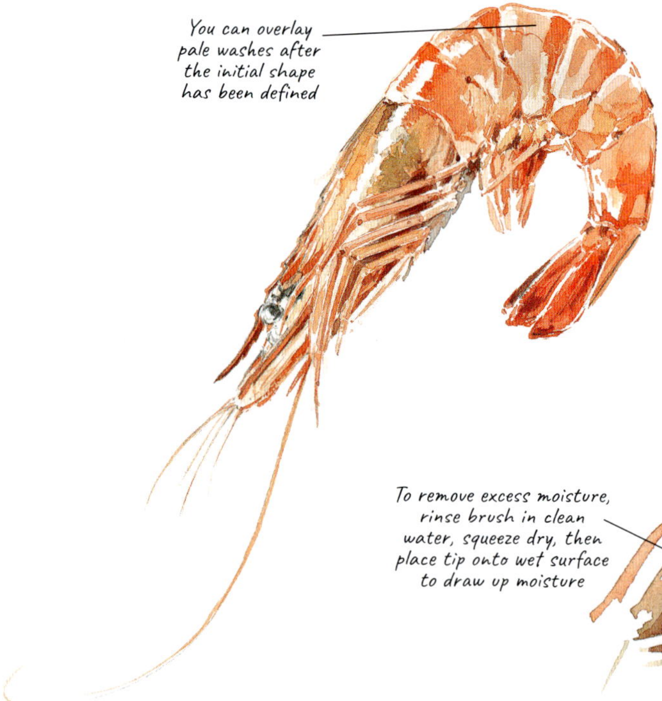

You can overlay pale washes after the initial shape has been defined

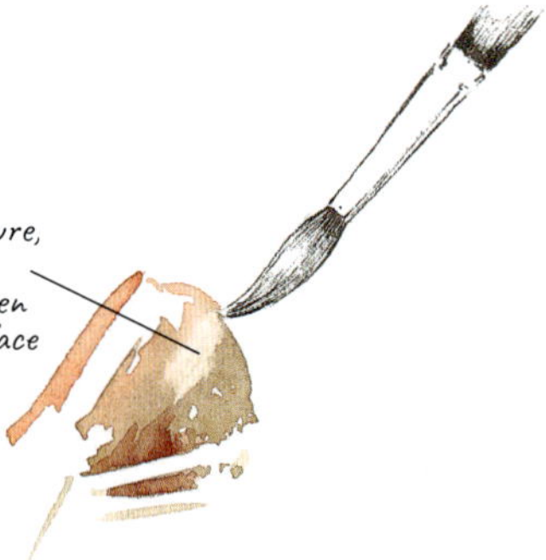

To remove excess moisture, rinse brush in clean water, squeeze dry, then place tip onto wet surface to draw up moisture

Blotting Off

As long as you are using plenty of water mixed with pigment, if you make an error you can quickly blot the surface to reduce the mark. Watercolor lightens when it dries, so the mark may be hardly noticeable and may be overpainted successfully.

Creating texture

The studies here show how blotting can be used to produce texture. Blotting produces subtle changes of tone with texture, and contrasts are essential for lively effects – gently drop darker pigment into damp textured areas. At all times keep the pigment fluid, paint onto a rough-surfaced paper and blot gently. Be careful not to dry the blotted area too much, or the final stages may not take.

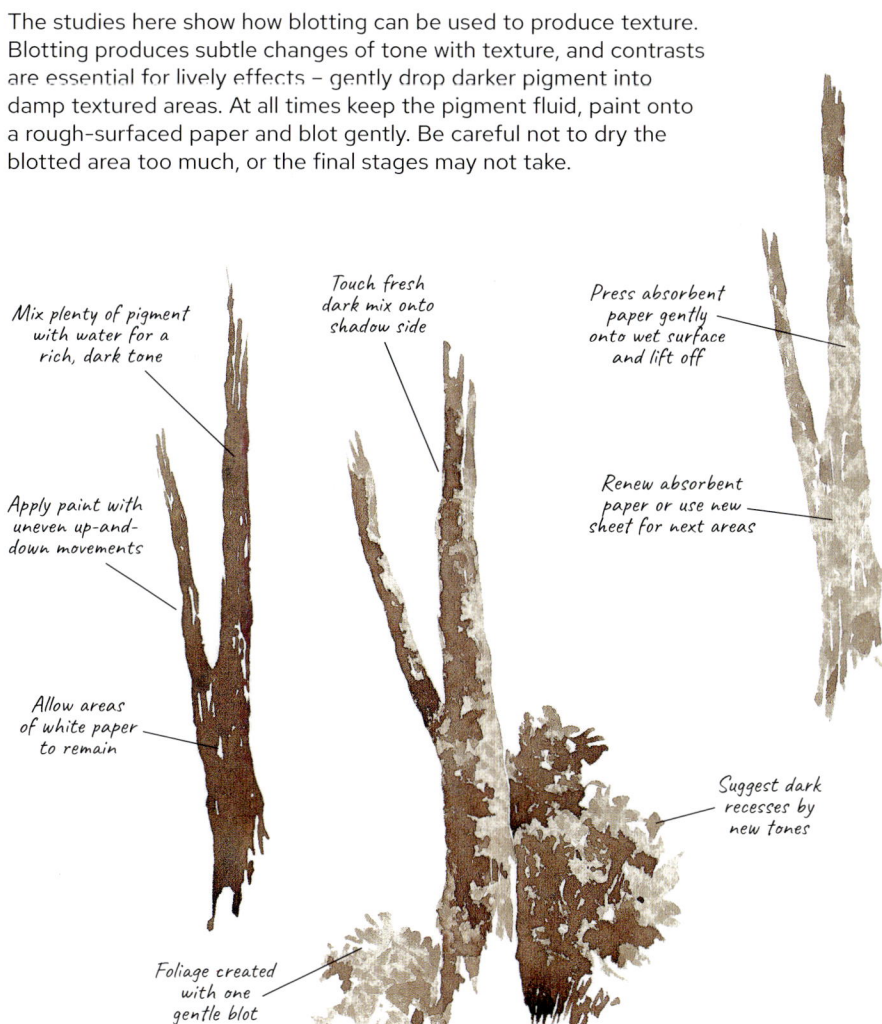

Mix plenty of pigment with water for a rich, dark tone

Touch fresh dark mix onto shadow side

Press absorbent paper gently onto wet surface and lift off

Apply paint with uneven up-and-down movements

Renew absorbent paper or use new sheet for next areas

Allow areas of white paper to remain

Suggest dark recesses by new tones

Foliage created with one gentle blot

Resists

*A resist method is when part of the paper's surface is
coated with a substance that prevents any overlaid washes
of pigment reaching the paper underneath it.*

Masking fluid

This fluid is applied to the paper with a
brush or pen. It dries to a rubbery film
over the areas covered, thus preventing
paint from marking the paper. You can
then paint normally around (or across)
the masking fluid in the knowledge that
once it is removed, the areas it covered
will appear as clean paper. When the
painting is thoroughly dry, you need only
gently rub the fluid with a finger or pull
the rubbery substance from the surface.

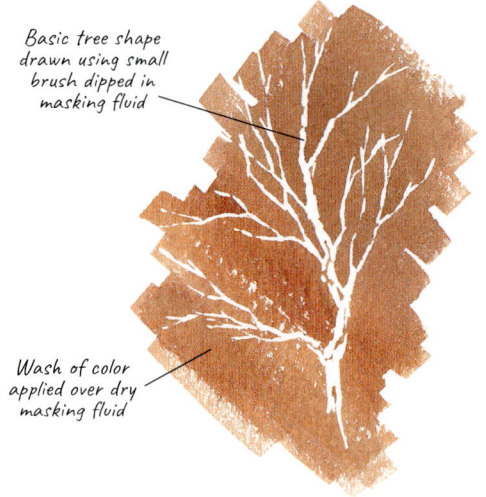

*Basic tree shape
drawn using small
brush dipped in
masking fluid*

*Wash of color
applied over dry
masking fluid*

Candle wax

Rub a white candle gently across the
paper, then apply paint over the area
and watch how the waxed area resists
the paint upon its surface. The texture
produced using this technique can be
used to depict many different surfaces,
and I have provided a sample study of
rocks among grass.

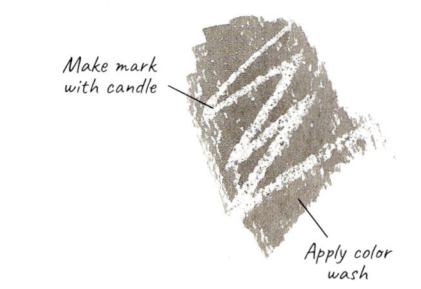

*Make mark
with candle*

*Apply color
wash*

Rocks among grass

Draw shapes with the candle to represent
smooth rocks, then sweep a wash of light
color over the waxed area. Any places
where the wax did not touch the surface
will take pigment in the usual way, as solid
color. Allow to dry before adding a darker
tone to indicate shadow areas.

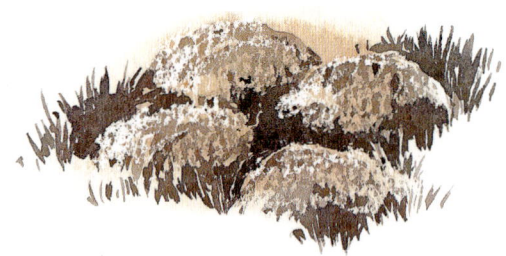

Creating Texture without Resists

Resists are not the only way to create texture in watercolor. Techniques such as drybrush work and leaving highlights can also be explored. The surface of the paper can be employed, too – look to see what it suggests.

Towelling, carpet and similar *(1)*

Through this method, work 'on your toes' to follow the texture that can be observed on the surface of the paper.

Wood grain *(2)*

This overall textured effect is achieved by drawing a series of slightly uneven lines, one beside the other, using a brush.

Rusty iron *(3)*

A rusty iron surface, with its cracks and indentations, can benefit from a stippling effect, for which you need to use the tip of your brush.

Underside of leaf *(4)*

This is a good example of how the surface of the paper can be used to great effect. Look closely at the paper's natural texture to note where the troughs occur. Apply the pigment in these 'pockets', leaving the raised areas as white paper.

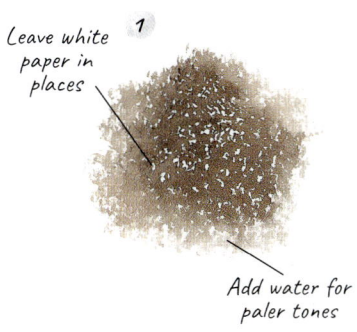

1

Leave white paper in places

Add water for paler tones

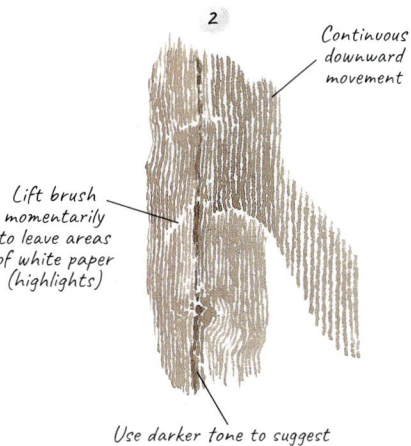

2

Continuous downward movement

Lift brush momentarily to leave areas of white paper (highlights)

Use darker tone to suggest recesses and shadow areas

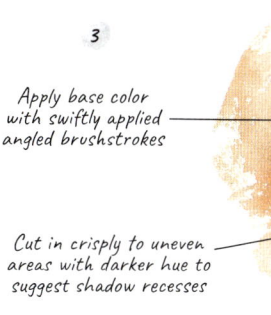

3

Apply base color with swiftly applied angled brushstrokes

Cut in crisply to uneven areas with darker hue to suggest shadow recesses

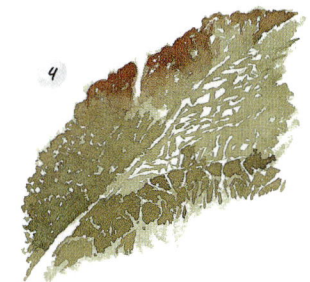

4

Understanding Color

Color enables you to create atmosphere in your paintings, and once you have mastered color mixing you will be able to express moods better. Explore colors to use together and which combinations to avoid by experimentation.

Color relationships

Colors affect each other – for example red and green, which are of equal intensity and are complementary colors, produce harmony when painted in equal proportions. By varying the proportions of these two colors within a painting you can create different effects. Paint a small square of green and surround it with a wide border of red. Compare this with a small square of red surrounded by a green border. Note how the green of the square appears lighter when surrounded by red, yet darker when green surrounds red.

The color wheel

A basic color wheel contains three primary colors, red, blue and yellow, with secondary colors, purple, green and orange, in between. On more comprehensive color wheels the intermediate colors are included – red-purple, blue-purple, blue-green, yellow-green, yellow-orange and red-orange – and the wheel can be subdivided again into further intermediates.

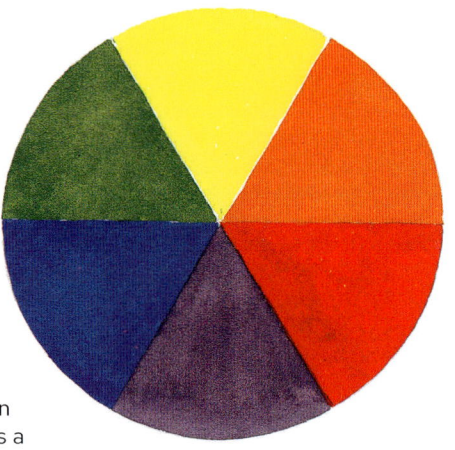

There is not actually a red, blue or yellow that is primary, as there are warm reds and cool reds for example. In the Winsor & Newton range an alizarin crimson or permanent rose is a cool red, whereas scarlet lake is a warm red.

Tonal scale

As with the pencil scale seen in Tone: Tonal blocks, we can also produce a tonal scale in color. Paint the darkest value first then, adding a little more water to the pigment for each block, work through to the lightest tone.

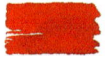 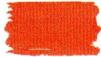 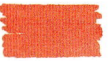  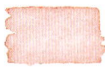  

Limited palette

Decorative stonework – in the form of a window frame or a statue – is a subject which lends itself to execution in a limited palette or in neutral colors. The stonework around the window to the right was painted using three colors – burnt sienna, yellow ochre and cobalt blue – mixed in varying quantities and strengths. The landscape subject explored in Developing Your Picture was also painted using the same palette, to show that a very few colors can be adapted for totally different subjects.

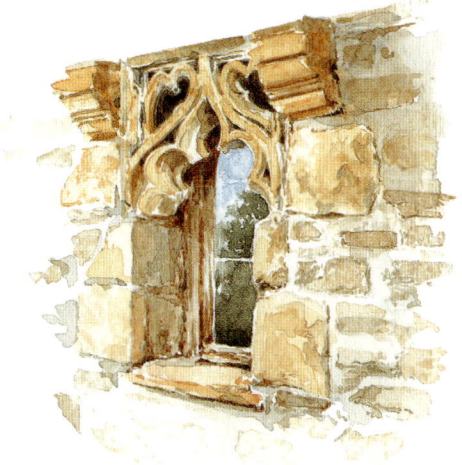

Neutral colors

When the three primary colors are mixed together in certain proportions they produce a neutral hue. A range of neutrals was used in this painting of an angel statue.

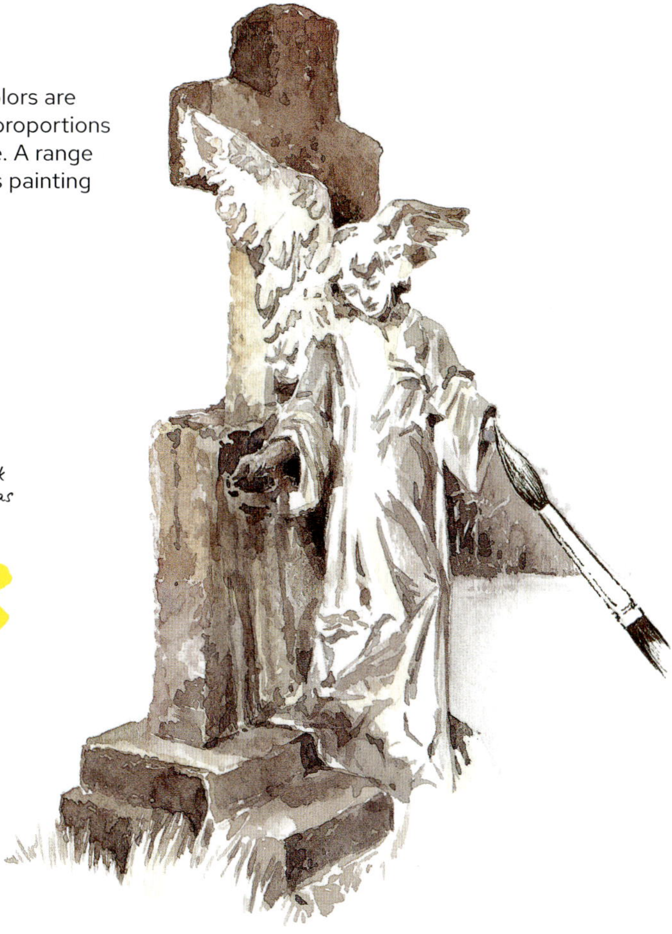

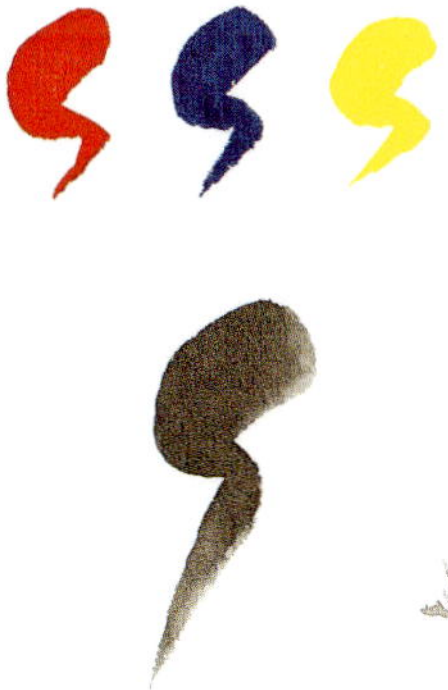

Concentrated mix produces very rich dark to enhance shadow areas

Developing Your Picture

Most watercolor paintings are created through a number of distinct preliminary stages. Be aware of, and think your way through, these stages in your work. This will ensure that you are in control as the painting develops.

Establishing composition

Make a preliminary sketch of your chosen subject, consciously looking for areas of interest. Here, the sheep on the ground, in neutral colors, blended into the surroundings, so I chose to concentrate on the strong shadows cast across the trees.

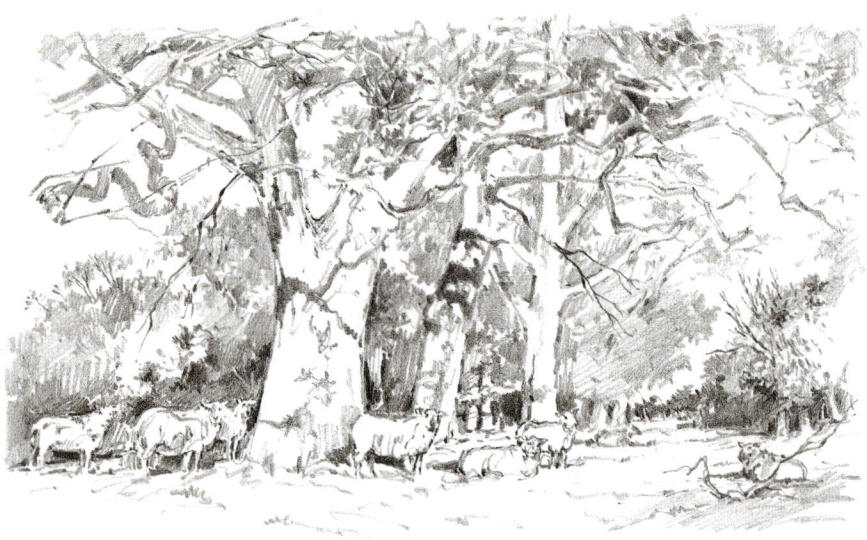

Drawing the tonal contrasts

A second sketch establishes the positions of negative and shadow shapes plus the areas of foliage mass. Once established, these basic shapes are then transferred onto watercolor paper as simple washes around the shapes of the trees.

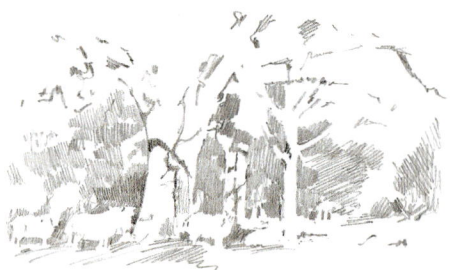
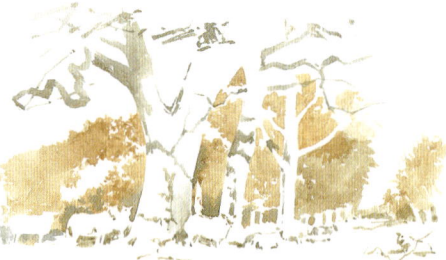

Painting the main areas

The palette is limited to three colors that, combined in varying quantities, also produce a range of subtle neutrals. The clear blue of the sky provides a cool contrast.

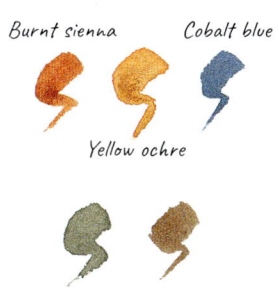

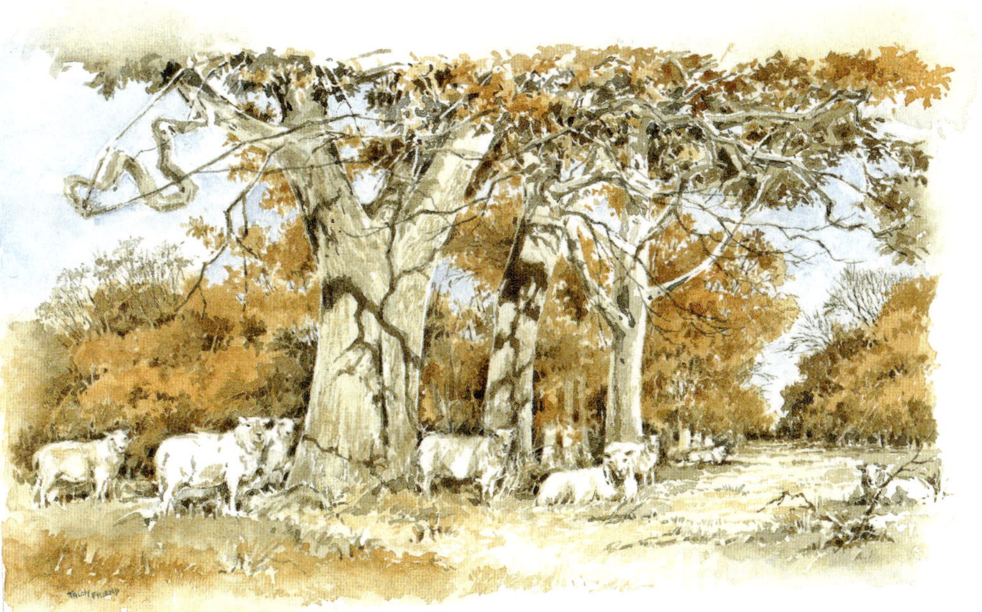

Burnt sienna   Cobalt blue

Yellow ochre

Blended colors

Build up painting with freely applied blocks of color and tone

Leave white paper to enhance contrasts

Blending

Crisp edges

Shapes between

Build up painting with freely applied blocks of color and tone

Leave white paper to enhance contrasts

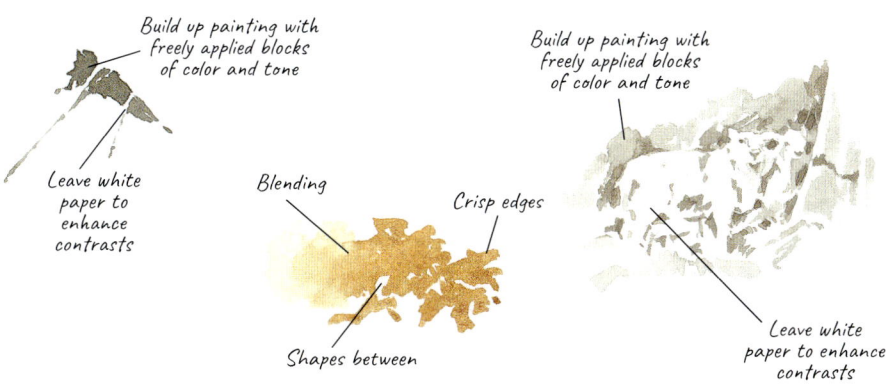

Rescuing Mistakes

The disappointment felt when a promising painting goes wrong after hours of work can be reversed with rescue techniques. First, assess the situation calmly and decide, is it the drawing or paint application that is at fault?

Thick paint

If you have produced a painting where the paint has been applied too thickly, you can rescue it with a wash-off method. This method also helps when too much white is exposed within the painting, as it mutes the colors and enables you to build them up again, as well as giving you another chance to alter any drawing deficiencies.

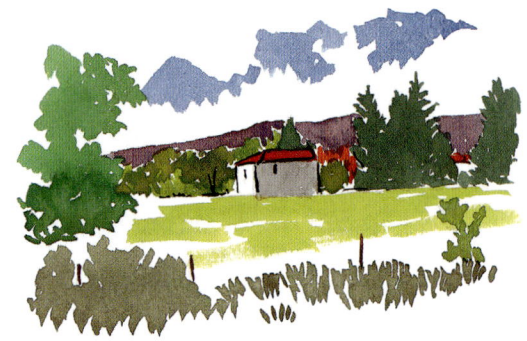

Back to drawing

Making a drawing helps you notice things that need to be corrected, so draw in a 'painterly' way, using tonal masses rather than outlines.

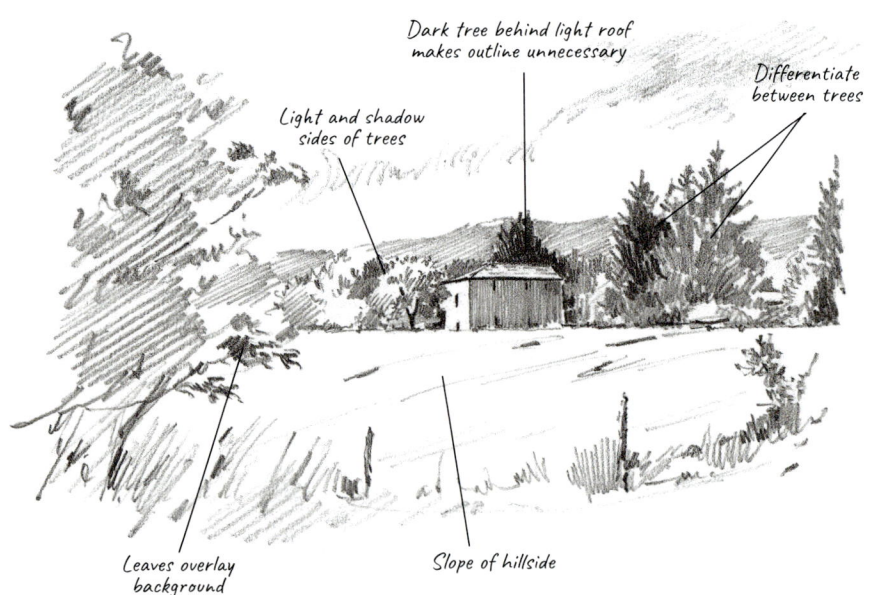

Dark tree behind light roof makes outline unnecessary

Differentiate between trees

Light and shadow sides of trees

Leaves overlay background

Slope of hillside

Washing paint off

Place your painting flat in a receptacle, and add clean running water. Gently stroke the surface with your finger, or brush or sponge off the pigment. Do this until there is no more pigment to be removed, only a residual tint staining the paper. Stretch the paper on a board and allow it to dry before continuing.

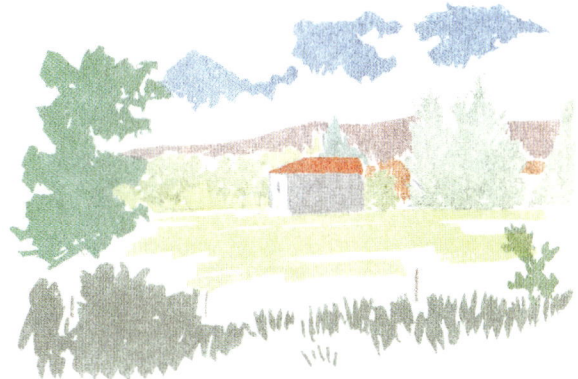

Cutting in and clarifying

Start by correcting the building, cutting in around the roof with a simple tree shape to give a dark color behind and thus bring the image forward. Establish the shapes of the nearby trees.

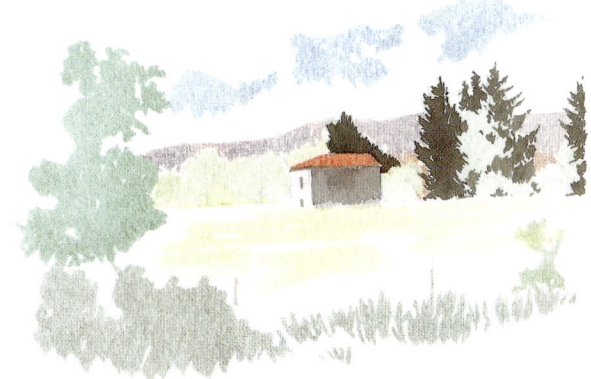

Relating the foreground

Establish the relationship between the foreground and background by introducing the smaller trees on the other side of the building. This will enable the composition to become set.

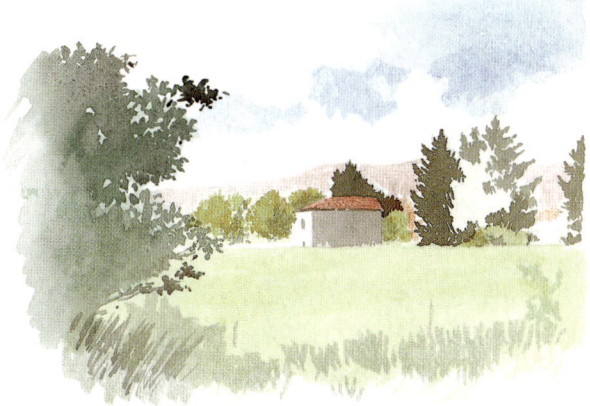

Final painting

Lightly apply washes to the grass area, to aid continuity.
Build up the painting with washes in the foreground and
background before adding the finishing details.

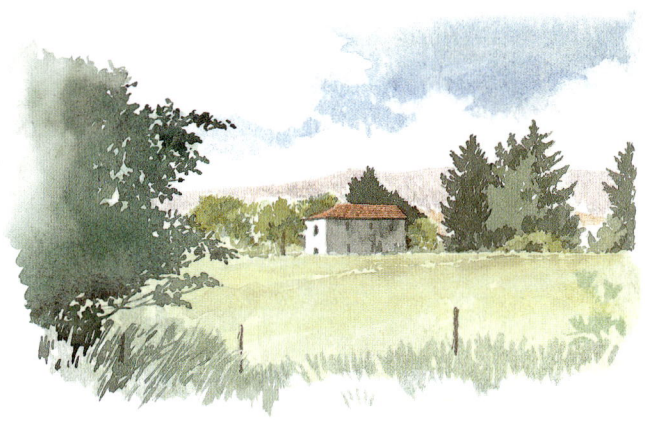

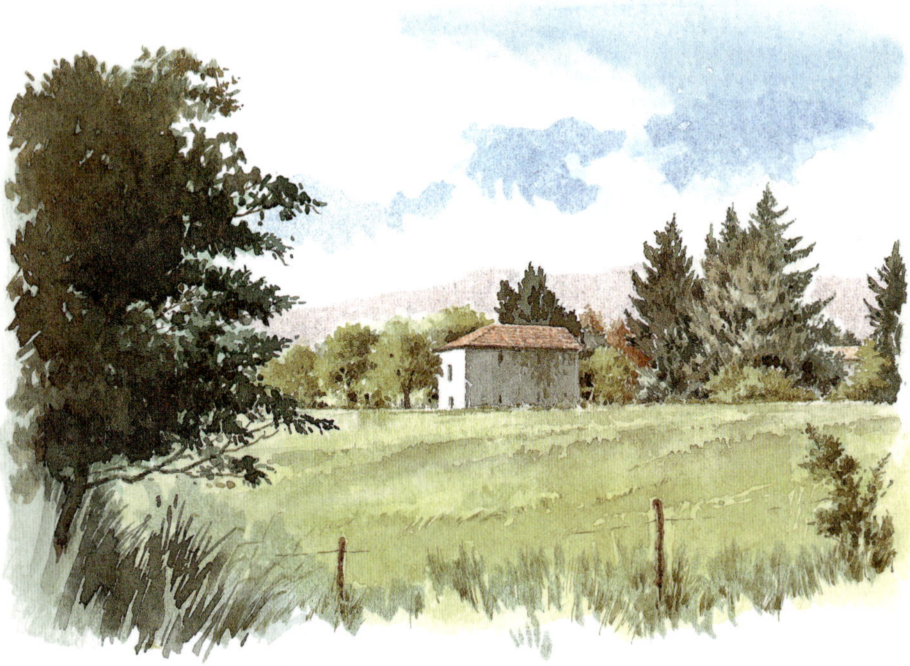

Using gouache

The problems with this bridge painting are the drawing (the right-hand side of the bridge slopes away too steeply), the greens (how to differentiate between them, and how much white paper to allow) and the muddled areas of shadow (the foreground area on the right-hand side is muddy and overworked, and lacks clarity within the shaded area).

Gouache allows you to reintroduce drawing to correct and eradicate an unsuccessful sky. You can also use the advantage of working on a tinted ground to correct and to apply thicker paint to alter areas.

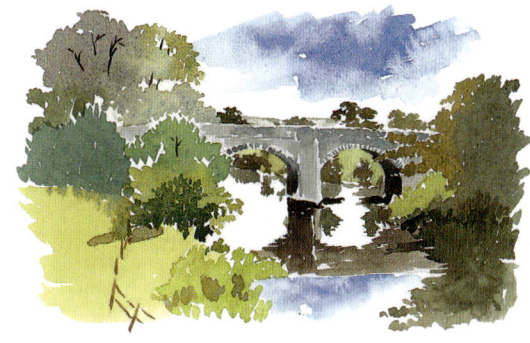

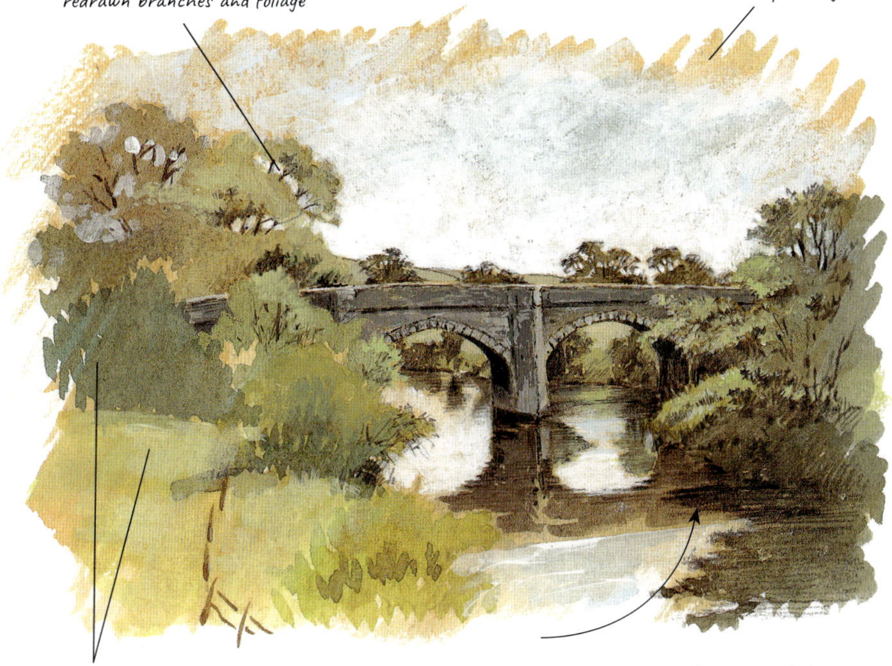

Establish areas of sky between redrawn branches and foliage

Lay warm (tint) wash over whole painting

Build up greens in relation to each other

Adjust tilt of picture and square off edges to lift bridge slightly, presenting more accurate perspective angle

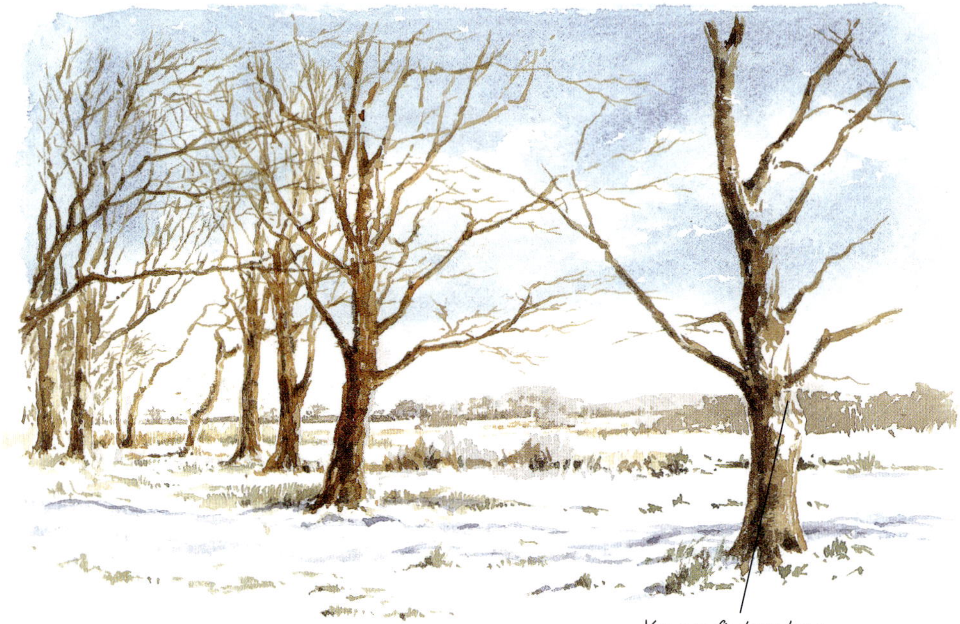

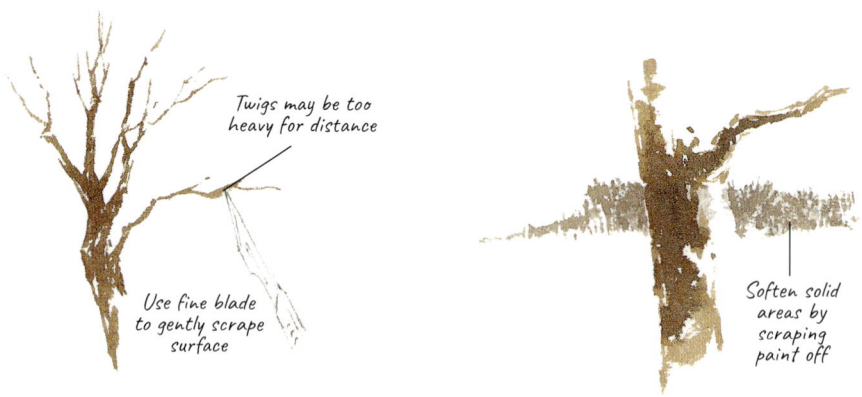

*You may find you have
painted an area which should
have remained white*

Scraping off

When painting a snow scene, you may find you have colored an area that
you feel you would prefer to keep white. There may also be occasions where
you wish to give the illusion of snowflakes, sea spray or sparkle upon a
surface. In this instance, scraping off is part of the method to use; make sure
that you use a sharp scalpel or craft-knife blade.

*Twigs may be too
heavy for distance*

*Use fine blade
to gently scrape
surface*

*Soften solid
areas by
scraping
paint off*

Scale and composition

If a painting's composition is becoming disjointed or you are having problems with relating the scale of one subject to another, you may find that excluding part of the picture is the answer. A simple method is to move a viewfinder around the picture until you find an area within the frame that presents a satisfactory composition, and then develop that area alone. If the painting was already completed and you were not satisfied with the overall effect, isolating a small area in this way can rescue many hours of hard work.

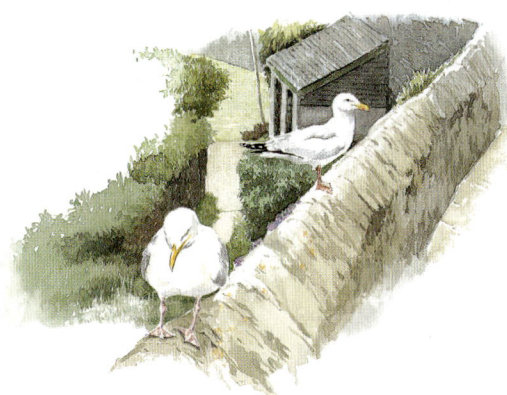

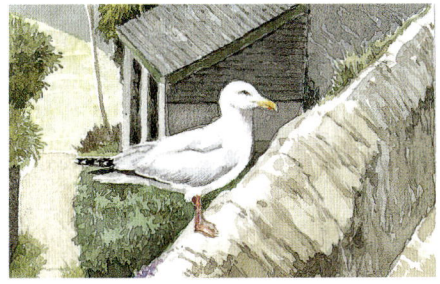

Using mixed media

Images that have lost clarity can be redrawn over the watercolor using another medium. Watercolor and pastel, or charcoal, or watercolor pencils are all examples of mixed media, but perhaps the most popular combination is watercolor and pen and ink, which is also an effective rescue technique because it allows you to clarify and re-establish the drawing aspect of your painting if this has been lost.

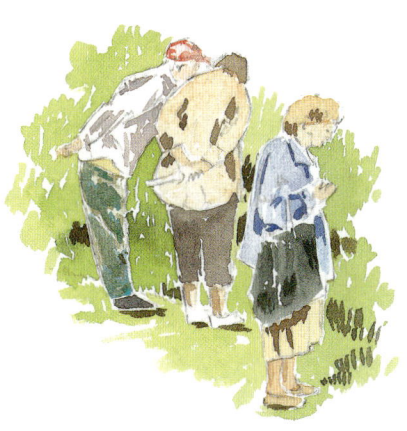

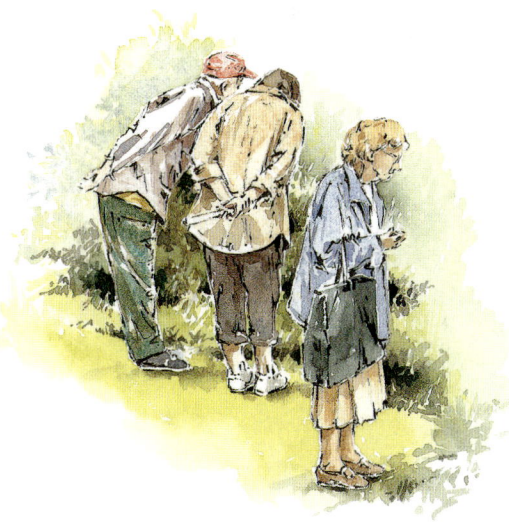

SKIES AND WATER
Basic Brushstrokes

These exercises are designed to help you learn to interpret movement of water and clouds, allowing the surface of white watercolor paper to play as important a part as the paint itself. There's also a flat wash included too.

Painting positions

The main brush positions for these examples are the normal painting angle (for the flat brush exercise) and one at a right angle to your hand (for the round brush exercise). Use a variety of angles for the cloud formation exercises shown below and opposite.

Sky and water washes

Practice glazing with this simple exercise. Wash a block of pale blue onto your paper and allow it to dry. Mix a paler wash of a second color, in this case raw sienna, and gently wash it over the blue to achieve a glazed surface.

Flat wash.

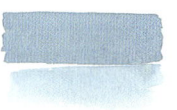

Blended with clean water

Cumulus clouds

Apply pigment with curved strokes to describe the edge of a cloud (right), and paint out and away from the cloud (left).

Flat brush exercise

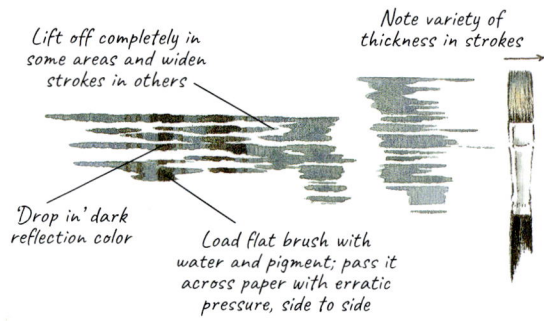

Note variety of thickness in strokes

Lift off completely in some areas and widen strokes in others

'Drop in' dark reflection color

Load flat brush with water and pigment; pass it across paper with erratic pressure, side to side

Round brush exercise

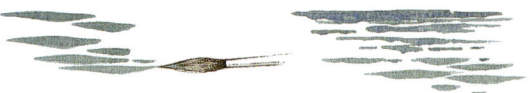

Hold brush at right angle to your body and touch; press as you travel and gently lift stroke

Make strokes narrower for distance, allowing to blend in places

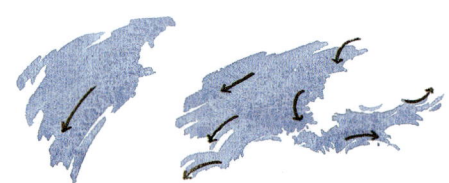

A variety of brush positions and directional strokes helps to create interesting cloud shapes

Developing Brushstrokes

These four exercises develop the strokes shown opposite. Remember to remain aware of the movement aspect when portraying water and skies, as well as employing the juxtaposition of crisp and blended edges.

Reflected image

The flat brush exercise is useful for broken reflections in rippling water. You can set it up yourself by placing an object that reflects onto water.

Different viewing angles

Choosing a viewpoint near the surface of the water produces variations on how you portray the water and reflections on it.

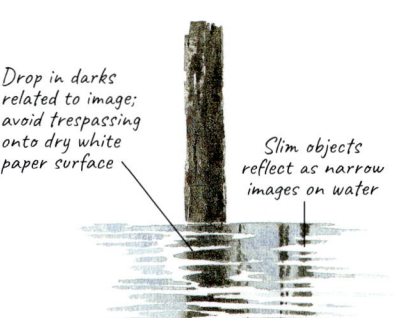

Drop in darks related to image; avoid trespassing onto dry white paper surface

Slim objects reflect as narrow images on water

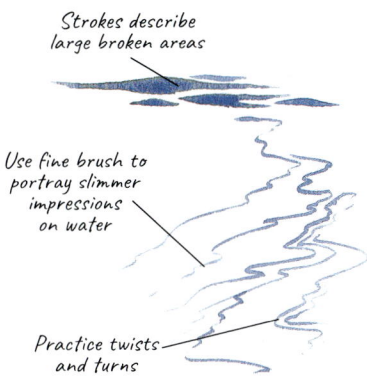

Strokes describe large broken areas

Use fine brush to portray slimmer impressions on water

Practice twists and turns

Blended wash

For painting tranquil skies you can create the desired effect by gradating a wash over another that has already dried (see Washes).

One-color sky

Developing the cumulus clouds exercise, you can practice painting cloud effects using only one color.

Paint a dilute raw sienna wash, allow to dry thoroughly, then paint a gradated wash over the first one

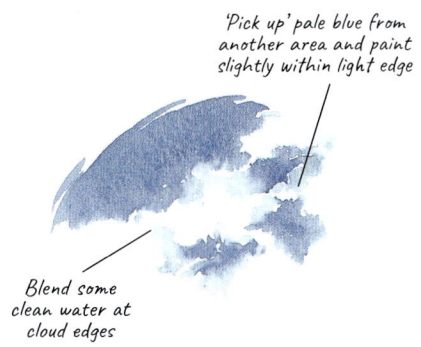

'Pick up' pale blue from another area and paint slightly within light edge

Blend some clean water at cloud edges

Still Water

To achieve spontaneity in your interpretation of water you need to restrict the number of washes applied. Without knowledge of the subject, however, adding washes at random cannot achieve satisfactory results.

Typical problems

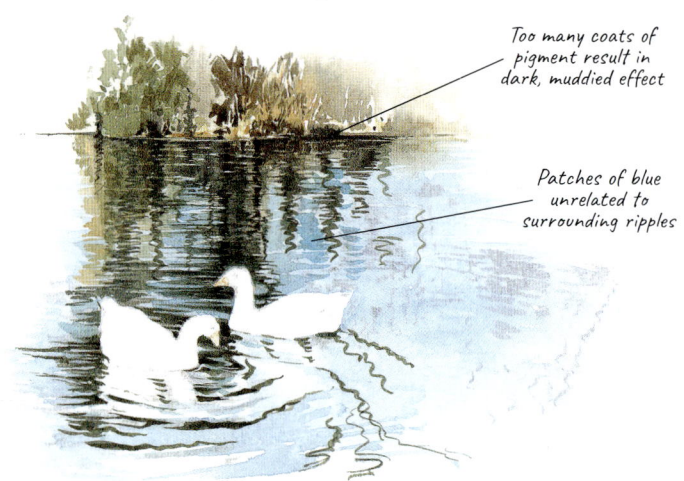

Too many coats of pigment result in dark, muddied effect

Patches of blue unrelated to surrounding ripples

Study detail using pencil

As water responds to its environment – stirred by a breeze or disturbed by birds or fish, for example – it creates interesting patterns within reflections on its surface.

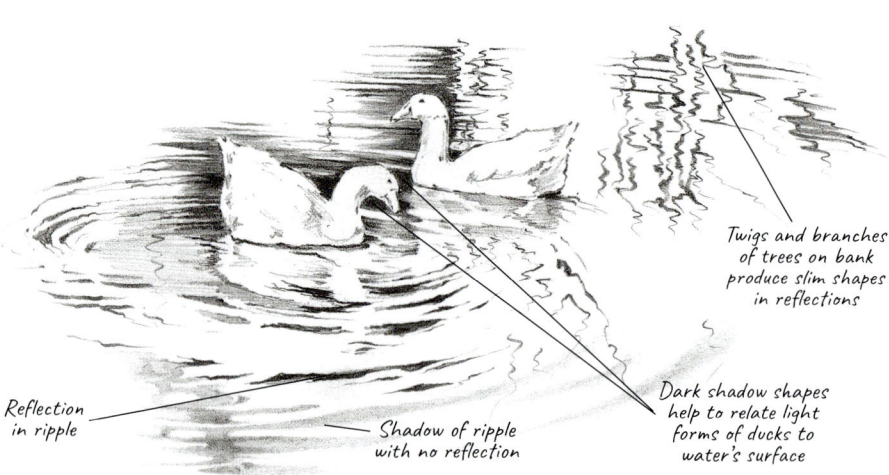

Twigs and branches of trees on bank produce slim shapes in reflections

Reflection in ripple

Shadow of ripple with no reflection

Dark shadow shapes help to relate light forms of ducks to water's surface

Solutions

An exercise in understanding

This exercise demonstrates wet-into-wet painting, representing distant reflections, and a controlled wet-on-dry interpretation for the close-up ripples. Once you understand the subject and have interpreted it in this controlled way, you will be able to achieve spontaneity in your personal style.

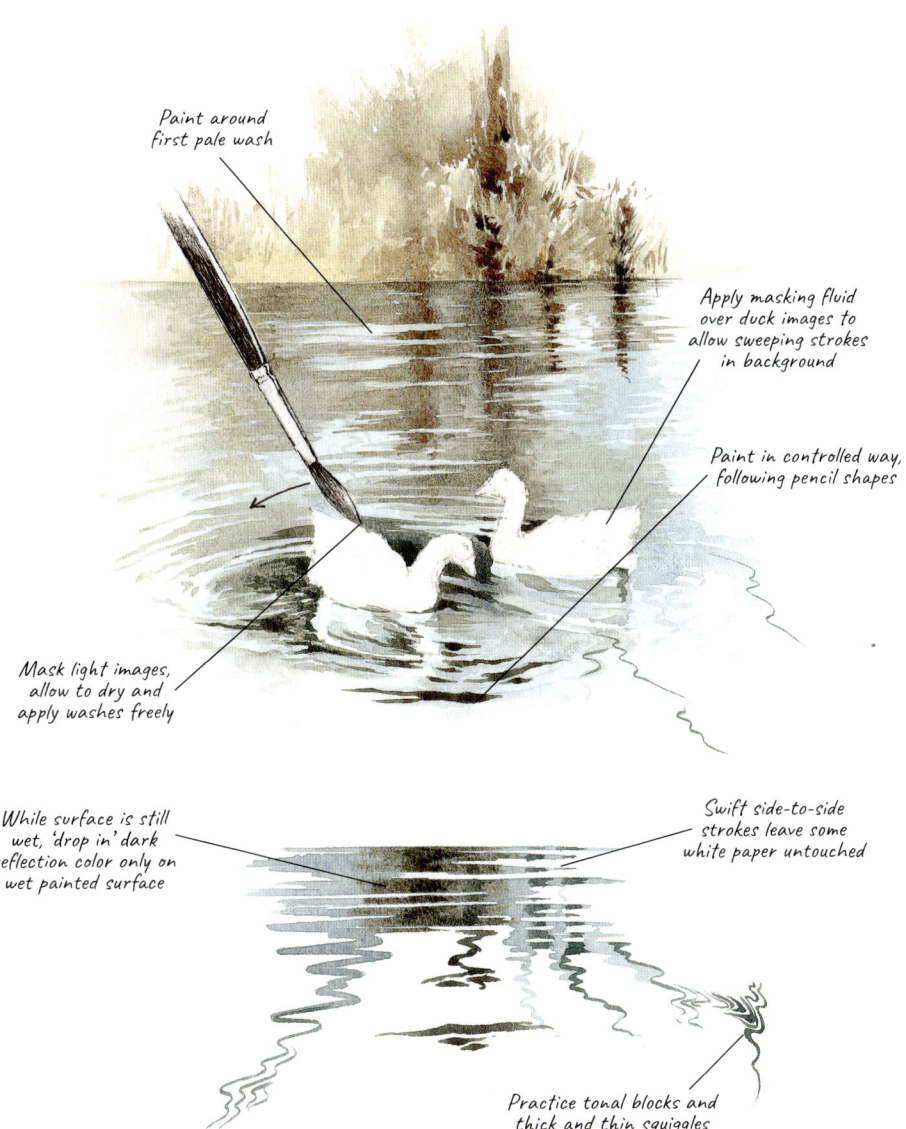

Paint around first pale wash

Apply masking fluid over duck images to allow sweeping strokes in background

Paint in controlled way, following pencil shapes

Mask light images, allow to dry and apply washes freely

While surface is still wet, 'drop in' dark reflection color only on wet painted surface

Swift side-to-side strokes leave some white paper untouched

Practice tonal blocks and thick and thin squiggles

Moving Water

*The complexities of falling water against a backdrop of rocks,
surrounded by ferns and other foliage, can be a daunting prospect
for a beginner, so take the time to observe closely first.*

Typical problems

You'll be looking not only at
an array of varying greens but
also at a vast variety of tonal
contrasts. It's a good idea to
separate one from the other
to understand the importance
of tonal relationships before
moving into full color to avoid
many of the problems seen in
this painting.

Observational study

Find a subject with water
falling a short distance.
Observe and draw the way it
flattens, twists and bubbles.
Pay particular attention to
tonal variations.

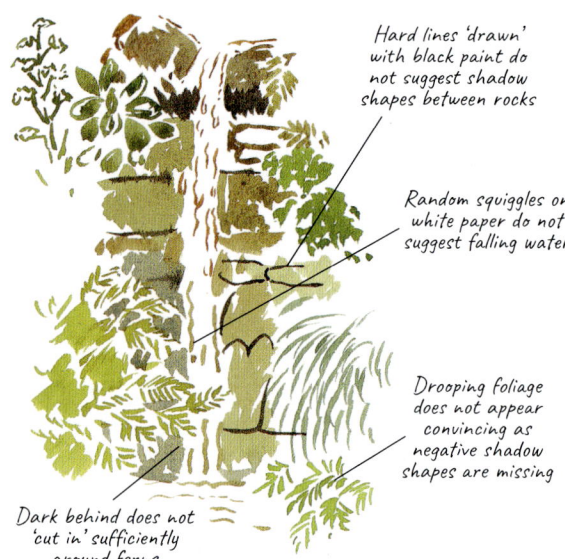

Hard lines 'drawn'
with black paint do
not suggest shadow
shapes between rocks

Random squiggles on
white paper do not
suggest falling water

Drooping foliage
does not appear
convincing as
negative shadow
shapes are missing

Dark behind does not
'cut in' sufficiently
around ferns

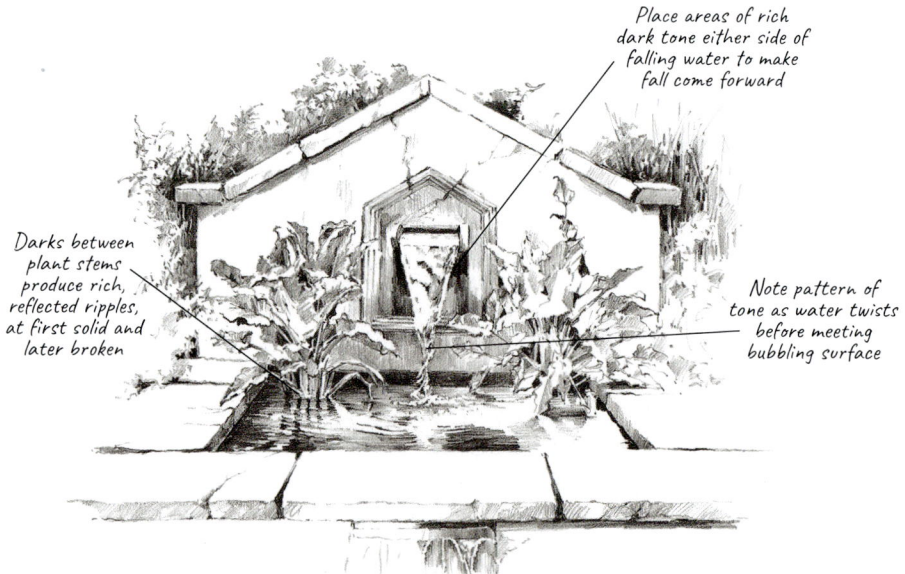

Place areas of rich
dark tone either side of
falling water to make
fall come forward

Darks between
plant stems
produce rich,
reflected ripples,
at first solid and
later broken

Note pattern of
tone as water twists
before meeting
bubbling surface

Solutions

The magic of monochrome

Working in monochrome means that you put any problems of using color to one side for the moment. This will allow you to take one learning step at a time. A number of points and methods mentioned in Materials and Techniques have been used in this study, including applying masking fluid to retain light areas while allowing freedom of brush movements, using drybrush techniques for rough rock surfaces, enhancing dark negative shapes, and making full use of the tonal scale.

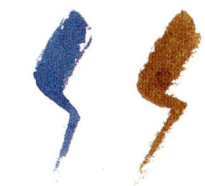

To make a monochrome, mix two colors together in plenty of water to create a pleasing neutral hue

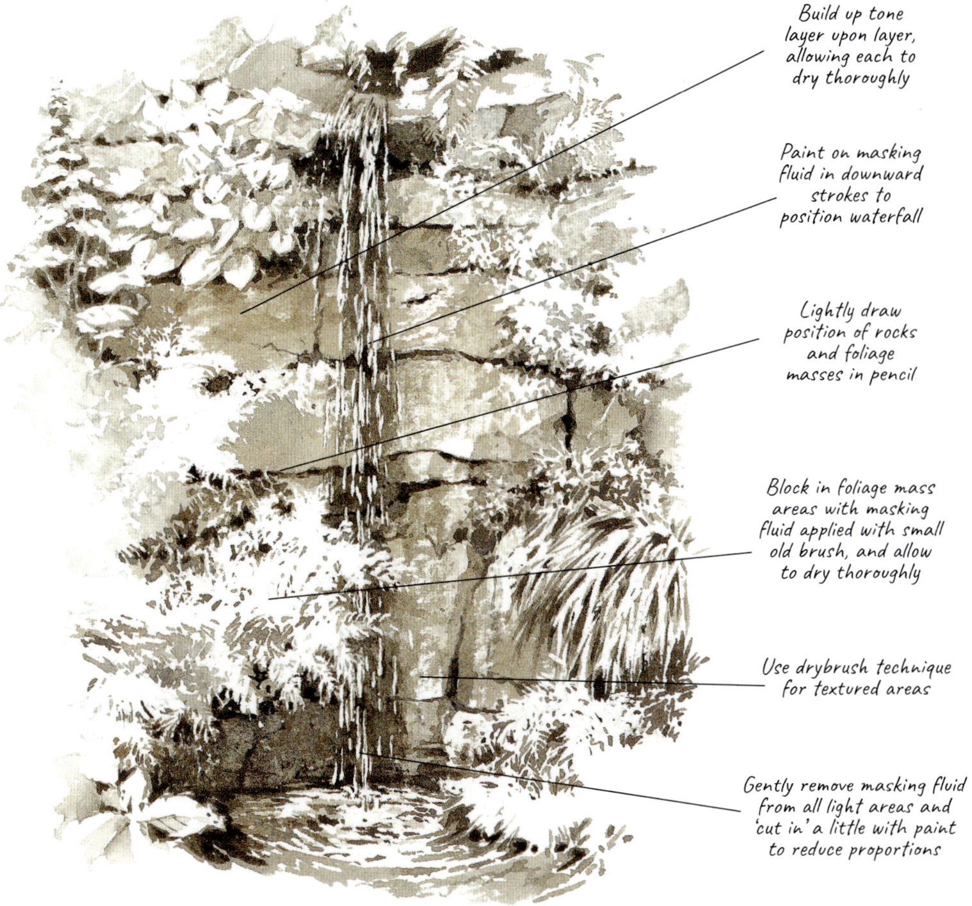

Build up tone layer upon layer, allowing each to dry thoroughly

Paint on masking fluid in downward strokes to position waterfall

Lightly draw position of rocks and foliage masses in pencil

Block in foliage mass areas with masking fluid applied with small old brush, and allow to dry thoroughly

Use drybrush technique for textured areas

Gently remove masking fluid from all light areas and 'cut in' a little with paint to reduce proportions

Cloudy Skies

Whether working wet into wet or using a rough, dry surface to produce interesting cloud edges, it's swiftness of paint application that produces the best results, although this doesn't allow time to consider the effects achieved.

Typical problems

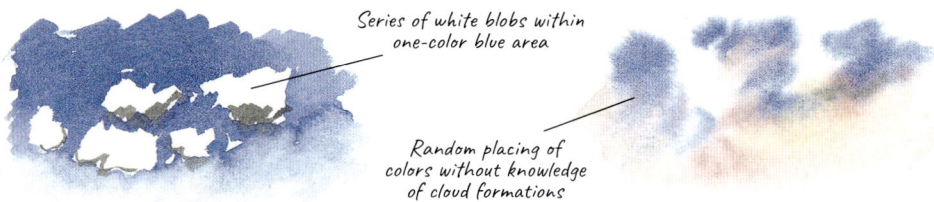

Series of white blobs within one-color blue area

Random placing of colors without knowledge of cloud formations

Playing with paint

Experiment with pushing the paint around before you start on your painting. Dampen the paper's surface with clean water. Either looking up at the sky, or at a photograph, paint the large shapes between the clouds. Make sure that the fluffy edges of the clouds that are to remain as white paper are interesting and appear natural. Mix some shadow color and apply to the underside of the cloud formations.

Mix each color separately in three separate palettes, using plenty of clean water, and have more palettes ready for mixing colors together to create different hues

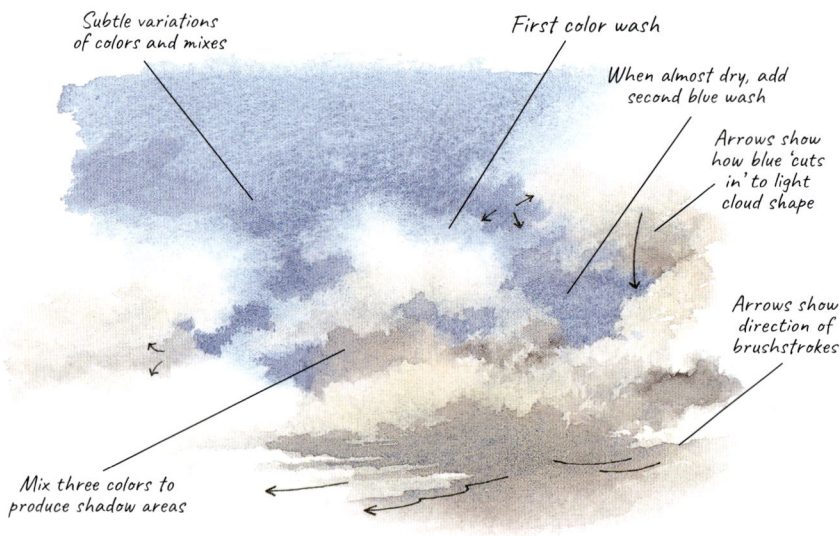

Subtle variations of colors and mixes

First color wash

When almost dry, add second blue wash

Arrows show how blue 'cuts in' to light cloud shape

Arrows show direction of brushstrokes

Mix three colors to produce shadow areas

Solutions

Cumulus clouds

When cumulus clouds are nearer to you they appear fuller than those in the far distance. The correct choice of paper helps – the surface of Saunders Waterford 300gsm (140lb) Rough paper is ideal as the pigment settles into the hollows.

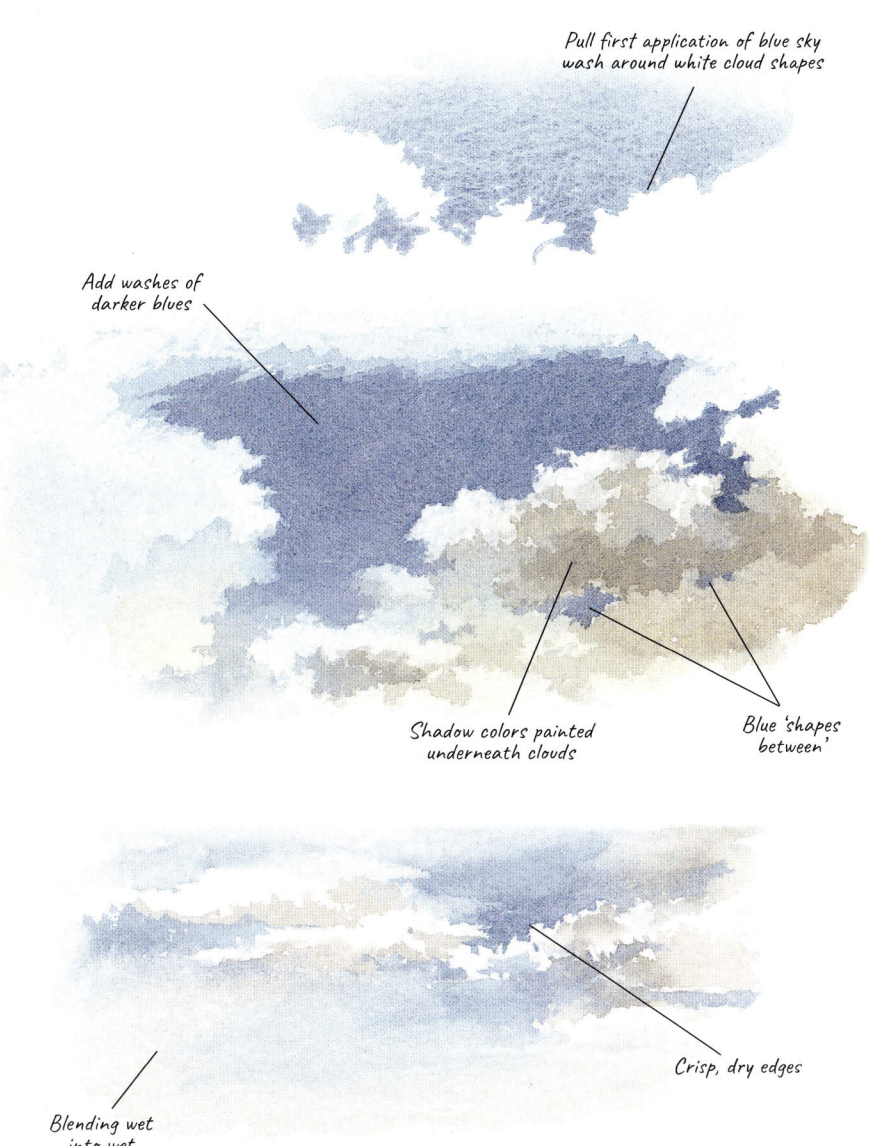

Pull first application of blue sky wash around white cloud shapes

Add washes of darker blues

Shadow colors painted underneath clouds

Blue 'shapes between'

Crisp, dry edges

Blending wet into wet

Calm and Clear Skies

Painting open landscape, or a wide expanse of sand and sea with a calm cloud arrangement is a chance to practice gradated washes. Let your hand and arm move smoothly, side to side, and use plenty of water in your washes.

Typical problems

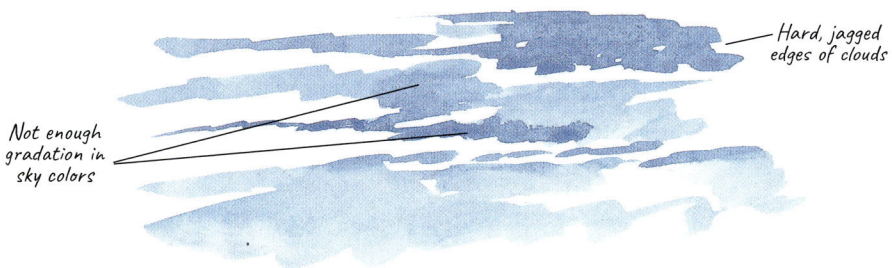

Hard, jagged edges of clouds

Not enough gradation in sky colors

A soft style of drawing

To get a feeling of space and tranquillity practice a calm approach to your painting and incorporate gentle blending. Get in the right frame of mind with a drawing first. Use a heavyweight quality cartridge paper and 2B pencil. Suggest subtle tones with light application of pencil pressure as you define the clouds' soft edges.

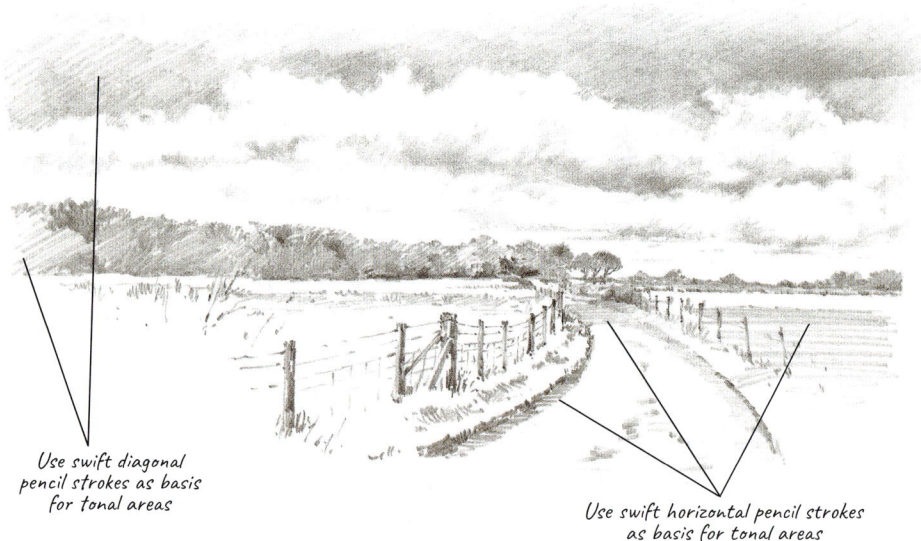

Use swift diagonal pencil strokes as basis for tonal areas

Use swift horizontal pencil strokes as basis for tonal areas

Solutions

Gradated sky

Subtle gradations of color and tone are essential for capturing the essence of a clear or calm sky. Note that the gradated washes in these exercises are shown darker than in the painting below, for the purpose of clarity.

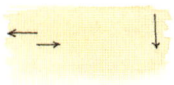

Invert your paper and work a raw sienna wash away from the horizon line

Creating distance

First the sky and distant coastline (see detail) were painted and allowed to dry. Darker foreground colors were then applied over the paler washes, and the sky was enhanced with cloud formations.

With the paper the correct way up, start a blue sky wash and work down, adding more clean water as you approach the horizon

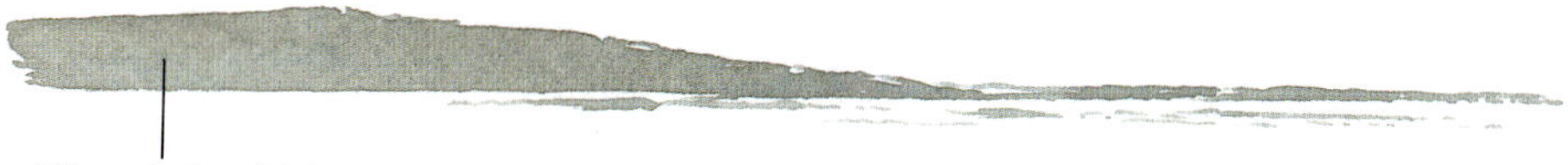

When sky has dried, paint in distant hill formations

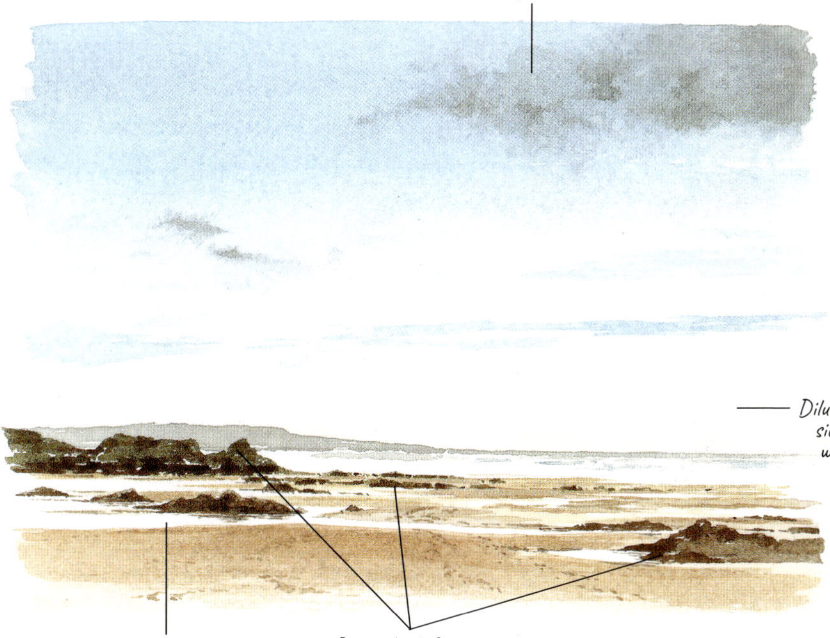

Overcast area of sky is directly overhead

Dilute raw sienna wash

Water left as white paper

Paint dark foreground shapes over lighter washes

TREES AND FOLIAGE
Basic Brushstrokes

These exercises are designed to help you achieve a variety of brushstrokes that will enable you to depict different types of foliage and bark textures.

Creating a foliage mass

This shows you how to start a foliage mass, individual leaves and textured bark. Hold the brush vertically for this exercise.

Directional leaf exercise

Hold the brush in a normal writing position for this exercise, but be prepared to vary the angle as you place individual strokes.

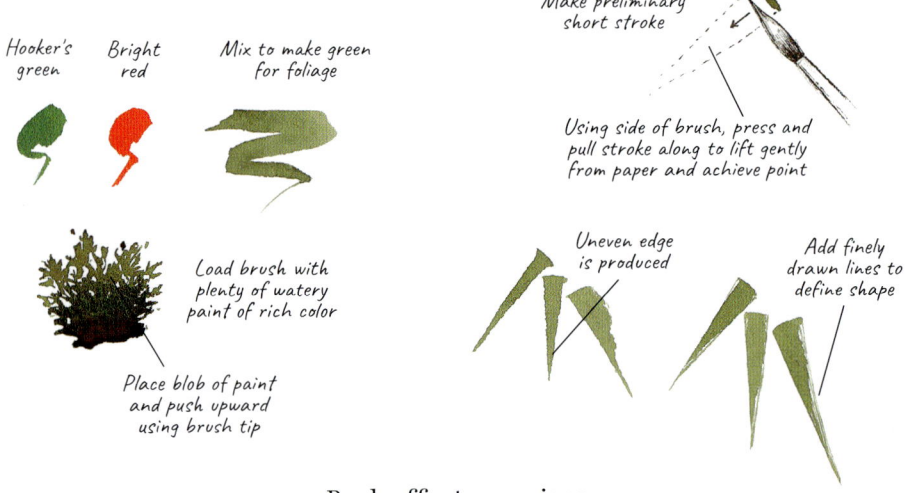

Hooker's green

Bright red

Mix to make green for foliage

Load brush with plenty of watery paint of rich color

Place blob of paint and push upward using brush tip

Make preliminary short stroke

Using side of brush, press and pull stroke along to lift gently from paper and achieve point

Uneven edge is produced

Add finely drawn lines to define shape

Bark effect exercises

The brush position varies for this exercise, using those shown for the directional leaf exercise and combining them with other ones.

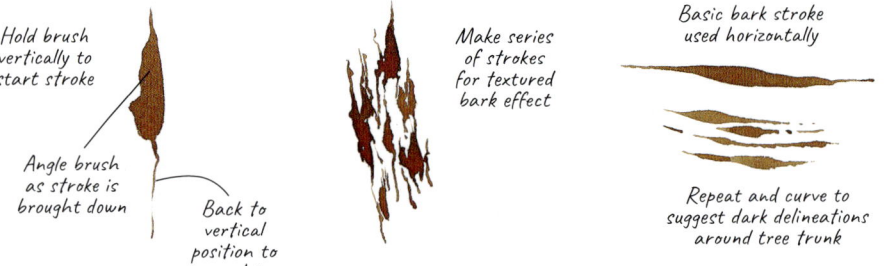

Hold brush vertically to start stroke

Angle brush as stroke is brought down

Back to vertical position to complete

Make series of strokes for textured bark effect

Basic bark stroke used horizontally

Repeat and curve to suggest dark delineations around tree trunk

Developing Brushstrokes

Four exercises to build on the basics. Practice varying brush pressure and the angles at which you work, and you will quickly learn to achieve impressions of individual leaves and masses of foliage against tree barks.

Foliage mass for distant trees and bushes

An extension of the creating a foliage mass ('blob and push') exercise, this shows you how to depict branches by pulling down individual strokes from a blob of paint.

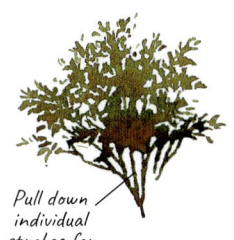 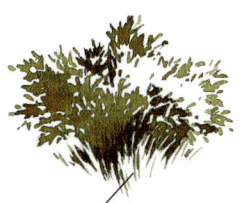

Pull down individual strokes for branches

Make repetitive downward strokes for grass in front of low shrub

Long-angled leaves

This is an extension of the directional leaf exercise.

Paint negative shapes seen between leaves

Paint additional leaves in darker tones

Creating light veins

Two more extensions of the directional leaf exercise; the second of these combines pencil and watercolor work.

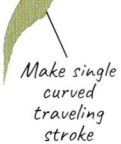 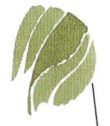

Make single curved traveling stroke

Repeat strokes alongside, leaving white paper between

Draw center vein and side veins in pencil

Paint between veins, allow to dry and erase pencil

Bark

This extension of the textured bark effect exercise shows how you can create bark patterns, using shadow lines and shadow shapes on textured paper.

Add darker tones near central vein and at edge of leaf to create highlights

Establish basic texture

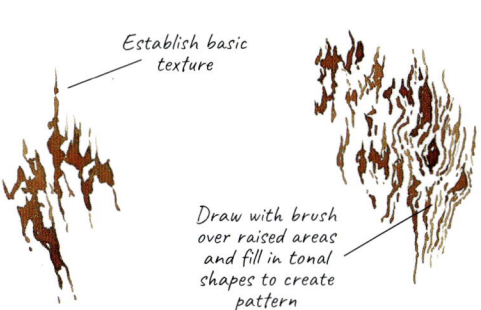

Draw with brush over raised areas and fill in tonal shapes to create pattern

Distant Trees

*Seen at a distance, trees often present a variety of problems
for beginners as they try to depict massed foliage, individual
branches and trunks of varying thickness.*

Typical problems

Remember, the colors of the
leaves and trunks may not be
as obvious when viewed from
a distance as they are when
placed in the middle ground
or foreground.

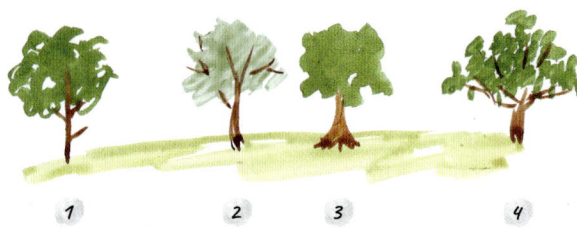

1. *Interpreted as scribble of
paint; too narrow at base*

2. *Diagonally applied strokes
with no regard for form;
branches do not join trunk*

3. *'Square' blob; base too
wide for narrow trunk*

4. *Unrelated blobs of paint;
lacking in structure*

Sketchbook drawings

Make preliminary drawings to
experiment with composition. In
the first drawing we see the view
through an opening between
bushes or hedgerows – almost as if
the composition has a natural frame,
that can be used in a painting.

In the second drawing
(below), we observe the
distant view through
sparse foliage but the
composition is not
contained and appears
to stretch away without
hindrance on either side.

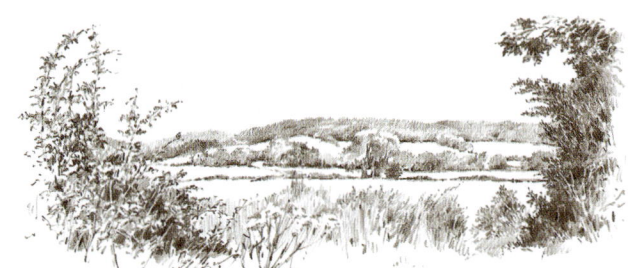

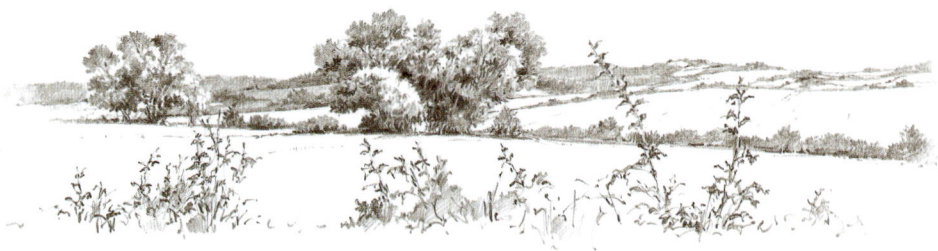

Solutions

Wet into wet

This technique uses the dampness of the paper surface to spread the first application of pigment. Make sure that you allow this to spread and dry enough to be able to control the later washes.

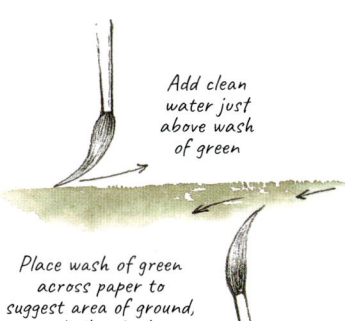

Add clean water just above wash of green

Place wash of green across paper to suggest area of ground, and allow to dry

Cut in crisply to create contrasts

Mix different green and gently touch damp surface, allowing it to spread and create tree foliage

As surface dries, add darker areas that can be controlled to suggest dark recesses

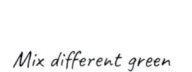

Blotting off

Taking up pigment and water with absorbent paper gives you a light base on which to drop in darker colors to produce a convincing impression of light and shade.

Paint trees and bushes in silhouette using dark, watery green

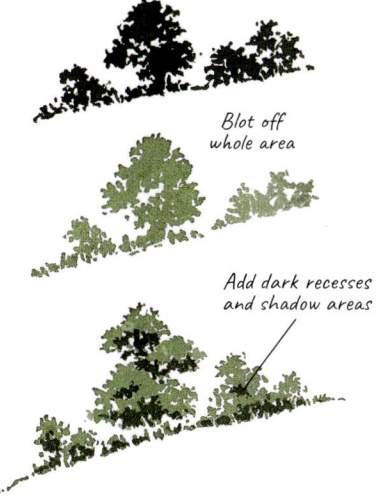

Blot off whole area

Add dark recesses and shadow areas

Building washes

After experimenting with wet into wet and blotting off first, try the method of building washes, one upon the other, allowing each to dry before the next is applied. This can also incorporate the other two methods by blotting off in some areas as necessary, and by allowing some 'bleeding' of the paint (wet into wet).

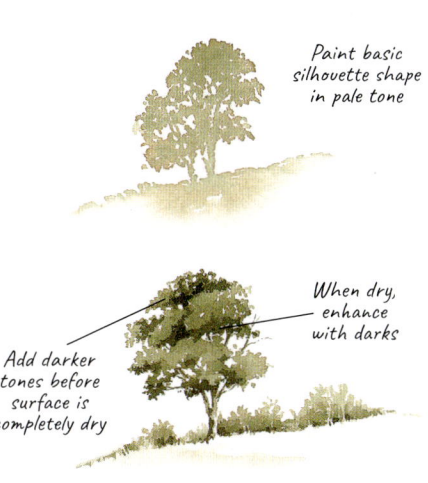

Paint basic silhouette shape in pale tone

When dry, enhance with darks

Add darker tones before surface is completely dry

Masses of Foliage

When painting masses of foliage, remember that you are not only trying to depict the prominent and obvious masses in the foreground but also those between and behind these masses.

Typical problems

One of the most common problems experienced by beginners is of how to give the impression of density – too much white paper is often exposed, almost like a halo around some images. There are also problems with repetition – leaves in a mass are often placed one after the other, at identical angles and in a formal, unnatural arrangement – and lack of structure, where leaves do not appear to be anchored in any way. These problems may be seen in this painting.

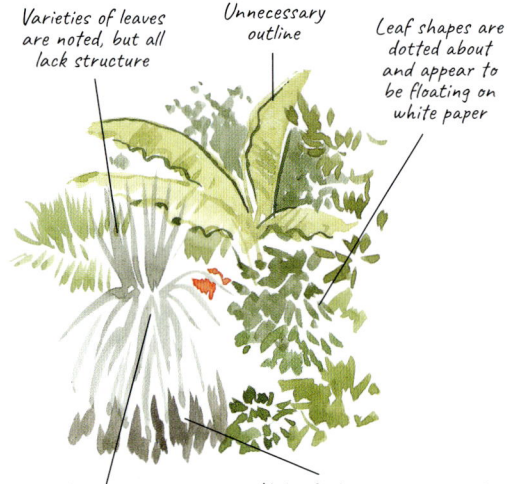

Varieties of leaves are noted, but all lack structure

Unnecessary outline

Leaf shapes are dotted about and appear to be floating on white paper

Positive shapes are depicted without any thought for negative shapes

Halo of white paper separates leaf from background, flattening image

Preliminary drawing

When observing a mass of foliage where different varieties are growing side by side, it is a good idea to concentrate on the largest, most obvious one first. Establish this then work away from the main mass, taking care to use any negative shapes between the leaves to place the leaves in correct relationship to each other. Note the amount of white paper – representing leaf shapes – that has been used in this study.

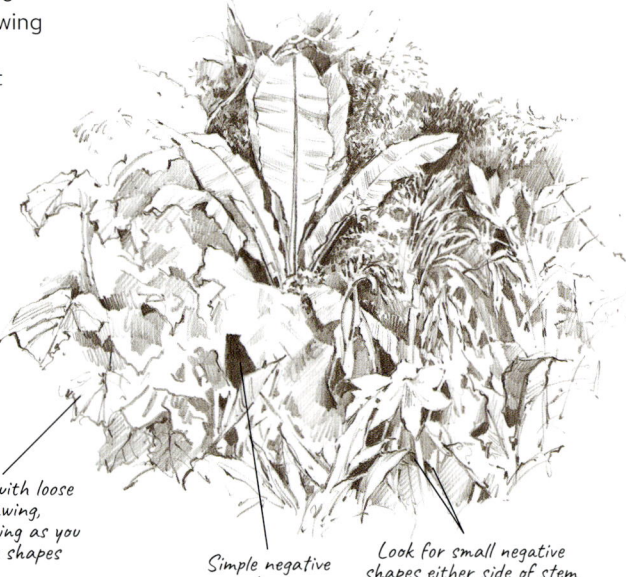

Start with loose drawing, tightening as you define shapes

Simple negative shape

Look for small negative shapes either side of stem

Solutions

Establishing the negative shapes

From closely observing where darker tones for the negative shapes between leaves and masses are depicted in the drawing, you will be able to create a medium-toned arrangement of these shapes. Practice a little study of one section to help you understand how this process works.

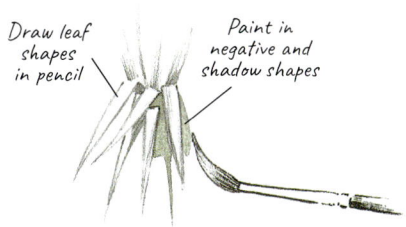

Draw leaf shapes in pencil

Paint in negative and shadow shapes

Developing the painting

The left-hand side of this study shows the 'undercoat' upon which the top layers are built. This comprises a series of negatives of various shapes and sizes, all in the same medium tone. Color-match the greens before you start painting rather than midway through, as you are unlikely to make a match in the later stages.

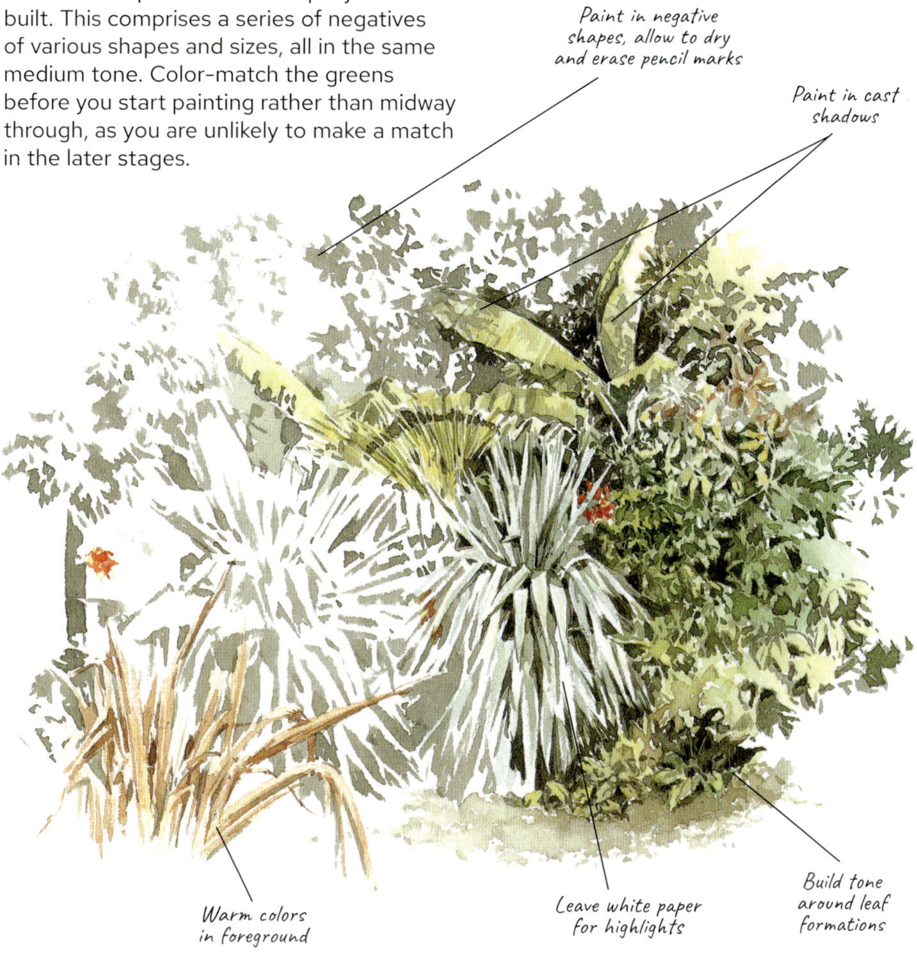

Paint in negative shapes, allow to dry and erase pencil marks

Paint in cast shadows

Warm colors in foreground

Leave white paper for highlights

Build tone around leaf formations

Individual Trees

Beginners can experience problems when trying to depict the structure of a single tree, especially when large areas of trunk and branches may be partially hidden by foliage masses. The structure then appears disjointed.

Typical problems

Another common problem is that of 'anchoring' the structure – the base of the trunk may be depicted as far too wide to give the correct proportions, or too narrow to support the structure above. Problems with treatment of the foliage occur when little thought is given to the direction of growth, resulting in a random placing of blobs of paint that do not represent leaves.

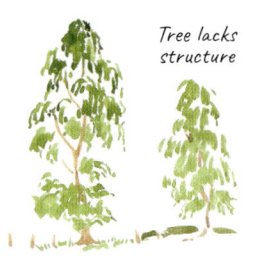

Tree lacks structure

Trailing leaves depicted with squiggle, not regarded as a mass

Foliage represented by blobs of paint

Using drawings to analyze problems

When you realize that something is wrong with the way that you have interpreted the subject, try to analyze the problem. Look at the edges of the tree silhouette and draw these as a flat pattern to start, then look within the mass and try to work out which areas appear light and which dark. Study the structure and leaf formations and determine the basic shape (silhouette) and growth pattern to familiarize yourself with the subject before starting to draw and paint.

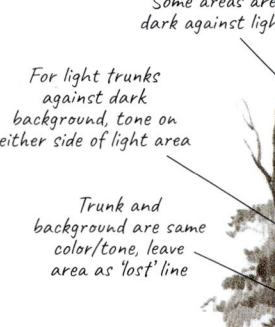

Some areas are dark against light

For light trunks against dark background, tone on either side of light area

Trunk and background are same color/tone, leave area as 'lost' line

Place darkest dark against lightest light for maximum contrast

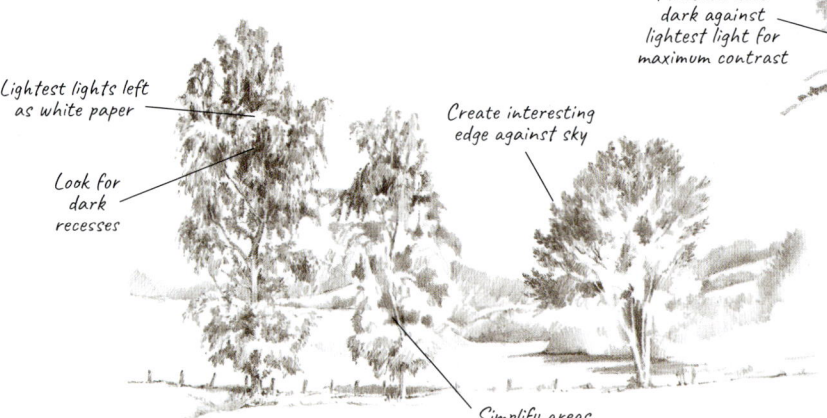

Lightest lights left as white paper

Look for dark recesses

Create interesting edge against sky

Simplify areas

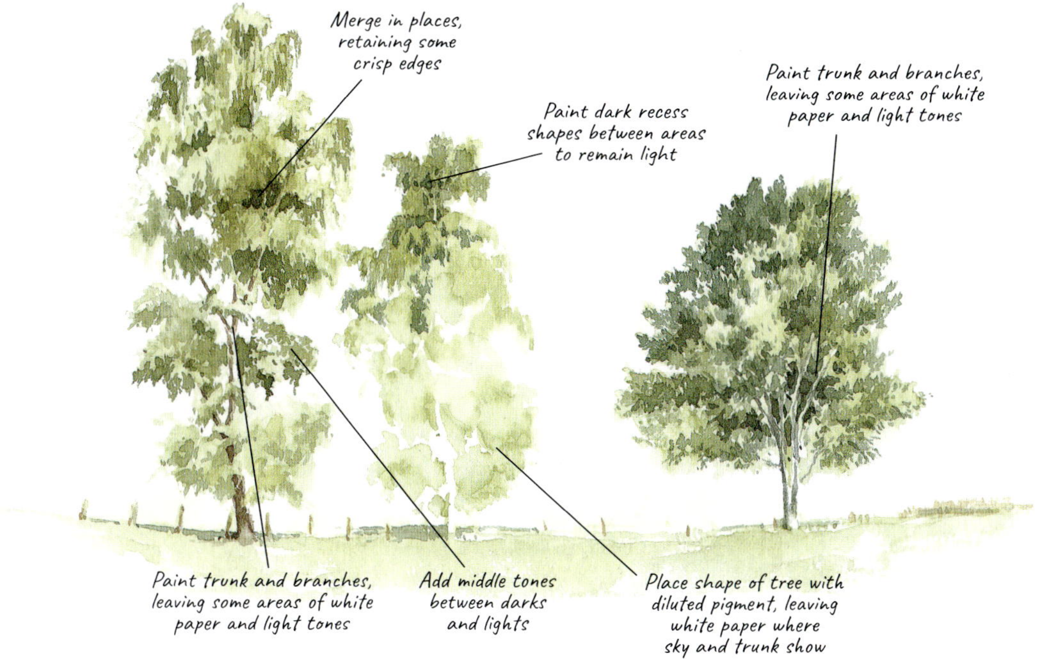

Merge in places,
retaining some
crisp edges

Paint dark recess
shapes between areas
to remain light

Paint trunk and branches,
leaving some areas of white
paper and light tones

Paint trunk and branches,
leaving some areas of white
paper and light tones

Add middle tones
between darks
and lights

Place shape of tree with
diluted pigment, leaving
white paper where
sky and trunk show

Solutions

Working diagrammatically

You will be well on the way to solving many of your tree painting problems if you approach some of your drawings in a diagrammatic way, and when you start painting, do so in stages, as this will enable you to be in control every step of the way. Remember that drawing in a 'painterly' way and painting in watercolor are very similar in approach. You need to use the white paper as part of the drawing/painting, so plan in advance which areas you intend to leave white or as light tones.

Basic stages

Here, the diagrammatic method is simplified to two basic stages. Look at a tree with a similar foliage mass silhouette to that shown in the first stage study and close your eyes a little, trying to see where dark masses show within the shape, as in the second stage study. The pale wash areas represent leaf masses touched by sunlight, and the dark shapes represent masses within shadow areas.

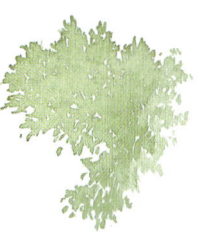

Stage 1: Paint first pale
color as silhouette block,
and allow to dry

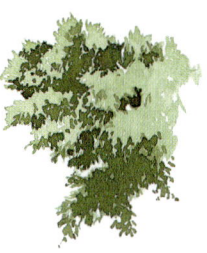

Stage 2: Paint in dark
recesses and shadow areas

TREES AND FOLIAGE

Leaf Shapes and Textures

By taking a detailed approach, learn to really look at subjects and be fully aware of their unique structure and form. As drawing and painting are so closely related, you can combine the two in one study.

Typical problems

One of the problems experienced by beginners with regard to detailed interpretations is that they may be too heavy-handed and this is not helped by the fact that often the pencil used is not sharp enough, or the brush does not have a sharp enough point for delicacy. Typical mistakes often made are seen in the illustrations to the right.

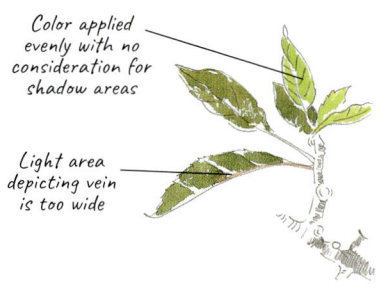

Color applied evenly with no consideration for shadow areas

Light area depicting vein is too wide

Drawing into paint

The illustration below shows leaves in relation to fruit, contrasting the busy interpretation of the leaves with the simple, smooth surface that is found on apples. You can see pencilwork on its own and areas of pure paint, but it is also interesting to carry one into the other and draw over your watercolor to add fine detail.

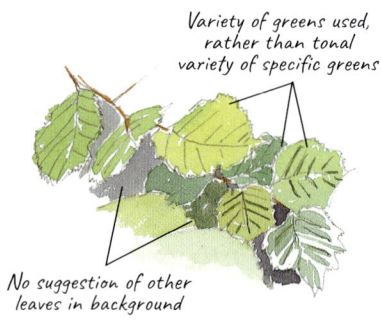

Variety of greens used, rather than tonal variety of specific greens

No suggestion of other leaves in background

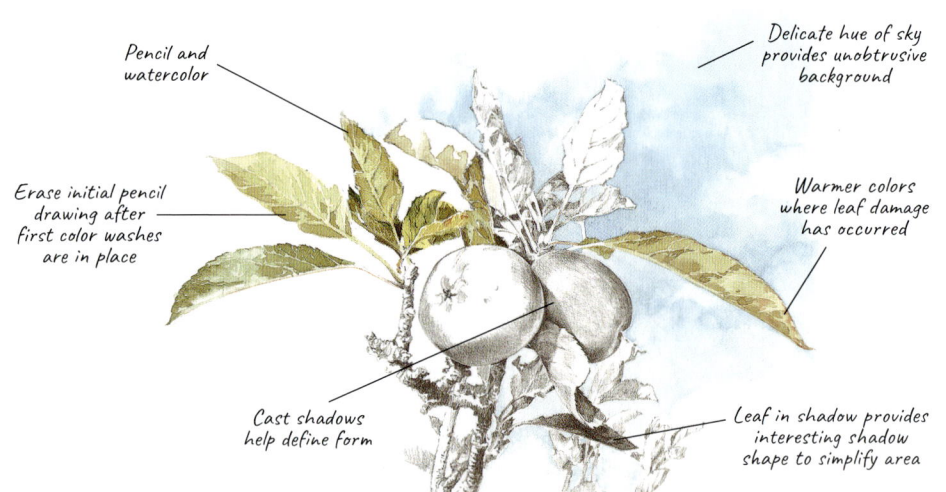

Pencil and watercolor

Delicate hue of sky provides unobtrusive background

Erase initial pencil drawing after first color washes are in place

Warmer colors where leaf damage has occurred

Cast shadows help define form

Leaf in shadow provides interesting shadow shape to simplify area

Solutions

Complementary combinations

This study combines watercolor pencil and watercolor, with the former dissolving into the latter and becoming lost as the watercolor washes take over. For this type of detailed work, a smoother surface paper is more suitable than some of the textured or rough varieties.

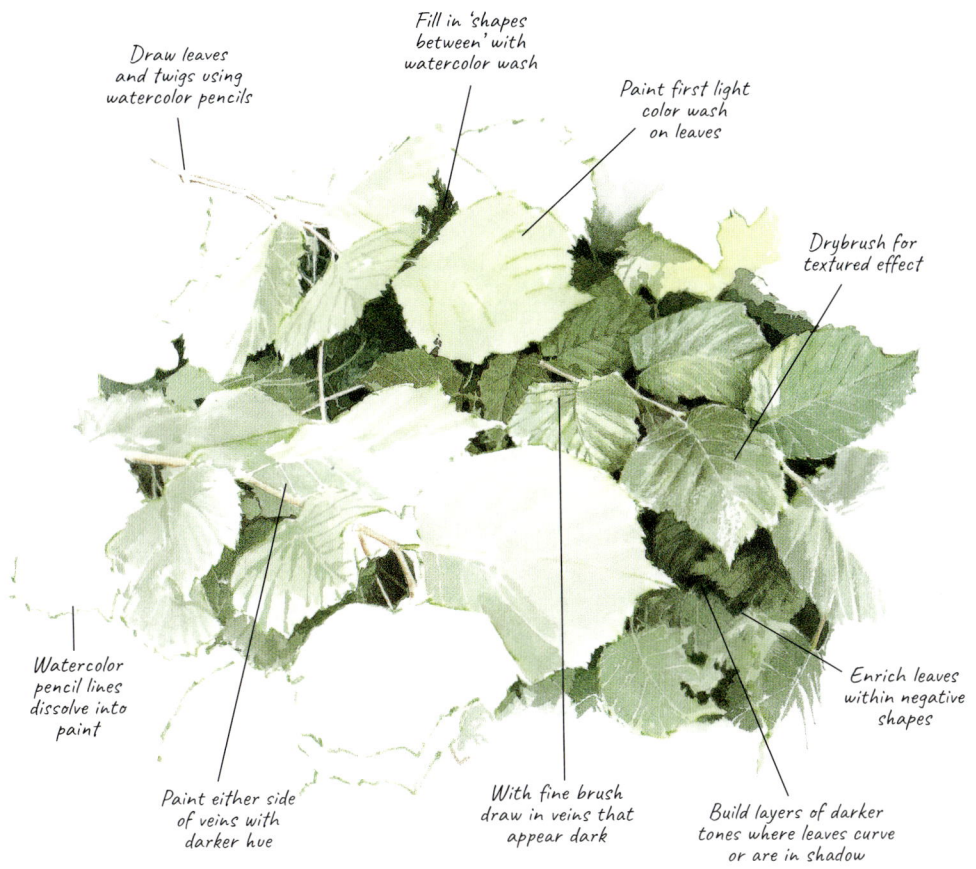

Fill in 'shapes between' with watercolor wash

Draw leaves and twigs using watercolor pencils

Paint first light color wash on leaves

Drybrush for textured effect

Watercolor pencil lines dissolve into paint

Enrich leaves within negative shapes

Paint either side of veins with darker hue

With fine brush draw in veins that appear dark

Build layers of darker tones where leaves curve or are in shadow

Bark Texture

The two obvious basic directions for bark texture – horizontal around the form, and vertical marks – have numerous variations (depending on the tree species) and can also play host to other textures.

Typical problems

The interesting contrasts of rough bark texture against smoother surfaced growths within a recess, provide opportunities for the inclusion of rich darks, resulting in full use of the tonal scale. One beginner's problem is how to use tones to full advantage – and an abundance of white paper, with a few dark blocks and squiggles, can be the result.

Put your thoughts on paper

You can approach these problems diagrammatically. For example, look at an area of tree bark directly in front of you and determine which texture line is exactly horizontal (on your eye level); notice when you raise your eyes slightly (above eye level) the bark texture lines curve downward and when you lower your gaze they sweep upward. This can be drawn as an arrow or series of arrows.

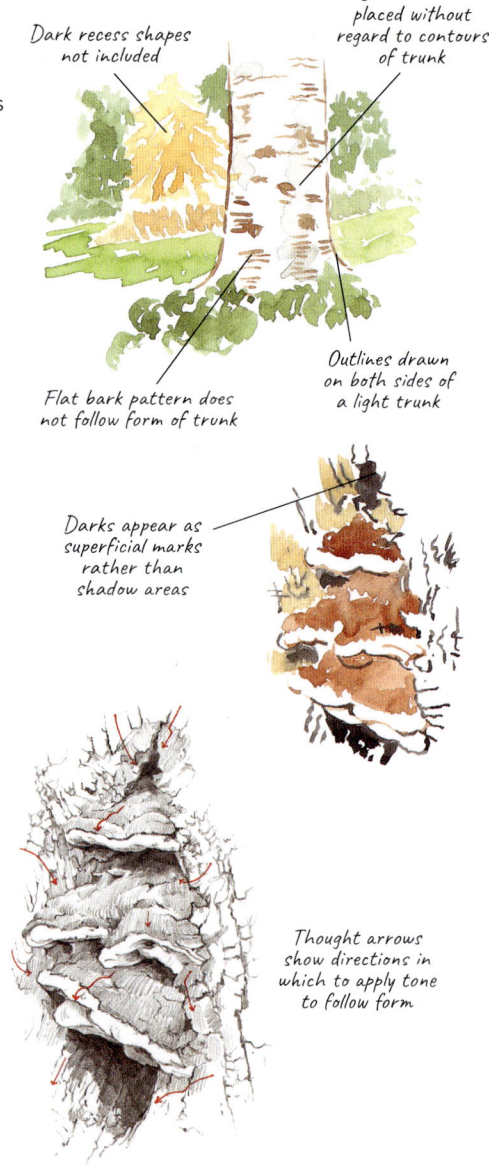

Shadow area placed without regard to contours of trunk

Dark recess shapes not included

Outlines drawn on both sides of a light trunk

Flat bark pattern does not follow form of trunk

Darks appear as superficial marks rather than shadow areas

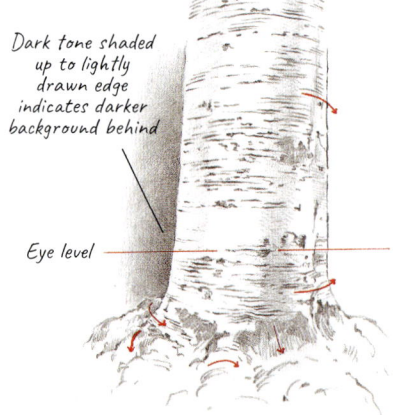

Dark tone shaded up to lightly drawn edge indicates darker background behind

Eye level

Thought arrows show directions in which to apply tone to follow form

Solutions

Contrasting bark textures

Here, a detailed, botanical-style illustration – where precision is of great importance – is contrasted with a looser style, used to depict a rough-textured bark with fungal growths (see below). A detailed style of drawing and painting encourages close observation and is best used to make precise marks depicting a species that should not be mistaken for another.

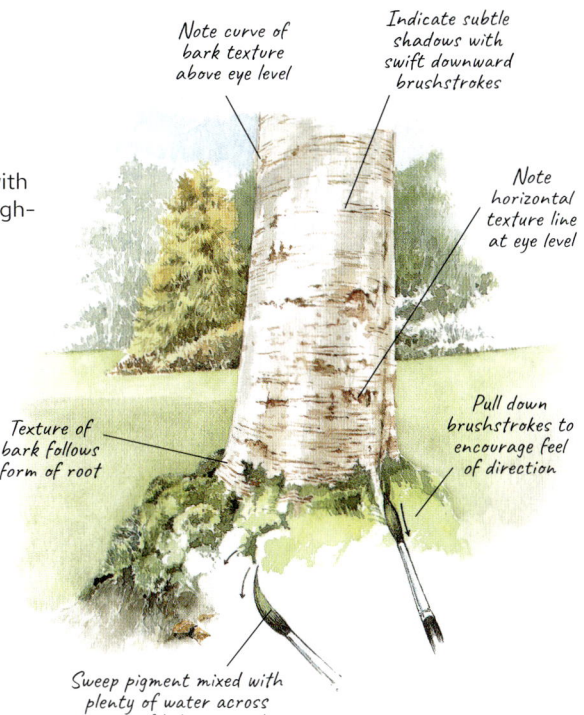

Note curve of bark texture above eye level

Indicate subtle shadows with swift downward brushstrokes

Note horizontal texture line at eye level

Texture of bark follows form of root

Pull down brushstrokes to encourage feel of direction

Sweep pigment mixed with plenty of water across areas of lichen growth

Using a loose approach

Rough-textured bark with interesting fungal growths can be depicted with a loose style of painting. This does not mean that it should be any less carefully observed, however, rather that observation should take in the fact that this surface possesses deep recesses with growths coming toward us.

Establish the darker recess, and the areas that are to remain as white paper, by painting around the shapes in medium tone. Slowly build up the intensity of tone and color, wash upon wash, enhancing the fine details by enriching tonal contrasts (darkening the darks against much lighter areas) and drawing shadow lines with the brush.

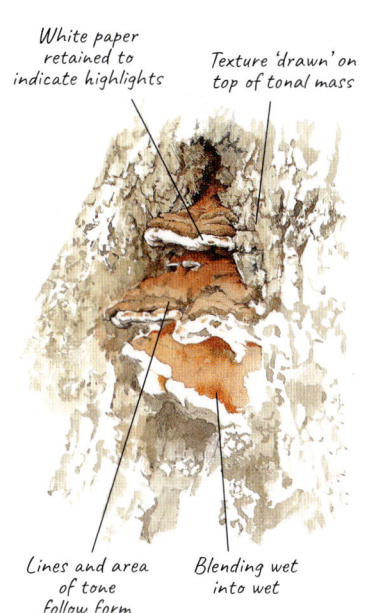

White paper retained to indicate highlights

Texture 'drawn' on top of tonal mass

Lines and area of tone follow form

Blending wet into wet

FLOWERS
Basic Brushstrokes

These exercises are designed to help you place leaf, petal and stem strokes with confidence – whether on detailed specimens or in a freely painted group. Here the basic strokes are shown in isolation.

One-stroke shape

The basic 'touch, press as you travel, lift and twist' stroke seen in Materials and Techniques: Getting to Know Your Brushes. The first stroke is upward, the second downward.

Short, curved strokes

A series of curved strokes, indicated by arrows, follows one after the other. Load the brush with plenty of water and pigment.

One-stroke 'press and lift' line

Use a standard working position to make a 'touch/travel, press to expand, then lift' stroke.

Touch tip of brush vertical to paper and angle end away from you

With brush position a little more vertical than normal, describe strokes using directional application

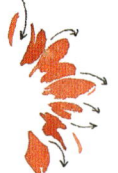

Place another stroke below, leaving thin strip of untouched paper between

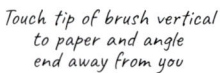

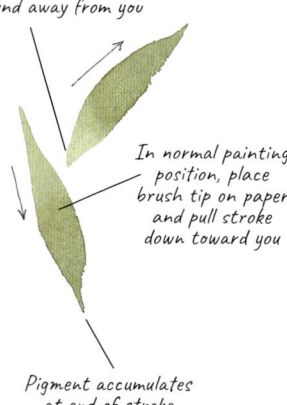

In normal painting position, place brush tip on paper and pull stroke down toward you

Positive and negative silhouettes

Use the normal painting position for these three exercises.

Pigment accumulates at end of stroke away from starting point

Touch tip of brush placed vertical to paper and angle end away from you

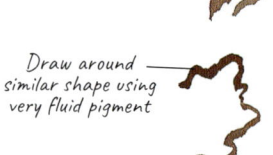

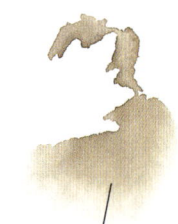

Draw around similar shape using very fluid pigment

While still wet, add clean water to blend pigment away from original outline

Developing Brushstrokes

These four exercises develop the basic brushstrokes within a painting.
Painted on a rough-surfaced paper, you should be able to achieve fine lines
if you use a good-quality brush that enables you to work with a fine point.

Leafy stem *(1)*

This is an extension of the one-stroke shape exercise (the 'touch, press as you travel and twist as you lift' stroke).

Mass of petals *(2)*

This is an extension of the short, curved strokes exercise. Remember the basic flower shape as you work.

One-stroke blending *(3)*

This is an extension of the one-stroke 'press and lift' line exercise. Note that a darker hue has been touched against a still wet area to produce a darker blended area.

Basic backgrounds *(4)*

This is an extension of the positive and negative silhouettes exercises.

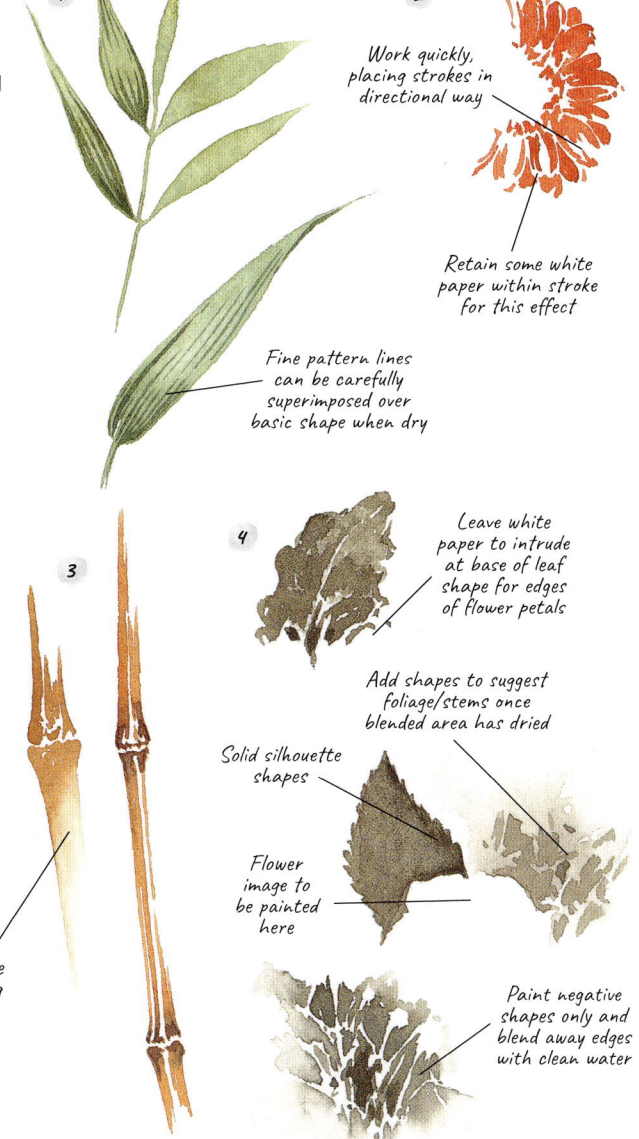

1

2

Work quickly, placing strokes in directional way

Retain some white paper within stroke for this effect

Fine pattern lines can be carefully superimposed over basic shape when dry

3

4

Leave white paper to intrude at base of leaf shape for edges of flower petals

Add shapes to suggest foliage/stems once blended area has dried

Solid silhouette shapes

Flower image to be painted here

Add clean water for pale color blending

Paint negative shapes only and blend away edges with clean water

Simple Shapes

The strong delicacy of lilies, where crisp crinkled edges of tapering petals can be clearly seen against the rich dark leaf shapes, provides a contrast to the more fragile rose seen in More Complex Shapes.

Typical problems

Here, simple trumpet shapes burst open to display their array of stamen around the central pistil, but it is this very arrangement that can prove to be problematic for beginners.

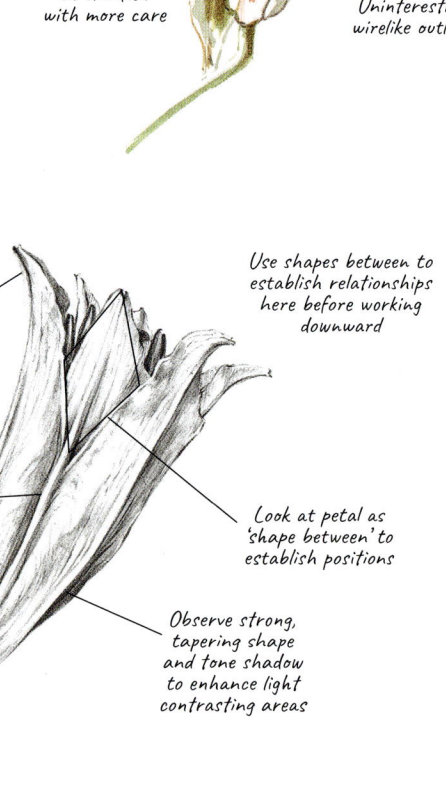

Area needs to be clarified with more care

Uninteresting, wirelike outlines

Beginning with a bud

This detailed drawing of a lily bud demonstrates how close observation can teach you much about structure and relationships. By drawing a single bud first you can begin to understand how the petals eventually open up to reveal the glory within.

Use shapes between to establish relationships here before working downward

Note slight correction where adjustment was made

Use long, sweeping strokes to position main vein

Look at petal as 'shape between' to establish positions

Observe strong, tapering shape and tone shadow to enhance light contrasting areas

Stem narrows here after being wider where it supports flower

Solutions

From drawing to painting

The main shapes in this study were drawn in both graphite and watercolor pencils on a rough-surfaced paper before watercolor was added. The combination works well and enhances blending techniques.

Note that the lower area demonstrates the first stages of the painting, where more emphasis is placed upon the background (negative) shapes to provide form to the lighter flowers.

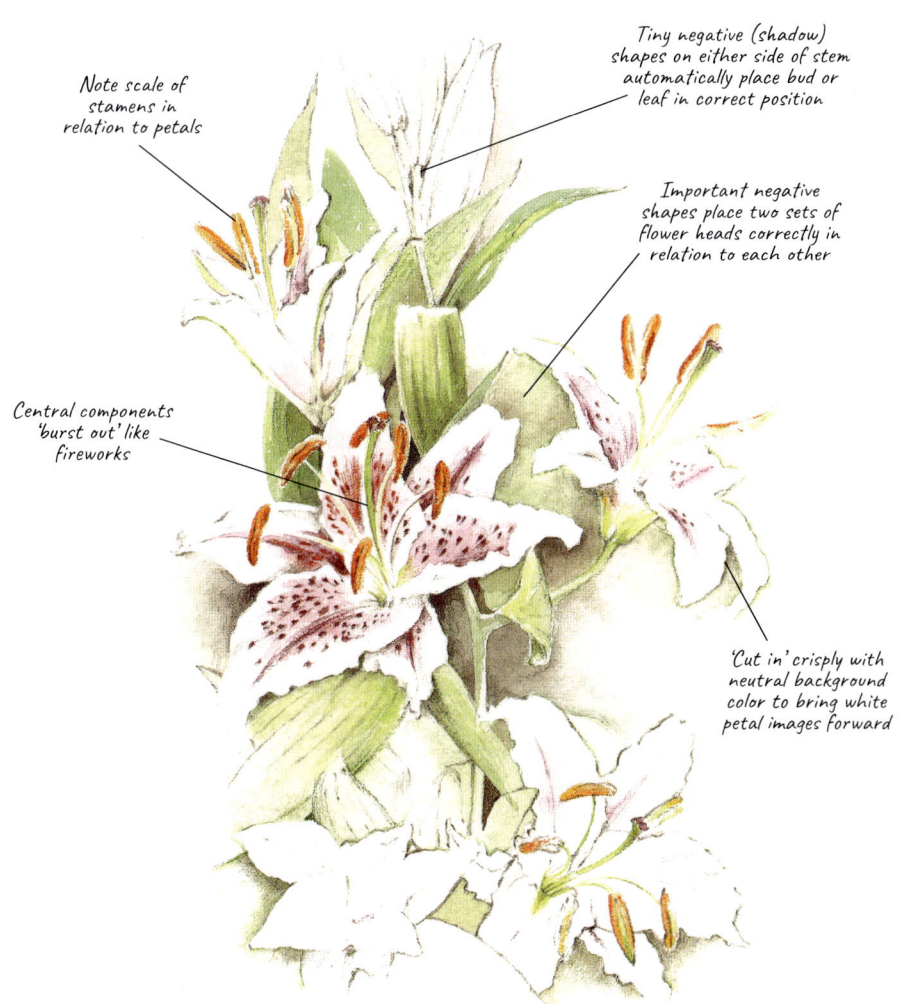

Note scale of stamens in relation to petals

Tiny negative (shadow) shapes on either side of stem automatically place bud or leaf in correct position

Important negative shapes place two sets of flower heads correctly in relation to each other

Central components 'burst out' like fireworks

'Cut in' crisply with neutral background color to bring white petal images forward

More Complex Shapes

*Delicate flowers can be painted in a free style, but
they will still rely on close observation and drawing
ability if your paintings are to be convincing.*

Typical problems

When painting pale colors, beginners
often resort to outlining petals or
placing contrasting colors behind
the image. Both of these methods
are acceptable when they are used
correctly, but they need to be applied
carefully. In this painting, the artist
has been rather heavy-handed for
such a delicate subject – a miniature
rose with fine, detailed leaves and
petals.

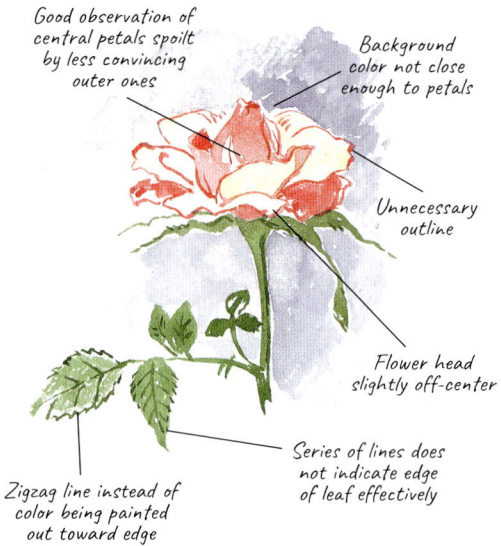

*Good observation of
central petals spoilt
by less convincing
outer ones*

*Background
color not close
enough to petals*

*Unnecessary
outline*

*Flower head
slightly off-center*

*Series of lines does
not indicate edge
of leaf effectively*

*Zigzag line instead of
color being painted
out toward edge*

Diagrammatic drawing

This sketch of a rose is
not intended as a finished
drawing but rather as a
finding-out exercise. The
lines around the edges have
been enhanced more than
usual, to help you understand
the shapes and reinforce your
knowledge prior to painting.

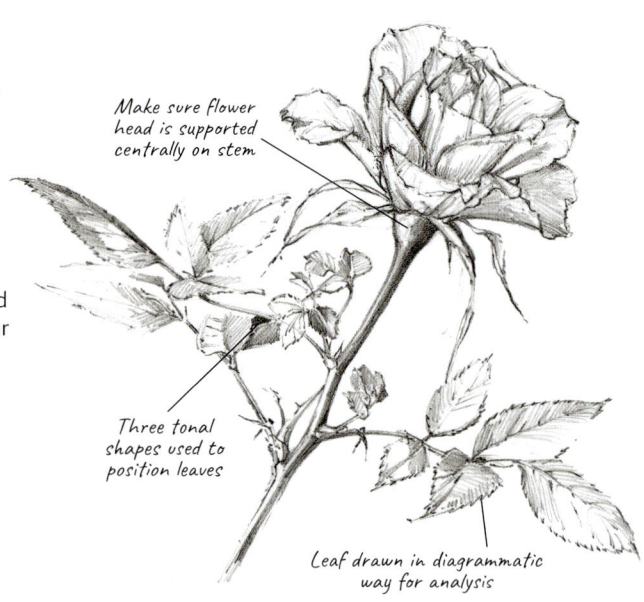

*Make sure flower
head is supported
centrally on stem*

*Three tonal
shapes used to
position leaves*

*Leaf drawn in diagrammatic
way for analysis*

Solutions

Color and form

Saunders Waterford 300gsm (140lb) Not paper was used for this subject, as it encourages free application while allowing fine detail to be achieved. In addition, gentle blending of background colors, that 'cut in' to describe the form, can help you to capture the essence of a rose.

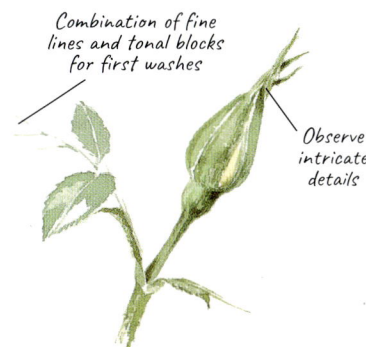

Combination of fine lines and tonal blocks for first washes

Observe intricate details

Start with tiny bud and observe simple shapes

Place dark leaf image behind light petal

Incorporate delicate background drawing with graphite pencil

'Cut in' behind light petal with background color and gently blend into white paper using clean water

Blend background color into leaf shape

Gently apply neutral background color to suggest leaf shapes

Different viewpoints

When painting your subject, observe the rose from various angles with an eye for the shapes of color and tonal blocks, rather than thinking of outlines.

Line and tone working together within form

Palm and Bamboo Types

The smooth surface of long, tapered leaves, particularly those of palms or bamboo types, comes as a contrast to the freely applied brushstrokes on the previous pages. Tradescantia leaves, although shorter, require similar treatment – long, sweeping brushstrokes from tip to base or vice versa. The studies on this page have been treated in a tighter, more controlled way, as it is the long slender lines that are important.

Typical problems

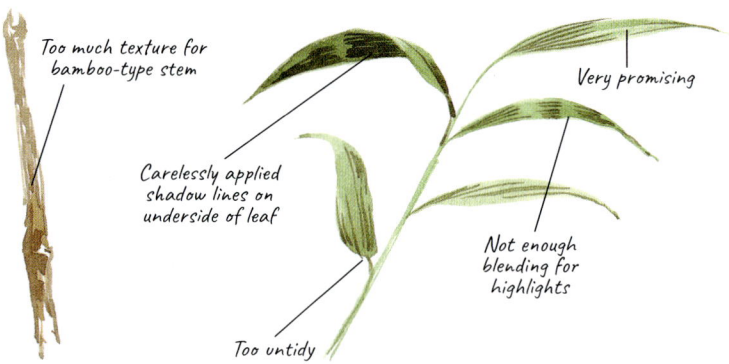

Too much texture for bamboo-type stem

Carelessly applied shadow lines on underside of leaf

Too untidy

Very promising

Not enough blending for highlights

Varied pressure drawing

Random, long leaf exercises give you the opportunity to practice 'press and lift' strokes with your pencil prior to starting brushstroke work, helping you learn how to create highlights.

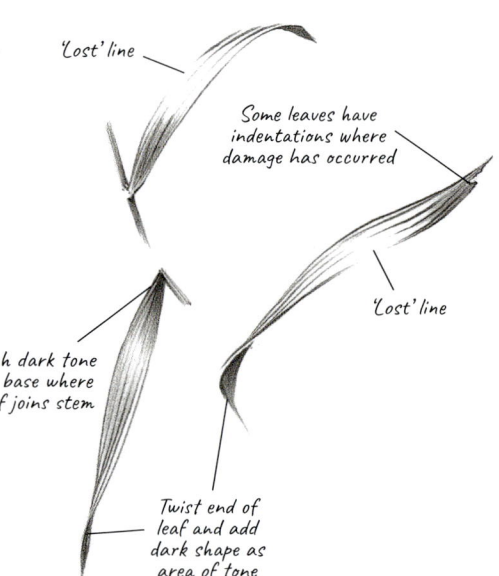

'Lost' line

Some leaves have indentations where damage has occurred

'Lost' line

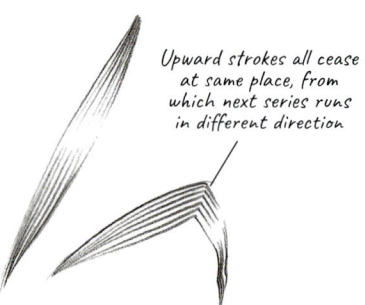

Upward strokes all cease at same place, from which next series runs in different direction

Rich dark tone at base where leaf joins stem

Twist end of leaf and add dark shape as area of tone

Solutions

Lines on leaves *(1)*

Tinted Bockingford paper is ideal for the basic sweeping strokes and thin lines of pattern in the leaves' surface – the paint flows on easily for the wider leaf shape, yet narrow lines can be just as successfully achieved using a fine brush for the delicate points on long, tapering leaves. The surface responds well to blending and, as it is tinted, background washes merge well into the tint.

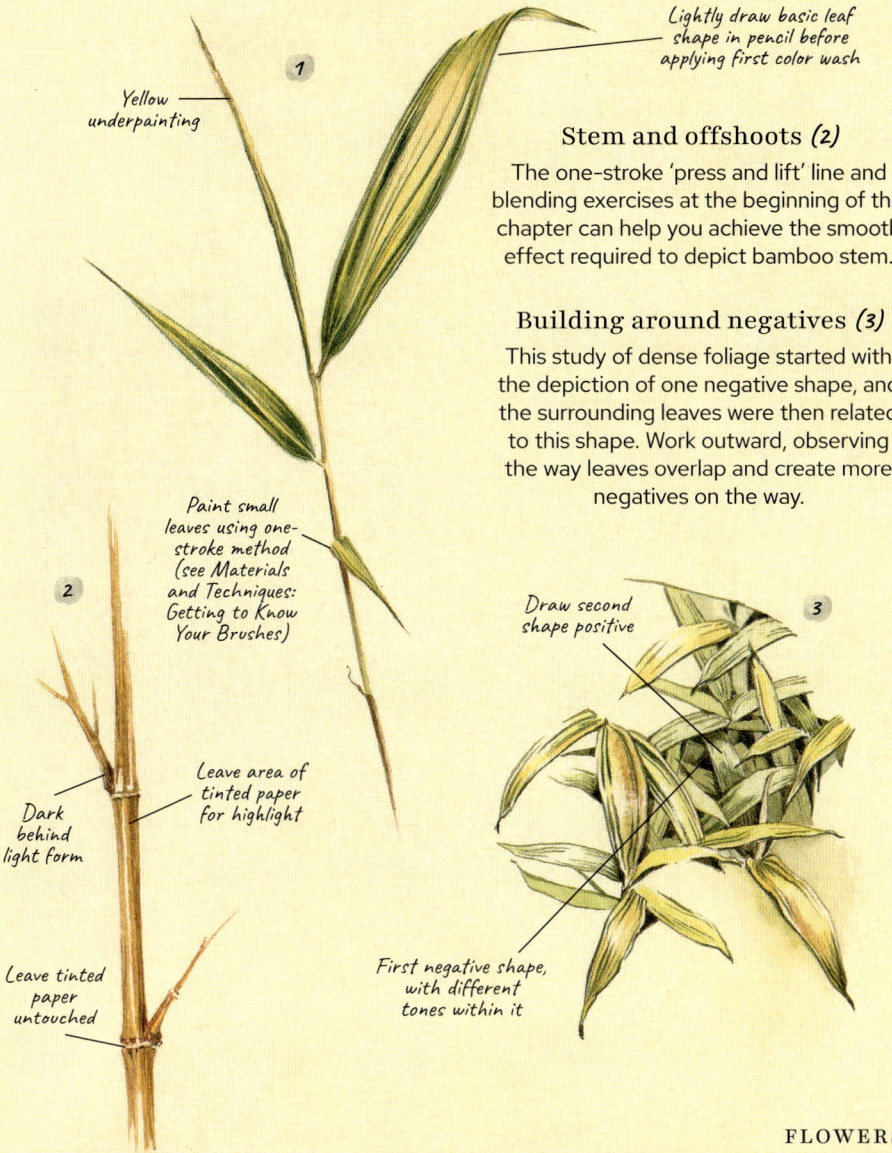

Lightly draw basic leaf shape in pencil before applying first color wash

Yellow underpainting

Stem and offshoots *(2)*

The one-stroke 'press and lift' line and blending exercises at the beginning of this chapter can help you achieve the smooth effect required to depict bamboo stem.

Building around negatives *(3)*

This study of dense foliage started with the depiction of one negative shape, and the surrounding leaves were then related to this shape. Work outward, observing the way leaves overlap and create more negatives on the way.

Paint small leaves using one-stroke method (see Materials and Techniques: Getting to Know Your Brushes)

Draw second shape positive

Dark behind light form

Leave area of tinted paper for highlight

Leave tinted paper untouched

First negative shape, with different tones within it

Bouquets

A floral bouquet supplies a profusion of brightly colored flower heads set against rich greenery, and this presents a range of challenges to capture their inevitable variety.

Typical problems

Light forms are thrown forward, creating crisp contrasts that rely upon a juxtaposition of interesting shapes to create the composition, and masses of stems and leaves behind the main flower heads provide contrasts of color, tone and form. Beginners are often unsure how to depict this greenery, as well as the intricate petals of the blooms.

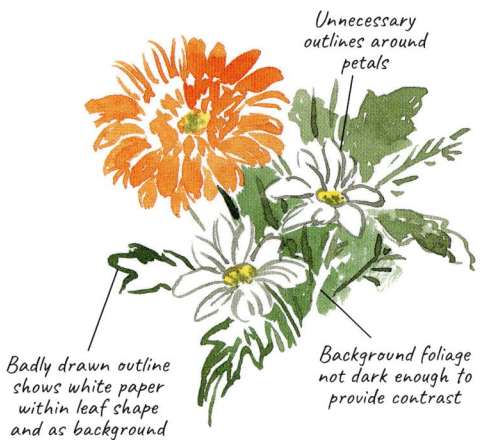

Unnecessary outlines around petals

Badly drawn outline shows white paper within leaf shape and as background

Background foliage not dark enough to provide contrast

Drawing the details

It is a good idea to familiarize yourself with the structure of the flower heads – this can be achieved by drawing details in order to analyze the forms. You can choose to draw the individual leaves and petals, or one or two in relation to each other.

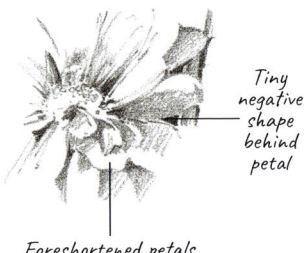

Tiny negative shape behind petal

Foreshortened petals

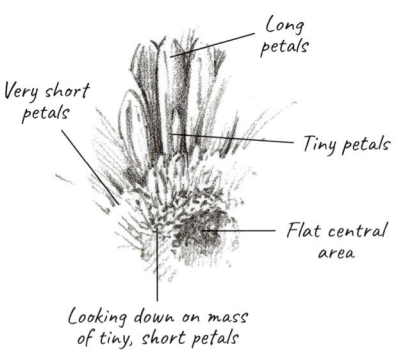

Long petals

Very short petals

Tiny petals

Flat central area

Looking down on mass of tiny, short petals

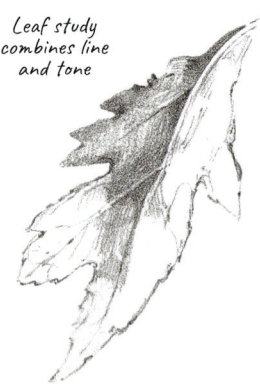

Leaf study combines line and tone

Solutions

Working from within

An exercise that encourages close observation is that of working from within a group of flowers, rather than arranging the composition as shapes around a central area or drawing them at random. Start with a single flower head and relate another to it. Add dark leaves and shadow shapes behind, and continue to work outward and away from the initial shapes. Saunders Waterford 300gsm (140lb) Not paper is ideal for this gentle blending technique.

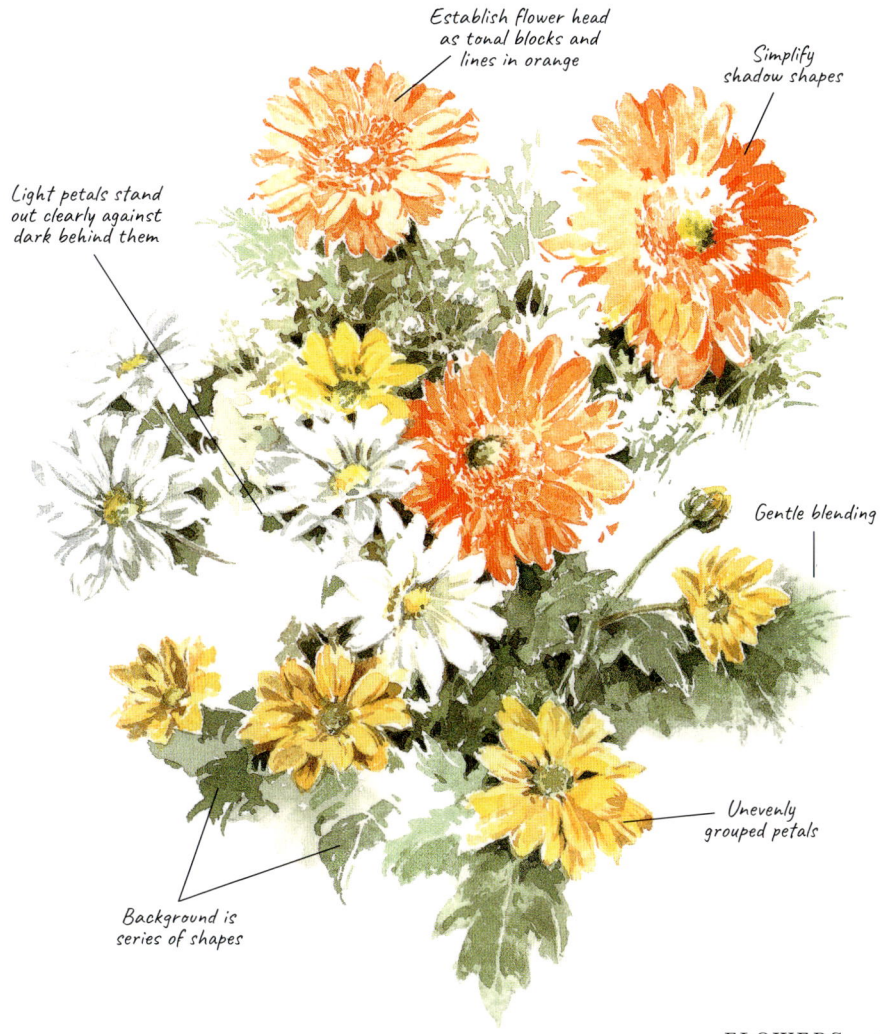

Establish flower head as tonal blocks and lines in orange

Simplify shadow shapes

Light petals stand out clearly against dark behind them

Gentle blending

Unevenly grouped petals

Background is series of shapes

Garden Scenes

*A garden scene, with flowers and foliage creating a 'busy' painting,
can benefit from the introduction of animal life. But its placement
and coloration can be key to the success of your work.*

Typical problems

It is important to consider both the
composition of the painting when
placing the animal subject and how
to make it clearly visible among the
foliage. These problems have arisen
in this painting, where the gray tabby
cat is 'lost' and not an obvious focal
point as intended.

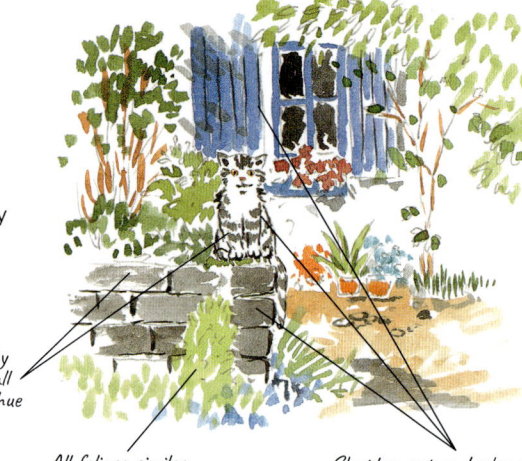

Gray of tabby
and stone wall
are of similar hue

All foliage similar
and appears
disjointed

Shutter, cat and edge of
wall all appear in line and
cut picture in two

Considering the cat

By changing the animal's
stance within the composition
you can break the line from
the shutter downward. You can
also increase the shadow area
behind the cat to bring its
form forward.

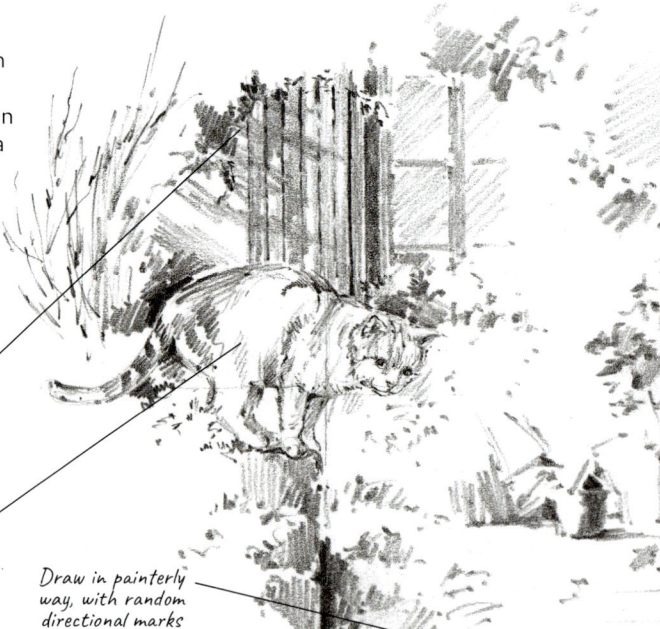

Include more intense
shadow shapes
to create strong
background

Leave part of cat as
white fur to simplify and
make form more obvious

Draw in painterly
way, with random
directional marks
suggesting background

Solutions

Improving the pictorial composition

You can make amendments throughout the picture, but often just one or two small changes can make all the difference. Here, deciding to change the cat's color to ginger and white, added to its new, animated and therefore more lively position, immediately improves both the composition and clarity of the painting.

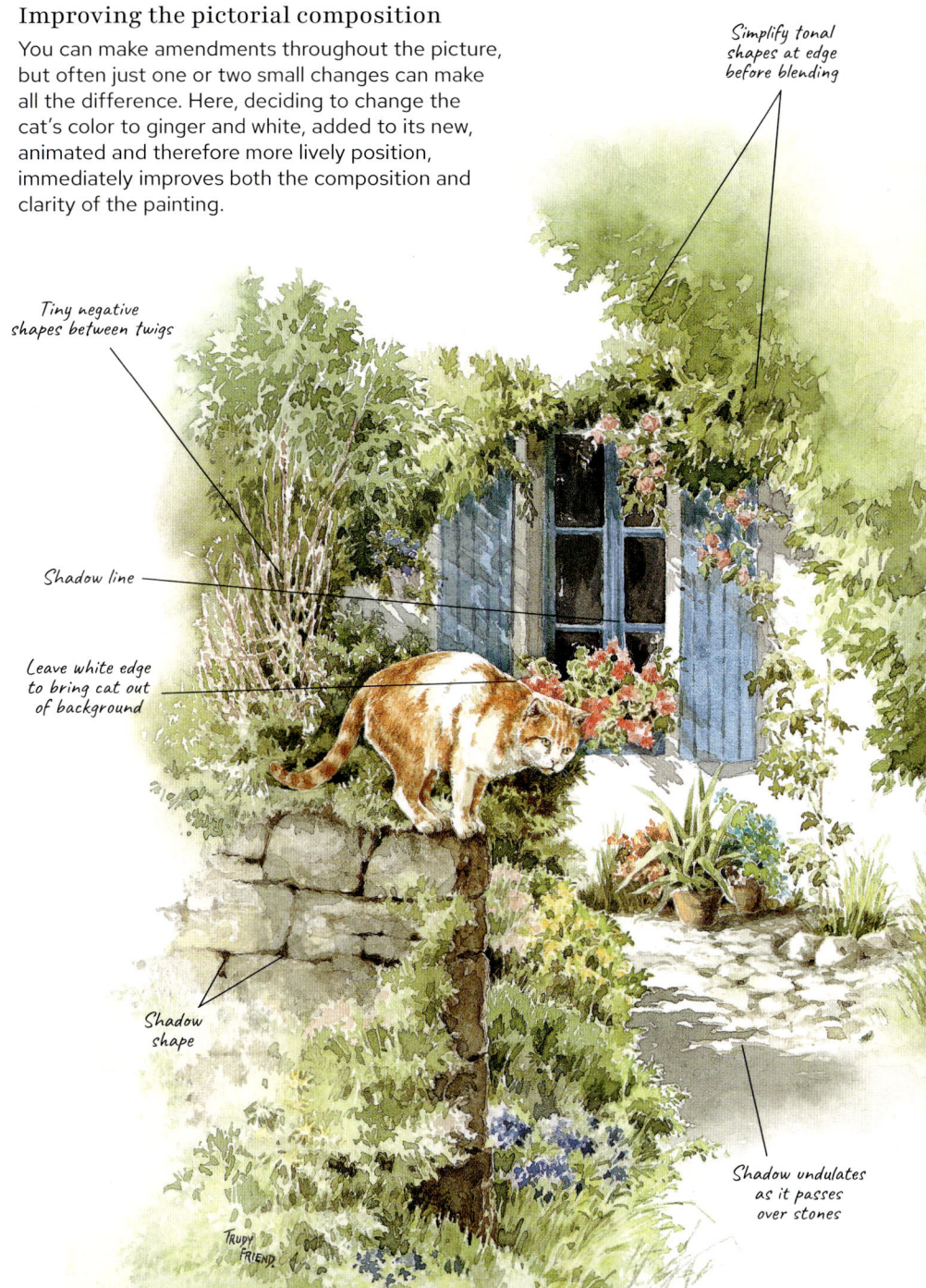

Simplify tonal shapes at edge before blending

Tiny negative shapes between twigs

Shadow line

Leave white edge to bring cat out of background

Shadow shape

Shadow undulates as it passes over stones

TRUDY
FRIEND

FRUIT AND VEGETABLES
Basic Brushstrokes

These exercises will help you to create textured effects for fruit and vegetables, with repetitious strokes for close texture and sweeping strokes for smoother surfaces.

'On your toes' painting position

This stroke pushes paint outward unevenly and is good for depicting the uneven, rough texture of citrus fruit skins.

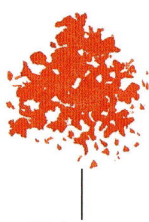

Make uneven blob and push paint outward, using texture of paper as guide

Add water to edges to blend and place tiny dots for indentations before blended area has fully dried

Place, sweep and curve stroke

This stroke, with the brush held at less of an angle, is suitable for depicting curved surfaces where shadow sides and highlights are required, for example on root vegetables such as carrots and parsnips. Note that some areas are solid color, with white paper cutting in. White (highlight) areas have contour lines drawn with a brush.

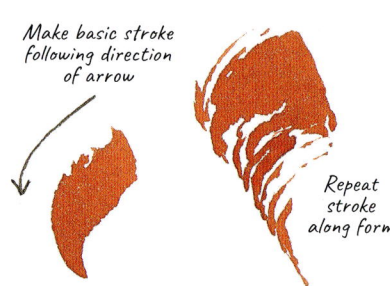

Make basic stroke following direction of arrow

Repeat stroke along form

Basic looped stroke

This looped stroke made in the standard writing position is suitable for depicting the fleshy, teardrop-shaped components of citrus fruit segments.

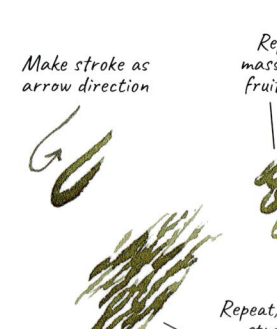

Make stroke as arrow direction

Repeat and mass for citrus fruit segments

Repeat, flattening strokes, for inside surface of bell pepper

Developing Brushstrokes

You can develop and adapt the basic brushstrokes for fruit and vegetable textures. Always study your subject closely before starting to paint, to establish brushstroke direction by following form and texture.

Citrus fruit skin *(1)*

Areas of highlight and shadow are required to give the impression of a 3D form. Building on the 'on your toes' exercise opposite, the edge of the fruit has been added, as well as the highlight positions and blending to dot in recesses.

Root vegetable texture *(2)*

With the place, sweep and curve stroke, this can be created easily within the sweep of the brushstrokes as they travel down the form, where white paper shows through pigment in places (particularly effective on a rough-surfaced paper).

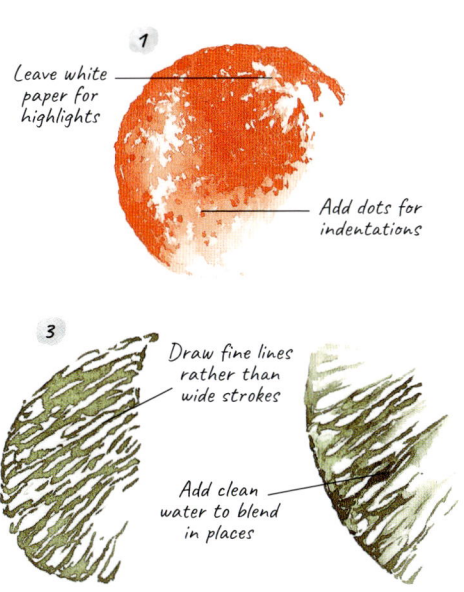

1

Leave white paper for highlights

Add dots for indentations

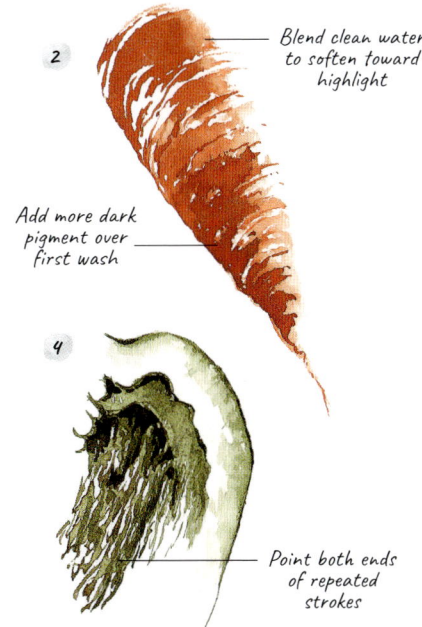

2

Blend clean water to soften toward highlight

Add more dark pigment over first wash

3

Draw fine lines rather than wide strokes

Add clean water to blend in places

4

Point both ends of repeated strokes

Internal segment highlights *(3)*

Repetitive, looped strokes form a mass to represent areas of highlight and shadow on a cut, flat surface of citrus (or side of separated segment). A more delicate interpretation of the place, sweep and curve stroke, it can be tightly looped.

Texture inside casing *(4)*

The inside casing of certain fruits, vegetables and in many cases nuts can receive the same treatment as demonstrated in the bell pepper example. This is another adaptation of the basic looped stroke.

Cross-Sections

You can build up your self-confidence by drawing and painting cross-sections of fruit and vegetables – these will present you with exciting, and sometimes surprising, patterns and textures.

Typical problems

A solution to many drawing and painting problems is to develop a deeper understanding and knowledge of your subject. For example, when observing the outer casing of a fruit or vegetable, it is sometimes difficult to imagine what lies within. Discovery leads to enlightenment, and this will help you to overcome many of the mistakes that beset beginners.

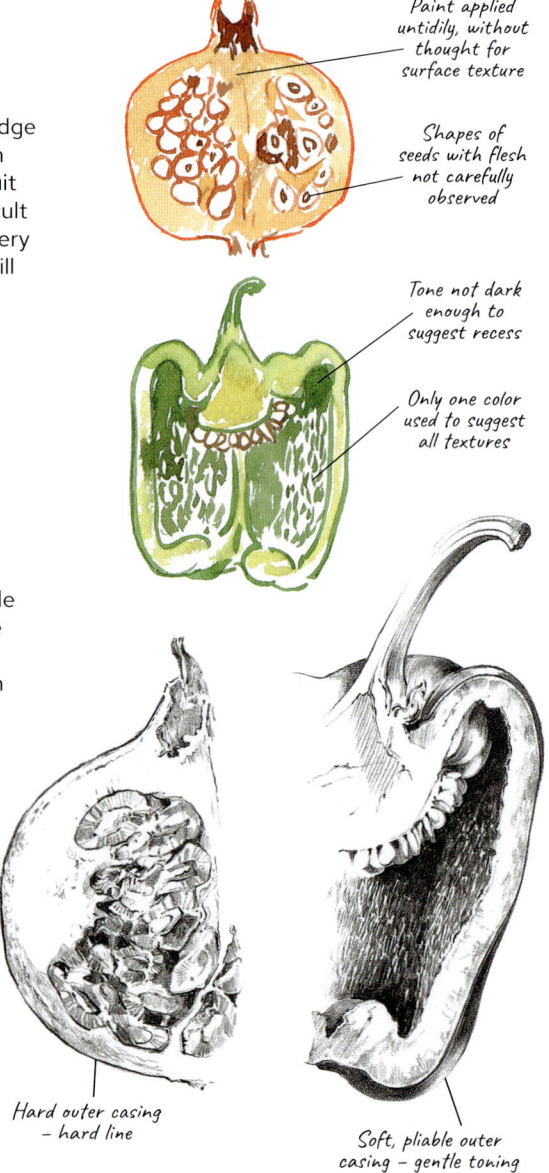

Paint applied untidily, without thought for surface texture

Shapes of seeds with flesh not carefully observed

Tone not dark enough to suggest recess

Only one color used to suggest all textures

Drawing the details

First draw a segment of a vegetable or fruit – such as the pomegranate on the left or the bell pepper (capsicum) on the right – and then note how the seeds are contained.

Hard outer casing – hard line

Soft, pliable outer casing – gentle toning

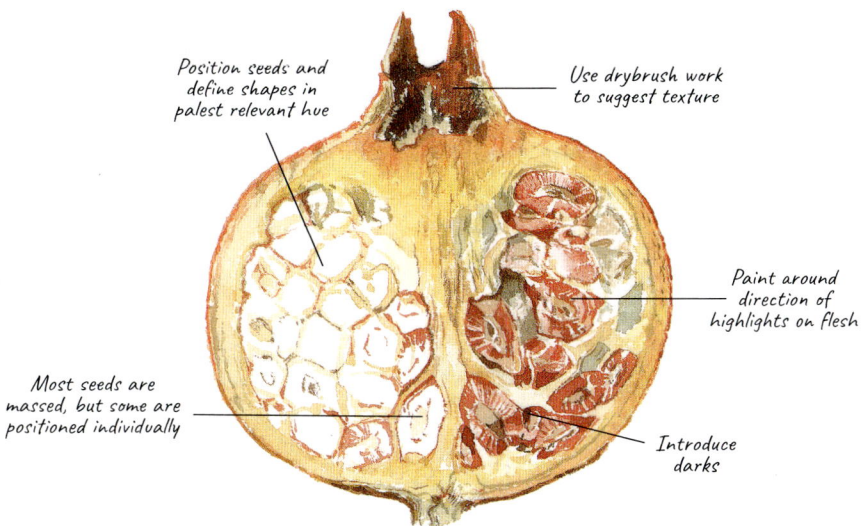

Position seeds and
define shapes in
palest relevant hue

Use drybrush work
to suggest texture

Paint around
direction of
highlights on flesh

Most seeds are
massed, but some are
positioned individually

Introduce
darks

Solutions

Pattern with texture – pomegranate

Be guided by weight before cutting fruit
in half. The solid feel of a pomegranate will
suggest the contents – numerous seeds
encased by flesh. The individual shapes
are dictated by the close proximity of the
neighboring ones, making interesting
patterns and textures. Note how the two
halves of this cross-section are different
in content and arrangement.

Hollow interior – bell pepper

The lighter weight of a bell pepper
suggests a hollow interior. The
uniformly shaped seeds cling to the
fleshy area at the base of the stem and
are surrounded by space.

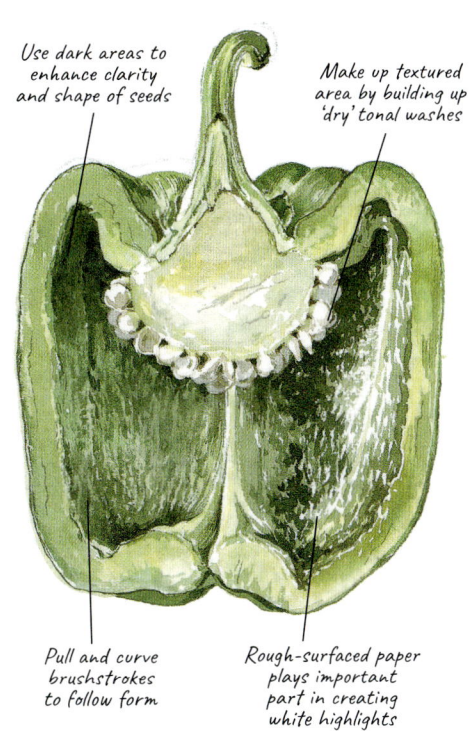

Use dark areas to
enhance clarity
and shape of seeds

Make up textured
area by building up
'dry' tonal washes

Pull and curve
brushstrokes
to follow form

Rough-surfaced paper
plays important
part in creating
white highlights

Three Dimensions

*Although you are inevitably working with a limited palette,
you also need to be sure you look for subtle color variations to
achieve a realistic rendition of the subject to be painted.*

Typical problems

The most common problem encountered
by beginners in drawing and painting fruit
and vegetables is creating something
that looks three-dimensional.

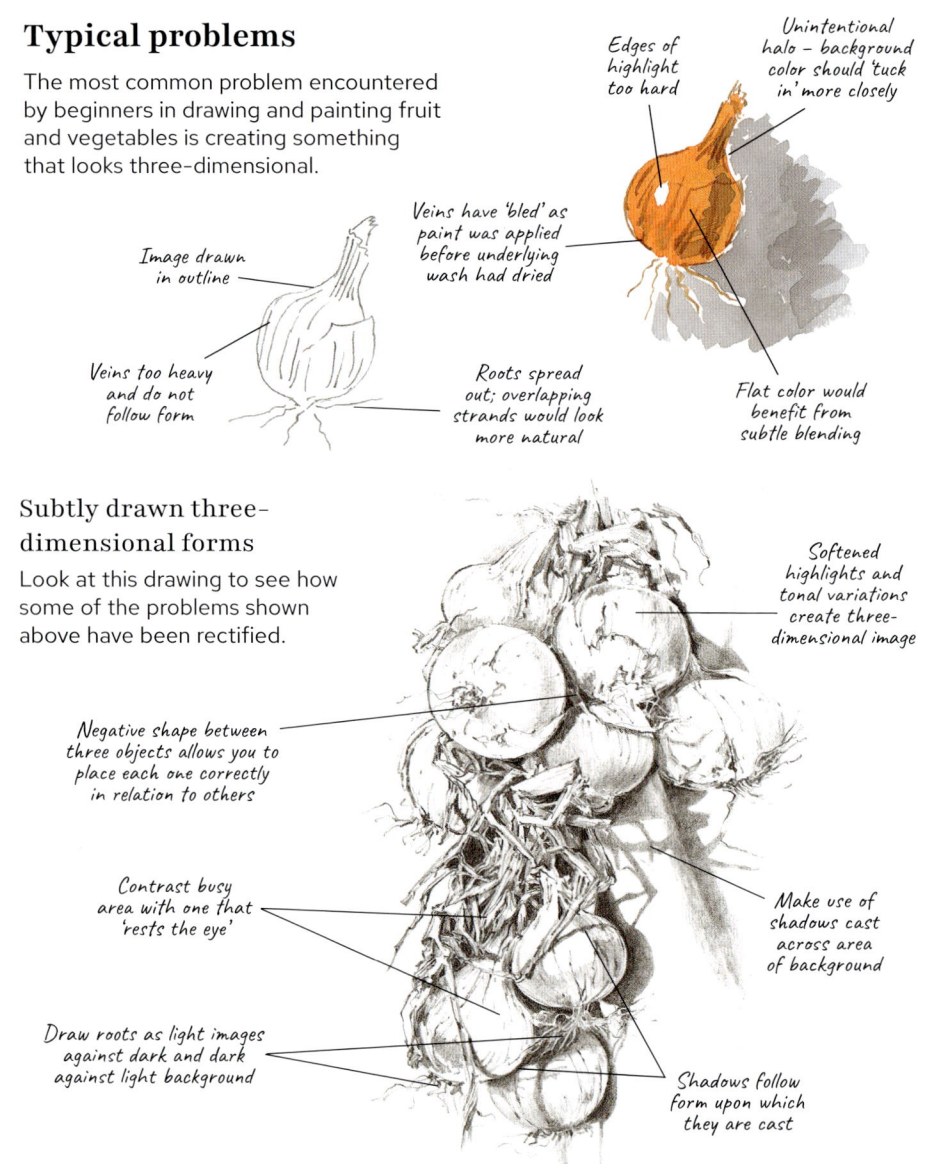

Edges of
highlight
too hard

Unintentional
halo – background
color should 'tuck
in' more closely

Veins have 'bled' as
paint was applied
before underlying
wash had dried

Image drawn
in outline

Veins too heavy
and do not
follow form

Roots spread
out; overlapping
strands would look
more natural

Flat color would
benefit from
subtle blending

Subtly drawn three-dimensional forms

Look at this drawing to see how
some of the problems shown
above have been rectified.

Softened
highlights and
tonal variations
create three-
dimensional image

Negative shape between
three objects allows you to
place each one correctly
in relation to others

Contrast busy
area with one that
'rests the eye'

Make use of
shadows cast
across area
of background

Draw roots as light images
against dark and dark
against light background

Shadows follow
form upon which
they are cast

Solutions

Creating a sense of form

Paint the form of an onion in a solid wash of very pale orangey-brown (mixed here from bright red and cadmium yellow), leaving paper untouched for the highlight. French ultramarine has been used to create the neutral tone, and when added with lemon yellow makes a green mix for the stem.

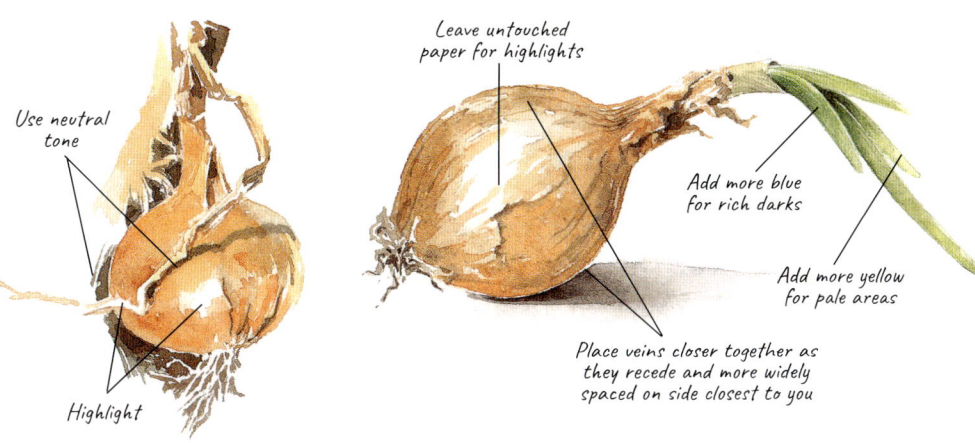

Use neutral tone

Leave untouched paper for highlights

Add more blue for rich darks

Add more yellow for pale areas

Place veins closer together as they recede and more widely spaced on side closest to you

Highlight

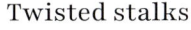

Twisted stalks

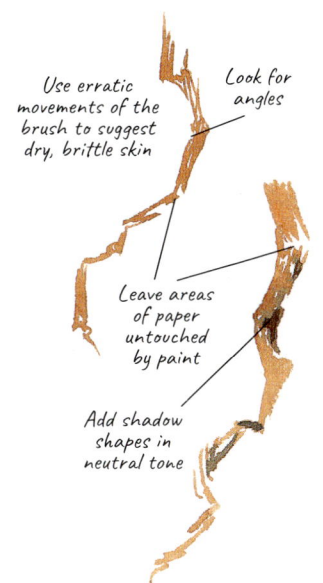

Use erratic movements of the brush to suggest dry, brittle skin

Look for angles

Leave areas of paper untouched by paint

Add shadow shapes in neutral tone

Painting the highlights and veins

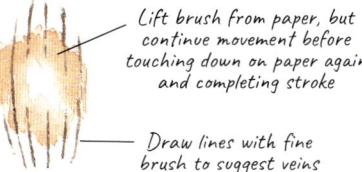

Before paint around highlight has dried, soften edges by adding clean water

Lift brush from paper, but continue movement before touching down on paper again and completing stroke

Draw lines with fine brush to suggest veins on curved surface

Shapes and Textures

The surface textures of some root vegetables are very similar to others; this occurs with the similarities between a parsnip and a carrot. In these instances, in order to differentiate between the two other than just with color, you need to be aware of the feel of the vegetable when holding it. Note the bands that curve around the form – their irregularities, indentations and protrusions – as these are the textures you should endeavor to portray.

Typical problems

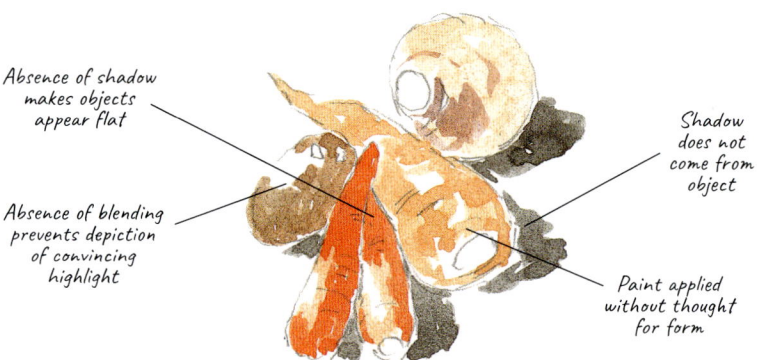

Absence of shadow makes objects appear flat

Absence of blending prevents depiction of convincing highlight

Shadow does not come from object

Paint applied without thought for form

Drawing to observe shape and form

It is important to see and depict the shape and form correctly, as the texture will need to 'follow the form'. Like anything else with drawing, this requires practice.

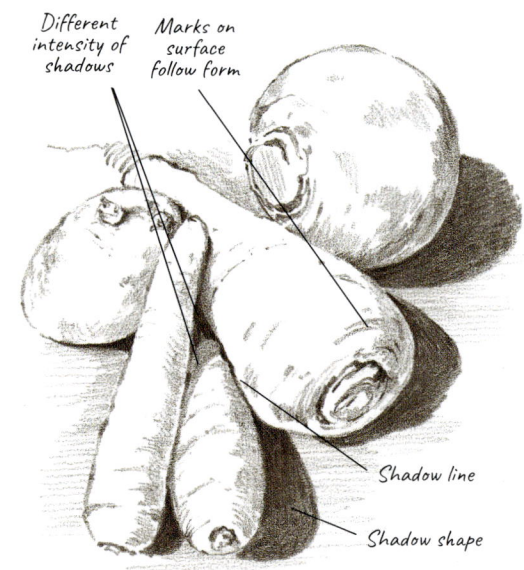

Different intensity of shadows

Marks on surface follow form

Shadow line

Shadow shape

Solutions

Blending textures

Crisp edges, where shadows overlap or cut in behind light forms, provide an interesting contrast to the subtle blending used on the surface of the potato here, and the gentle 'bleeding' required to paint the rutabaga (swede).

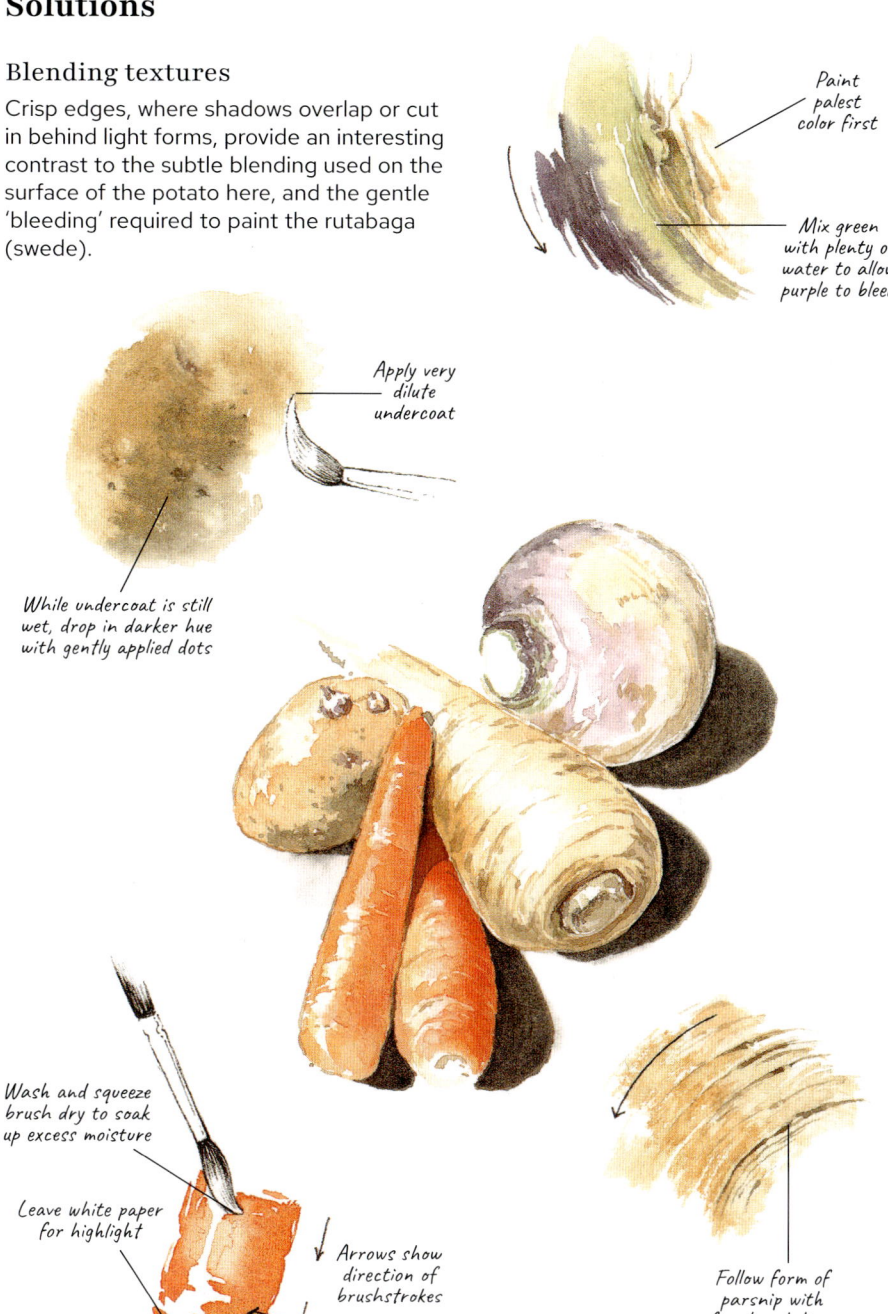

Paint palest color first

Mix green with plenty of water to allow purple to bleed

Apply very dilute undercoat

While undercoat is still wet, drop in darker hue with gently applied dots

Wash and squeeze brush dry to soak up excess moisture

Leave white paper for highlight

↓ Arrows show direction of brushstrokes

Follow form of parsnip with fine brush lines over base color

Color

The vibrant colors of citrus fruit and contrasting highlights can sometimes prove to be a problem. Keep your colors fresh and unmuddied by limiting the number you use, mixing only one or two together and trying them out on a separate sheet of paper before applying them as translucent washes.

Typical problems

If colors are too dull or highlights are positioned incorrectly, you may end up with a flat, patterned image instead of a 3D impression of form. With a flat image of cut fruit, you need to look closely at the exposed texture, where highlights also play an important part.

Drawing with watercolor pencils

You can remain aware of the colors while working on your drawing by using watercolor pencils, either dry or with water added to solidify the color.

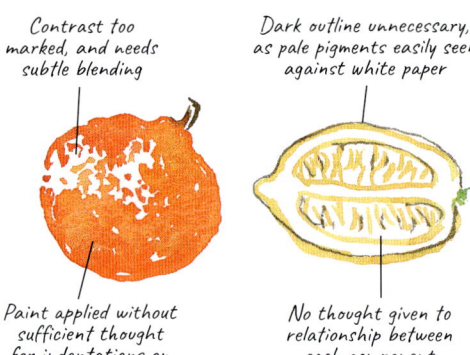

Contrast too marked, and needs subtle blending

Dark outline unnecessary, as pale pigments easily seen against white paper

Paint applied without sufficient thought for indentations on surface texture

No thought given to relationship between each component

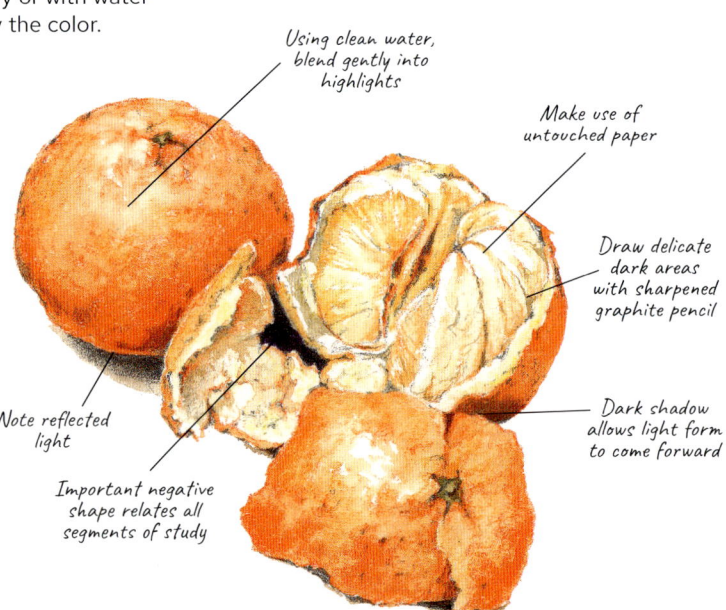

Using clean water, blend gently into highlights

Make use of untouched paper

Draw delicate dark areas with sharpened graphite pencil

Dark shadow allows light form to come forward

Note reflected light

Important negative shape relates all segments of study

Solutions

Single study

Painting a study of a single fruit allows you to concentrate fully on the color of an individual specimen. The texture on the surface of this lime was achieved by working wet pigment onto a damp surface and allowing it to bleed.

Citrus group

In a group of similar-shaped and colored citrus fruits, you need to consider perspective and angles in addition to textures.

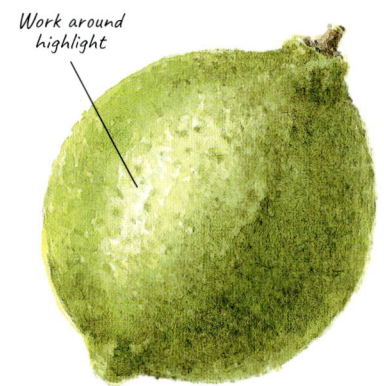

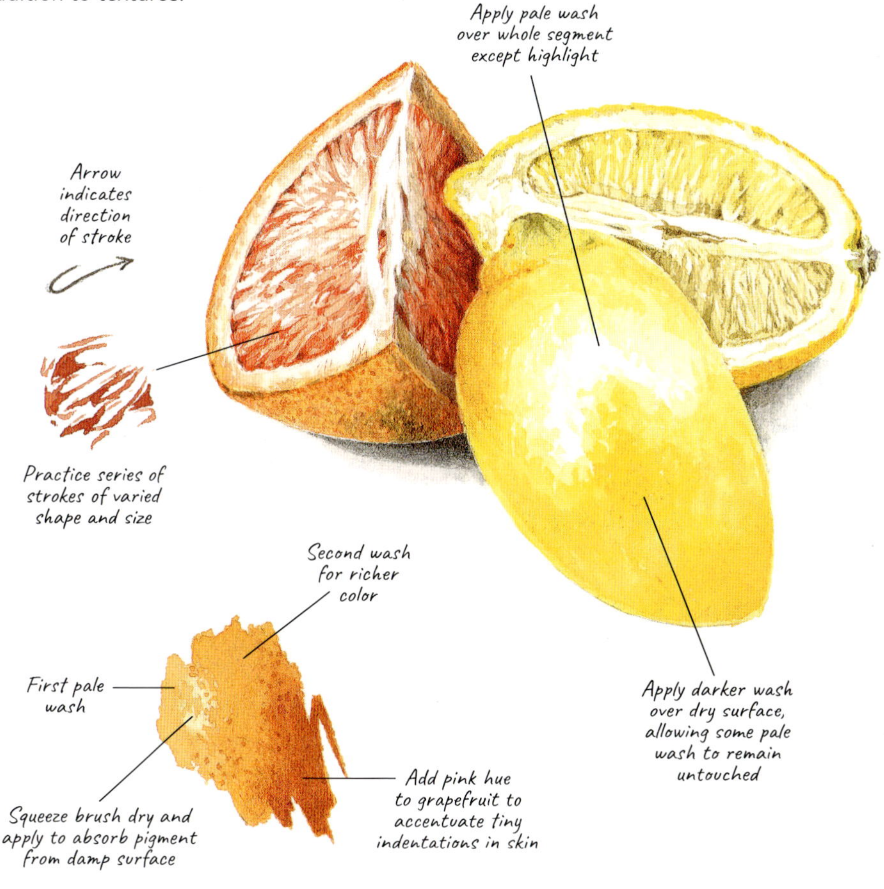

Work around highlight

Apply pale wash over whole segment except highlight

Arrow indicates direction of stroke

Practice series of strokes of varied shape and size

Second wash for richer color

First pale wash

Apply darker wash over dry surface, allowing some pale wash to remain untouched

Add pink hue to grapefruit to accentuate tiny indentations in skin

Squeeze brush dry and apply to absorb pigment from damp surface

Tones in Monochrome

When an object lacks color we have an opportunity to become fully aware of tonal variations. Mushrooms, with their interesting forms and rich contrasts of tone, from surface light to gill recesses, and their rich darks encourage you to consider the tonal scale.

Typical problems

Beginners often experience problems with a tonal scale, limiting their range to such an extent that the subsequent painting appears dull and uninteresting. They also find it difficult to rely solely on tone to create forms, and resort to unnecessary outlines to differentiate one form from another.

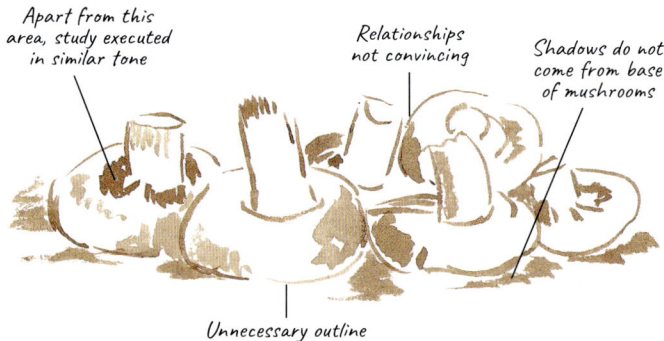

Apart from this area, study executed in similar tone

Relationships not convincing

Shadows do not come from base of mushrooms

Unnecessary outline

Limiting outlines in drawing

Try to use an area of dark tone against a light form without resorting to an outline. Find opportunities to 'lose' these lines.

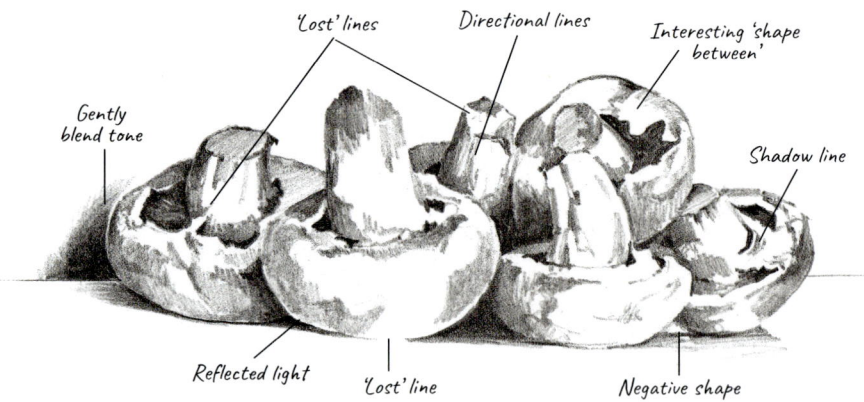

Gently blend tone

'Lost' lines

Directional lines

Interesting 'shape between'

Shadow line

Reflected light

'Lost' line

Negative shape

Solutions

Tonal scale

A good exercise to help understand the tonal scale is to use one color only – in this example, sepia – diluting the pigment little by little as you paint tonal blocks. In this way you can produce a variety of tones, ranging from intense to weak.

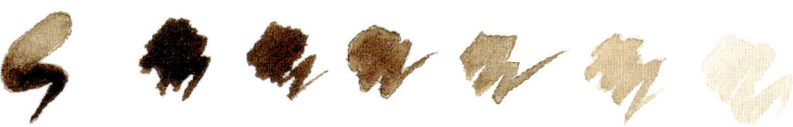

Placing dark behind

Placing a dark tone against a light area produces an exciting tonal contrast. These contrasts are very important within a painting to add interest and bring work to life. Enrich the dark areas (the negative shapes and shadows) to allow untouched white paper (from the other end of the tonal scale) to be used to full advantage and produce strong contrasts.

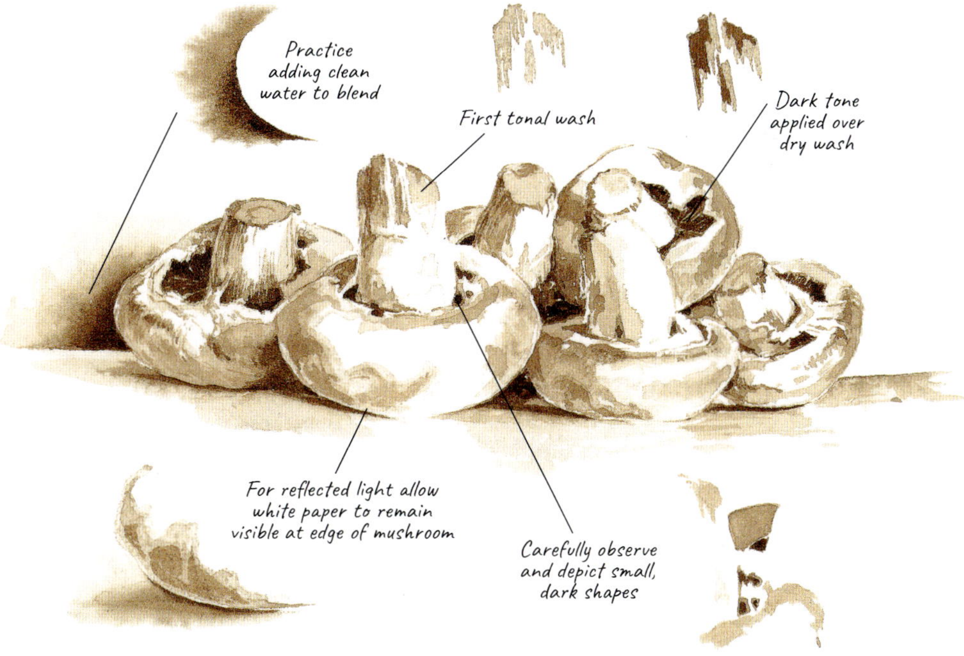

Practice adding clean water to blend

First tonal wash

Dark tone applied over dry wash

For reflected light allow white paper to remain visible at edge of mushroom

Carefully observe and depict small, dark shapes

ANIMALS
Basic Brushstrokes

The following exercises are designed to help you develop an understanding of how to create different textures of animal fur. This page shows the basic brushstrokes in isolation, while the facing page demonstrates how to develop them further in the context of an animal painting.

Three painting positions

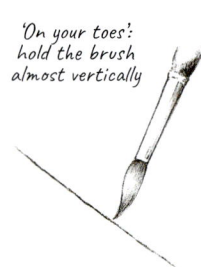

'On your toes': hold the brush almost vertically

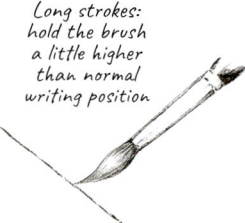

Long strokes: hold the brush a little higher than normal writing position

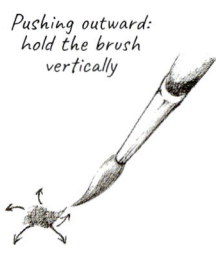

Pushing outward: hold the brush vertically

Curved strokes

Load the brush with slightly less water and pigment

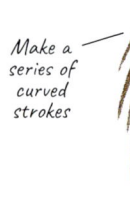

Make a series of curved strokes

Place curved strokes closer together

Blending exercise

Load the brush with plenty of water mixed with pigment

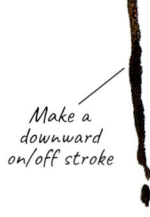

Make a downward on/off stroke

While line is still wet, add clean water on one side to blend

Pushing paint outward

Load the brush with plenty of water mixed with pigment

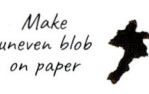

Make uneven blob on paper

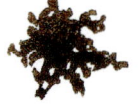

Push paint away from the blob with uneven movements

Developing Brushstrokes

You can very quickly learn how to build on the basic brushstrokes to create the texture of hair or fur. The key to success – which comes with practice – is knowing when to apply clean water to achieve the desired effect.

Glossy, smooth-haired animals

An extension of the blending exercise, this wet-into-wet effect can be used to depict the sheen on an animal's coat.

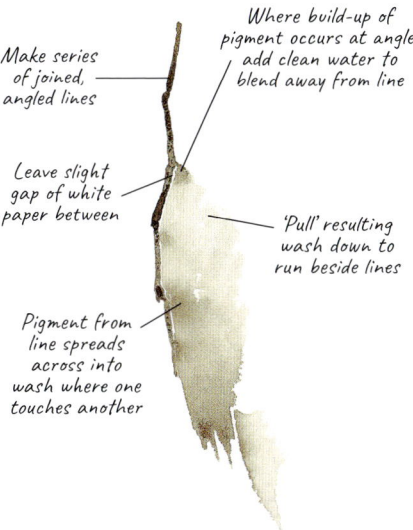

Make series of joined, angled lines

Where build-up of pigment occurs at angle, add clean water to blend away from line

Leave slight gap of white paper between

'Pull' resulting wash down to run beside lines

Pigment from line spreads across into wash where one touches another

Dense hair or fur

This is an extension of the curved strokes exercise. Paint initial strokes in one direction, for the undercoat. Once dry, add darker tones to suggest long, dense hair or fur.

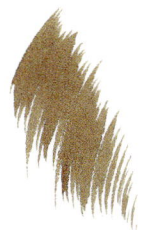
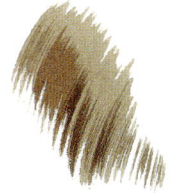

Join curved strokes together to form a mass

When dry, add further strokes of a different color or tone

Woolly coats

Pushing paint outward to develop shapes from a blob is a useful way of depicting woolly-coated animals such as sheep and some breeds of cattle and dogs.

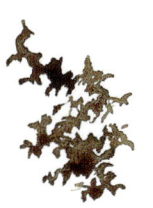
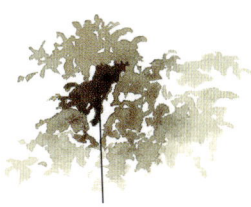

Initial shapes

Lighten tone by adding water so dark areas suggest shadows

Highlights

A variation on the curved strokes exercise, showing how to leave white paper untouched to suggest highlights by 'cutting in' with the darker tones. It is suitable for use on tails and manes.

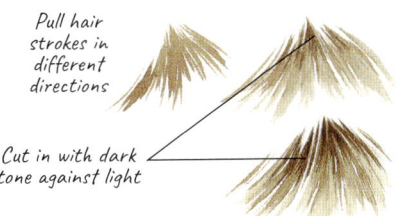

Pull hair strokes in different directions

Cut in with dark tone against light

Introducing Ink

Pen and ink used with watercolor washes is a popular choice. Practice this combination using a limited palette, so that you can control the tonal values without having too many colors to think about. A pig possesses neutral or subtle hues naturally; place the animal in a setting where the same range of colors may be adapted for the background.

Typical problems

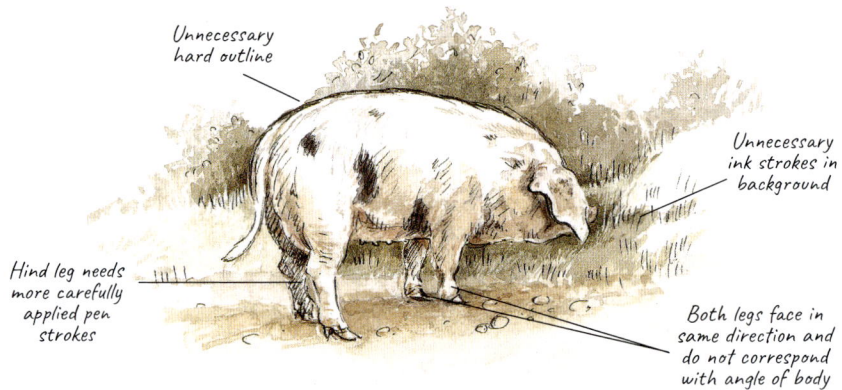

Unnecessary hard outline

Unnecessary ink strokes in background

Hind leg needs more carefully applied pen strokes

Both legs face in same direction and do not correspond with angle of body

From pencil into ink

A preliminary drawing in pencil using guidelines establishes the scale and position of the subject. Draw the same image alongside in ink, omitting your guidelines and positional marks but being careful to achieve the right proportions. You can use a tracing for this.

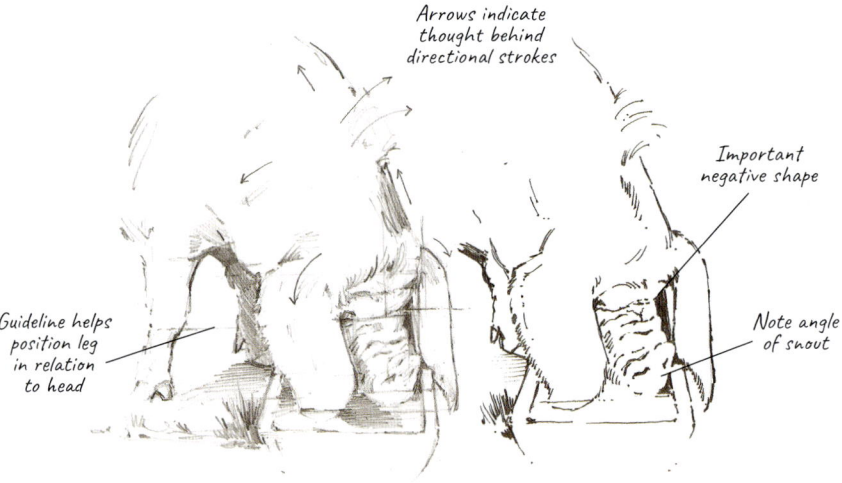

Arrows indicate thought behind directional strokes

Important negative shape

Guideline helps position leg in relation to head

Note angle of snout

Solutions

Working with a limited palette

Before choosing colors for a limited palette, it is a good idea to practice your color-mixing proportions. By adding a little more of one color than the other, a monochrome hue can move from the warm range into the cool, and vice versa.

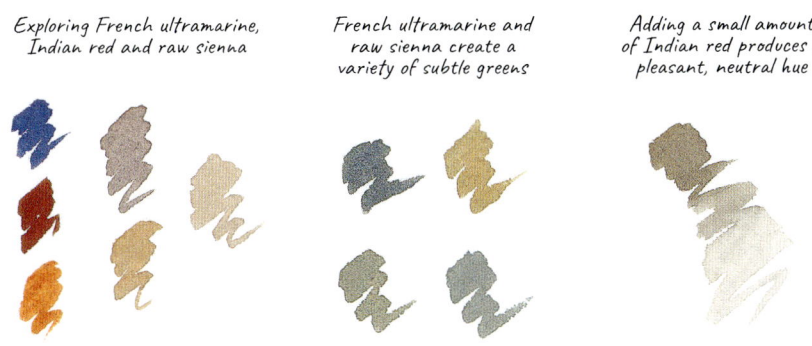

Exploring French ultramarine, Indian red and raw sienna

French ultramarine and raw sienna create a variety of subtle greens

Adding a small amount of Indian red produces a pleasant, neutral hue

Ink over watercolor

Executing a watercolor painting on rough-surfaced paper enables you to drag your pen lightly across the surface and achieve delicate lines that do not overpower the painting.

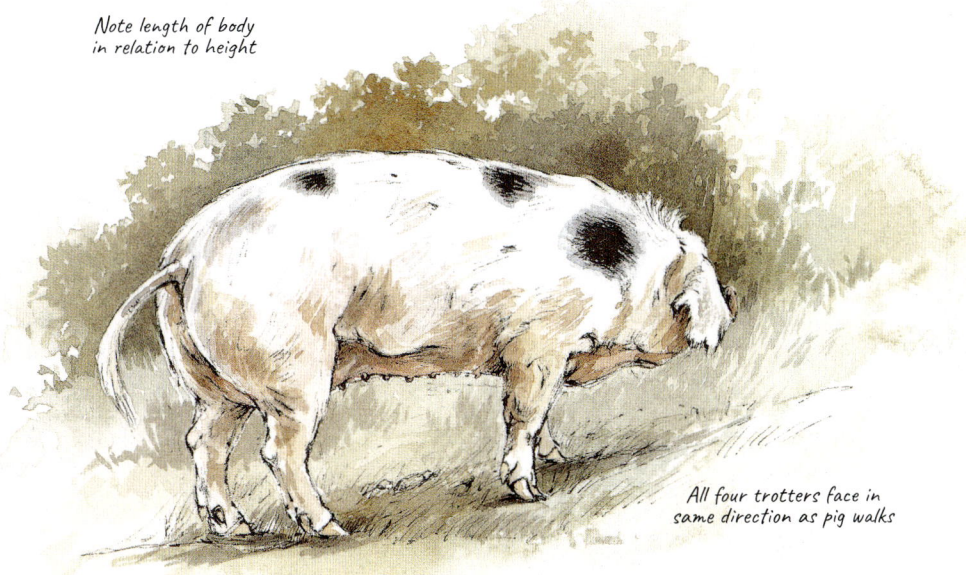

Note length of body in relation to height

All four trotters face in same direction as pig walks

Contexts

*It is very important, when painting animals that spend time outdoors,
such as ponies and cattle or sheep, that you include some of the background
or context. Very often the contrast between the hair of the animal and
the foliage of a landscape, or farm building, can enhance a painting.*

Typical problems

Failure to establish a realistic
background makes it harder to
realize the correct proportions
of the pony.

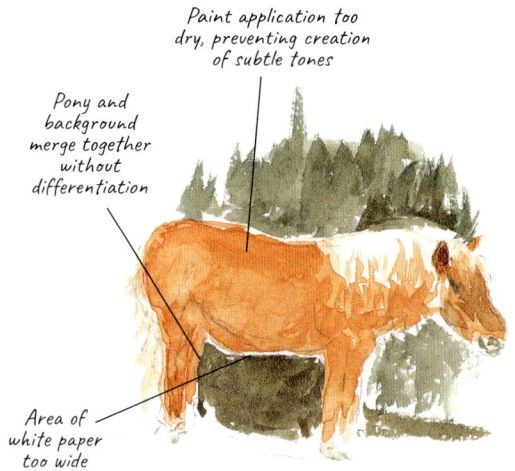

Paint application too
dry, preventing creation
of subtle tones

Pony and
background
merge together
without
differentiation

Area of
white paper
too wide

Preliminary drawing to establish proportions

Try to take as much care of
shadow and negative shapes as
you do over the positives. Think of
it as a jigsaw – fit one piece into
another until the content of the
whole drawing is placed correctly.

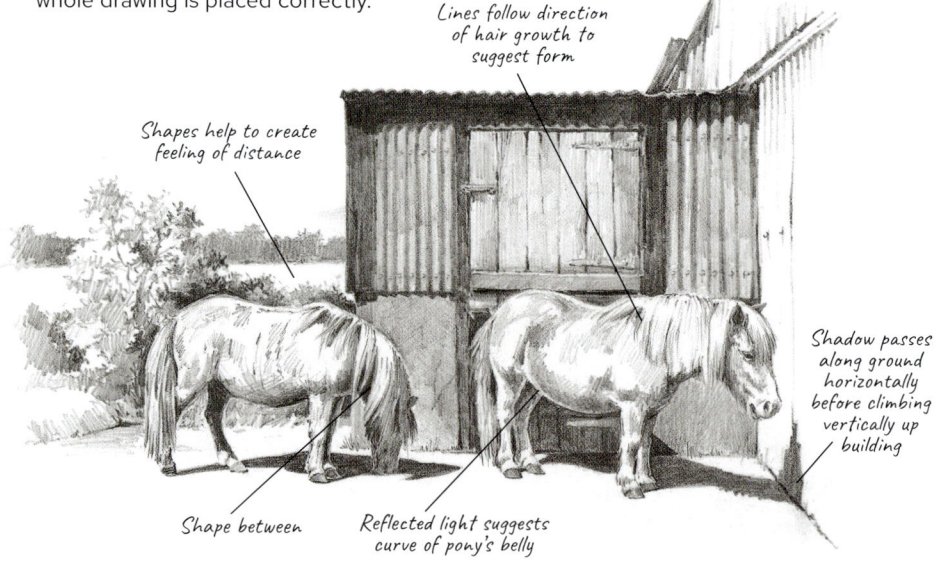

Lines follow direction
of hair growth to
suggest form

Shapes help to create
feeling of distance

Shadow passes
along ground
horizontally
before climbing
vertically up
building

Shape between

Reflected light suggests
curve of pony's belly

Solutions

Placing your subject in context

Clearly differentiate your subject from its background through careful consideration of the tones – light against dark, dark next to light and so on.

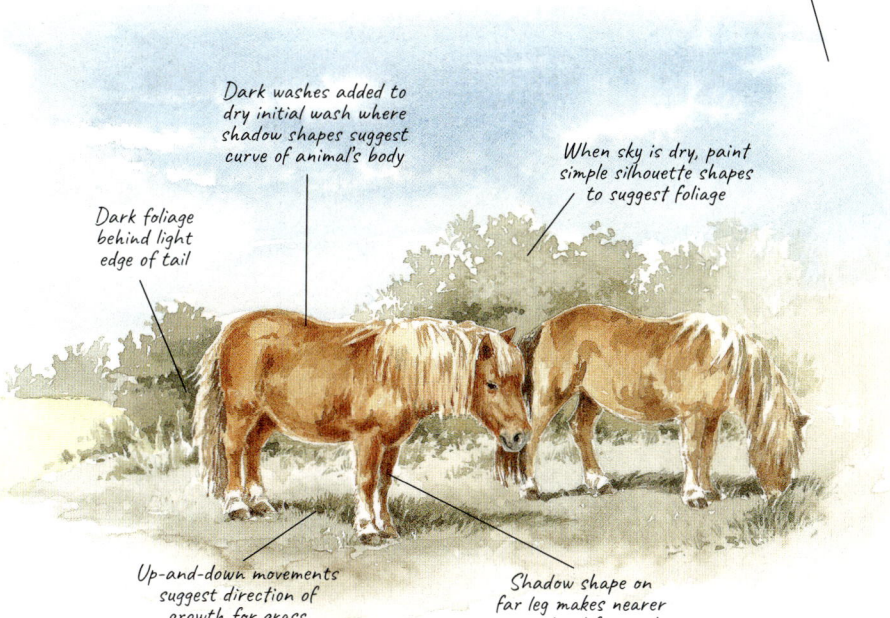

Dampen the paper, load your brush with a mix of cobalt and cerulean blue, and drop color onto the surface, leaving some areas white to suggest clouds

Dark washes added to dry initial wash where shadow shapes suggest curve of animal's body

When sky is dry, paint simple silhouette shapes to suggest foliage

Dark foliage behind light edge of tail

Up-and-down movements suggest direction of growth for grass

Shadow shape on far leg makes nearer one stand forward

Fine detail

This study demonstrates how, by building darker tones one upon the other and using delicate, 'directional' brushstrokes, you can create a three-dimensional impression.

Small, but essential, shadow shapes suggest form

Angle of eye neither straight line nor circle

Light tones and areas of white paper suggest highlights

Directional Strokes

A common problem experienced when painting horned animals is that of how to relate the horn growth to the animal's head. This also applies to the depiction of hooves, whether it be the round hoof of a pony or that of a cloven-footed animal. The most important thing to remember with all of these is the direction involved of both the growth rings on horns and hooves and the hair growth, which itself can cause problems.

Typical problems

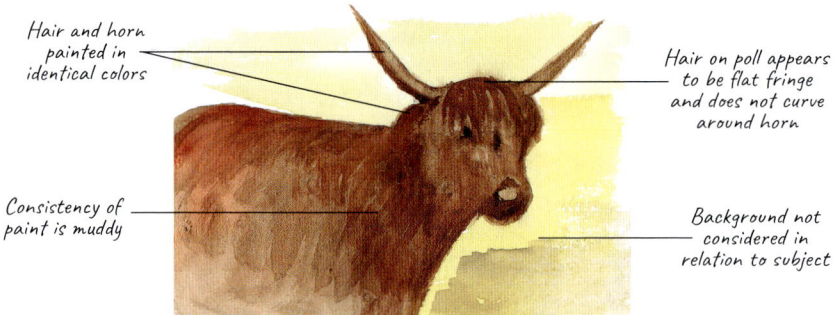

Hair and horn painted in identical colors

Hair on poll appears to be flat fringe and does not curve around horn

Consistency of paint is muddy

Background not considered in relation to subject

Detail studies

Studies of detail may be made in your sketchbook. One method is to stand by an animal and look down at the feet to draw them singly, in relation to a small area of ground.

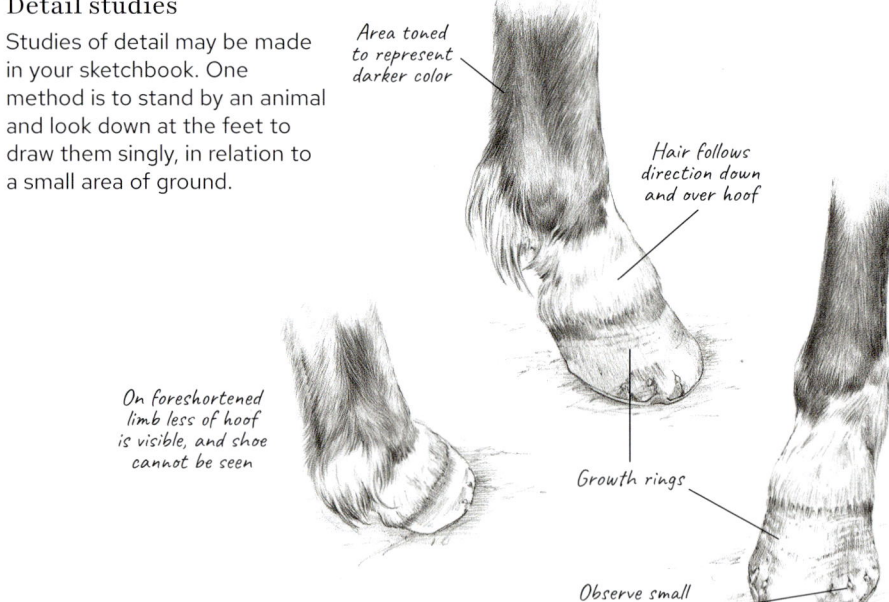

Area toned to represent darker color

Hair follows direction down and over hoof

On foreshortened limb less of hoof is visible, and shoe cannot be seen

Growth rings

Observe small details

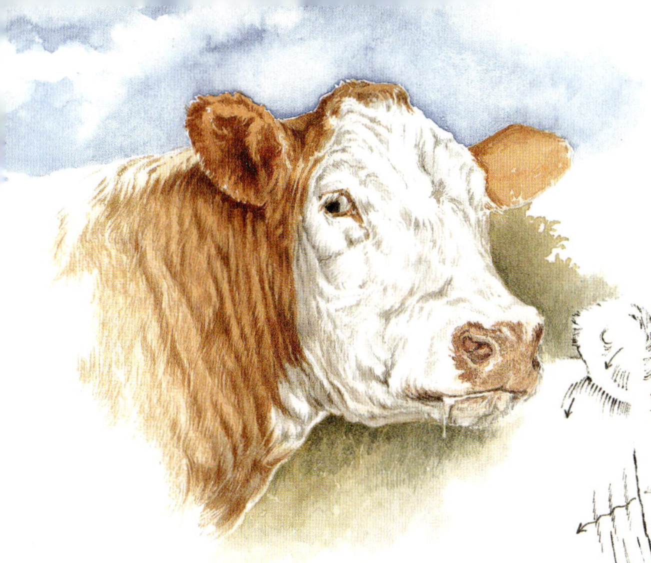

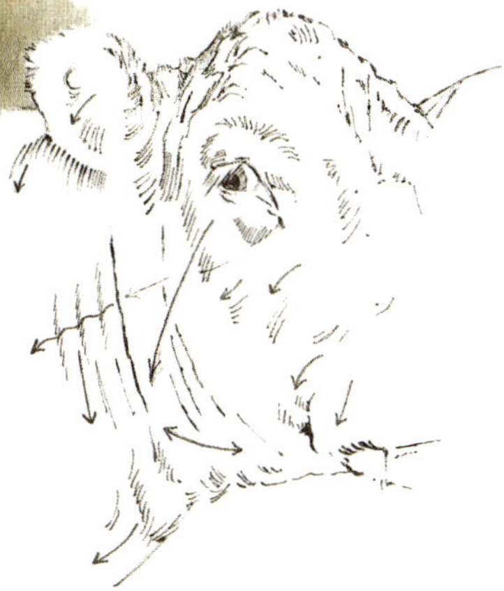

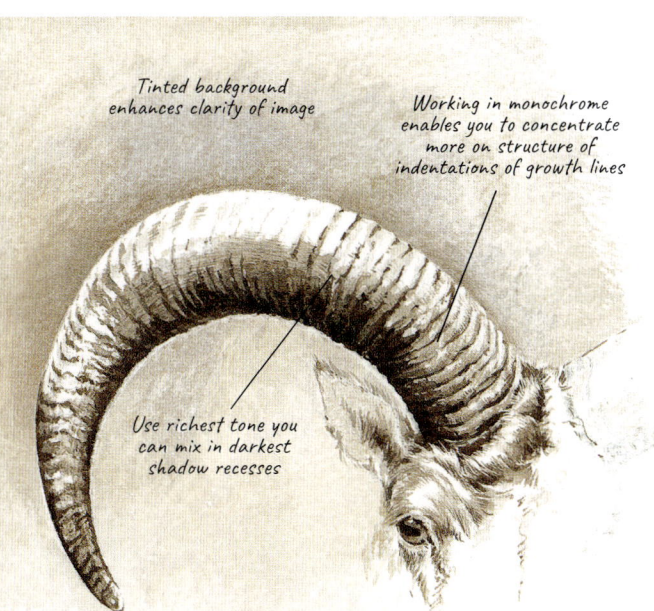

Strokes follow down line of neck and undulate over folds of skin

Solutions

Concentrating on hair

For safety reasons, some farm animals are de-horned. In the cow study there are no horns to focus on hair growth direction over the strong bone structure of the head.

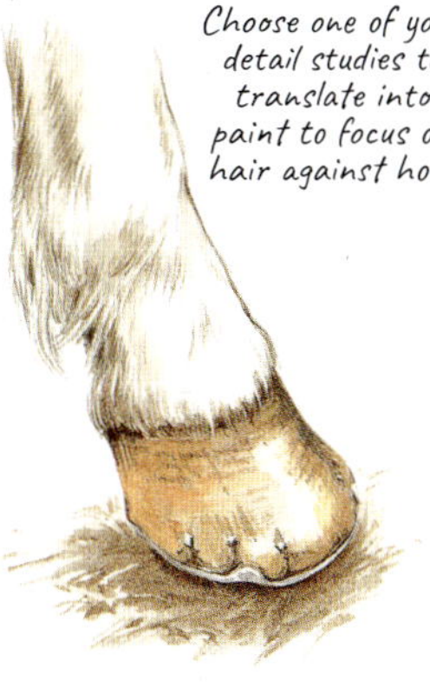

Choose one of your detail studies to translate into paint to focus on hair against hoof

Tinted background enhances clarity of image

Working in monochrome enables you to concentrate more on structure of indentations of growth lines

Use richest tone you can mix in darkest shadow recesses

Disproportionate horn growth

The magnificent curved horns of some varieties of sheep twist and turn, with highlights accentuating the direction.

Woolly Textures

The dense texture of thick wool is a problem for some beginners to depict for a number of reasons. In the drawing and painting below, the problems are clearly visible, both in the drawing of the subject, where the neck has been elongated and the back legs placed unconvincingly, as well as with the texture of the animal's coat.

Typical problems

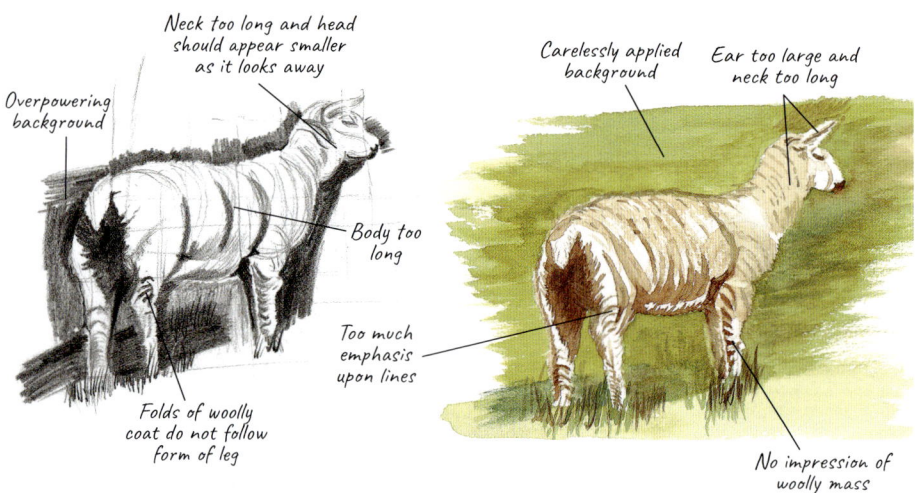

Neck too long and head should appear smaller as it looks away

Overpowering background

Body too long

Folds of woolly coat do not follow form of leg

Too much emphasis upon lines

Carelessly applied background

Ear too large and neck too long

No impression of woolly mass

Grouping subjects

Sheep are usually seen as a flock, so the darks of shadows behind and between their forms allow white paper to play an important role.

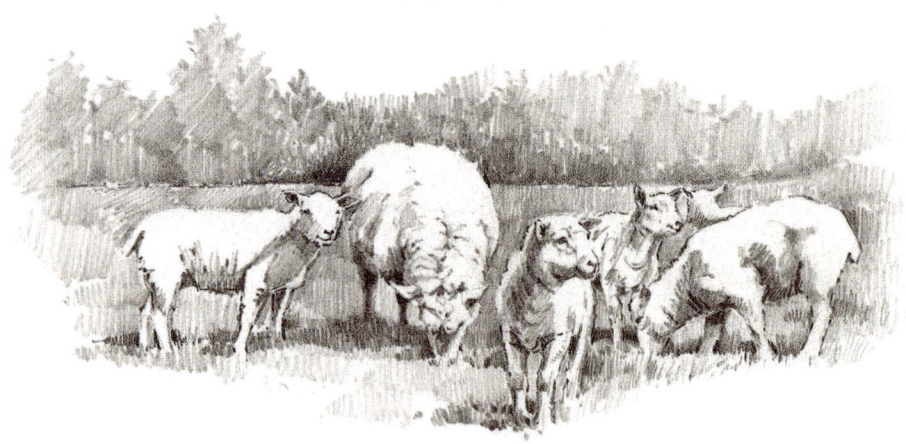

Solutions

Drawing wool

Animals seen at a distance appear as light shapes against a darker background. So, when drawing wool avoid filling in the image with too much pencil work.

Painting exercise

Transfer the image onto watercolor paper with gentle pressure on your pencil strokes, then place a watery wash of olive green around the drawing.

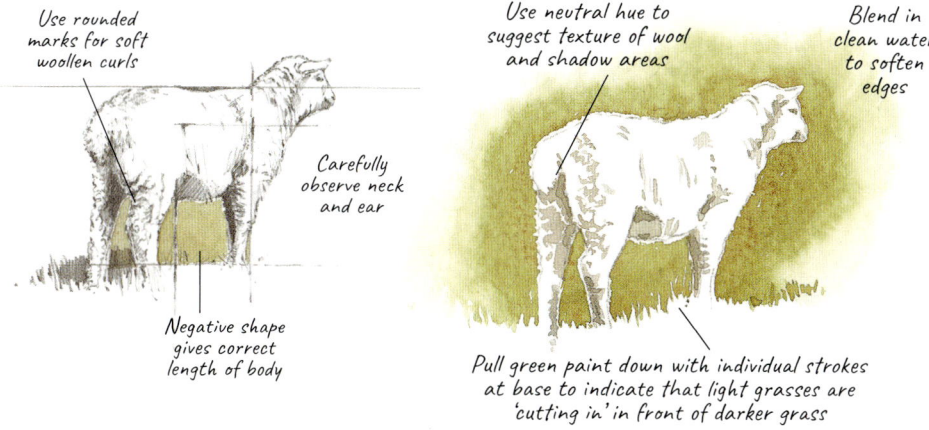

Use rounded marks for soft woollen curls

Carefully observe neck and ear

Negative shape gives correct length of body

Use neutral hue to suggest texture of wool and shadow areas

Blend in clean water to soften edges

Pull green paint down with individual strokes at base to indicate that light grasses are 'cutting in' in front of darker grass

Building up the washes

After the drawing had been transferred lightly onto watercolor paper, a wash of green was painted around the subjects to represent the grass and distant bushes. Care was taken to leave areas of white paper to suggest sunlight upon the sheep, and the shadow sides were painted in textured washes.

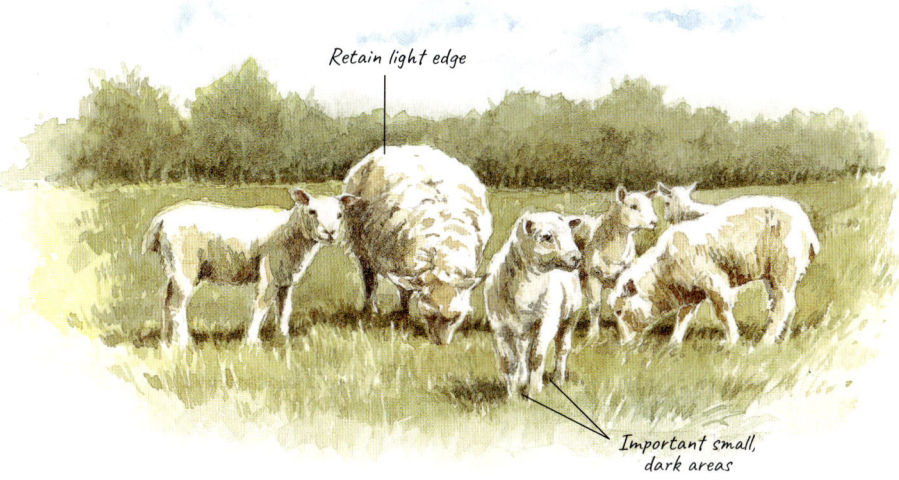

Retain light edge

Important small, dark areas

STILL LIFES IN THE LANDSCAPE

Basic Brushstrokes

These exercises are designed to help you understand brush movements and pressures for common thematic effects. For instance, superimposing lines can suggest wood grain, or the grille of an old car; while curved brushstrokes of uneven pressure recreate tyre tread, or overlapping planks on a boat. Sideways sweeps of the brush depict flat panels and sheets of glass, or can be adapted to indicate curved panels with dark recesses behind.

Superimposing grain

Hold the brush sideways against the paper in a horizontal position.

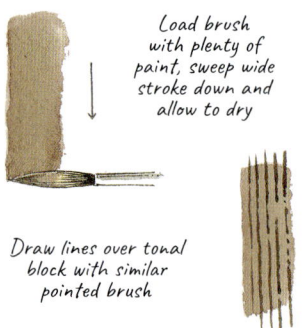

Load brush with plenty of paint, sweep wide stroke down and allow to dry

Draw lines over tonal block with similar pointed brush

Sideways sweeping strokes

Hold the brush at less of an angle to the paper; with swift movements, make a series of diagonal sweeps.

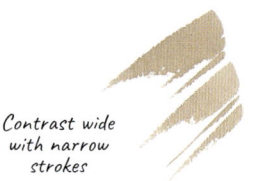

Contrast wide with narrow strokes

Curved lines

A normal writing position is the best one to adopt for this exercise.

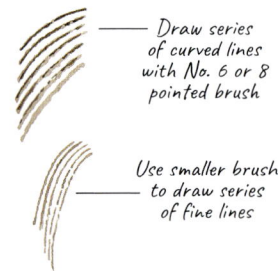

Draw series of curved lines with No. 6 or 8 pointed brush

Use smaller brush to draw series of fine lines

Curved metal surfaces

To suggest highlight areas, enhance controlled sweeps of the brush by adding fine lines.

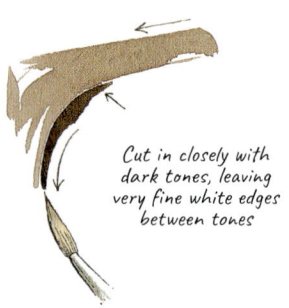

Cut in closely with dark tones, leaving very fine white edges between tones

Developing Brushstrokes

The exercises here are developments of the basic brushstrokes. They demonstrate varied pressure on the brush, angles of application and superimposed marks, and are designed to help you become aware of the importance of following the form of an object in order to create a three-dimensional impression of your subject.

Wood grain

This is an extension of the superimposing grain exercise. You can also use it to suggest the grille on a car, but the strokes will need to be straighter.

Curved strokes following form

Overlapping planks on boat and tyre treads follow the form of the object. This is an extension of the curved lines exercise.

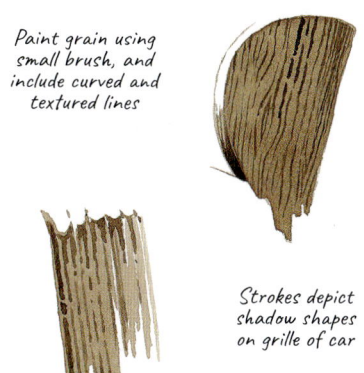

Paint grain using small brush, and include curved and textured lines

Strokes depict shadow shapes on grille of car

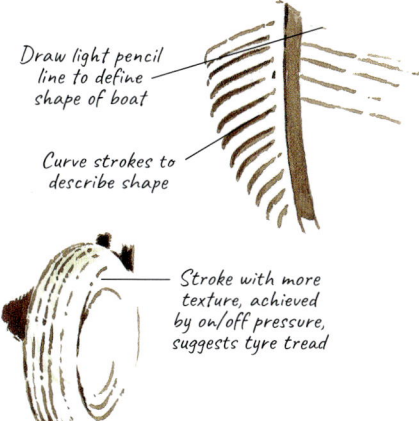

Draw light pencil line to define shape of boat

Curve strokes to describe shape

Stroke with more texture, achieved by on/off pressure, suggests tyre tread

Sweeping strokes

Use sideways sweeping strokes to suggest a flat metal panel on the side of a trailer, for example, or glass in the windows of a vehicle or a boat.

Strokes for curved metal surfaces

Sweeping strokes, applied swiftly, or at varying angles and of different lengths, for curved metal areas on the bonnet of a motor vehicle.

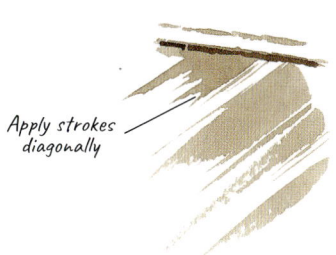

Apply strokes diagonally

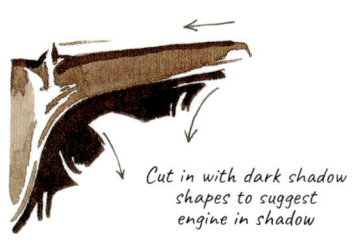

Cut in with dark shadow shapes to suggest engine in shadow

Garden Benches

It is only by making comparisons with certain subjects/objects that we can develop a deeper understanding of methods. For instance, the fencing in a landscape is made up of both vertical and horizontal posts and rails – by observing the elongated shapes between these you can achieve scale, proportion and perspective accurately.

Typical problems

When drawing a bench, beginners often experience problems with perspective and proportions when they consider only the positive shapes.

Sketchbook composites

The freedom of using a sketchbook allows you to place objects of varying scale, seen at different angles of perspective, in close proximity to each other. You can draw the object against a relevant background, or portray it simply as the object. In both cases it is most important to relate it to the ground – in other words, anchor it.

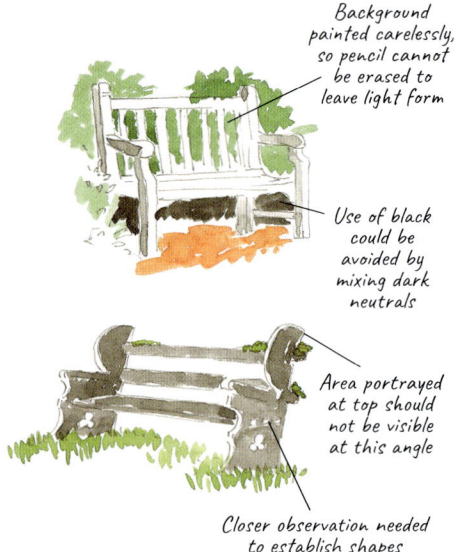

Background painted carelessly, so pencil cannot be erased to leave light form

Use of black could be avoided by mixing dark neutrals

Area portrayed at top should not be visible at this angle

Closer observation needed to establish shapes

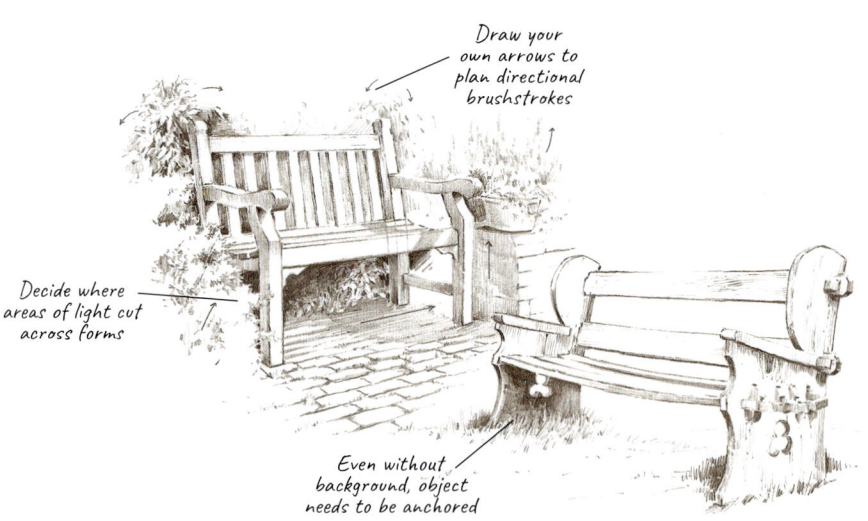

Draw your own arrows to plan directional brushstrokes

Decide where areas of light cut across forms

Even without background, object needs to be anchored

Solutions

Learning from comparisons

The upper painting demonstrates how crucial it is to consider the background and paint around the form when you decide to paint your subject in a setting. In the lower painting, the bench is made of darker wood and can be presented as a study without background. Both studies demonstrate how observing and drawing the negative shapes between the vertical and horizontal slats leads to accurate placing of the positive shapes.

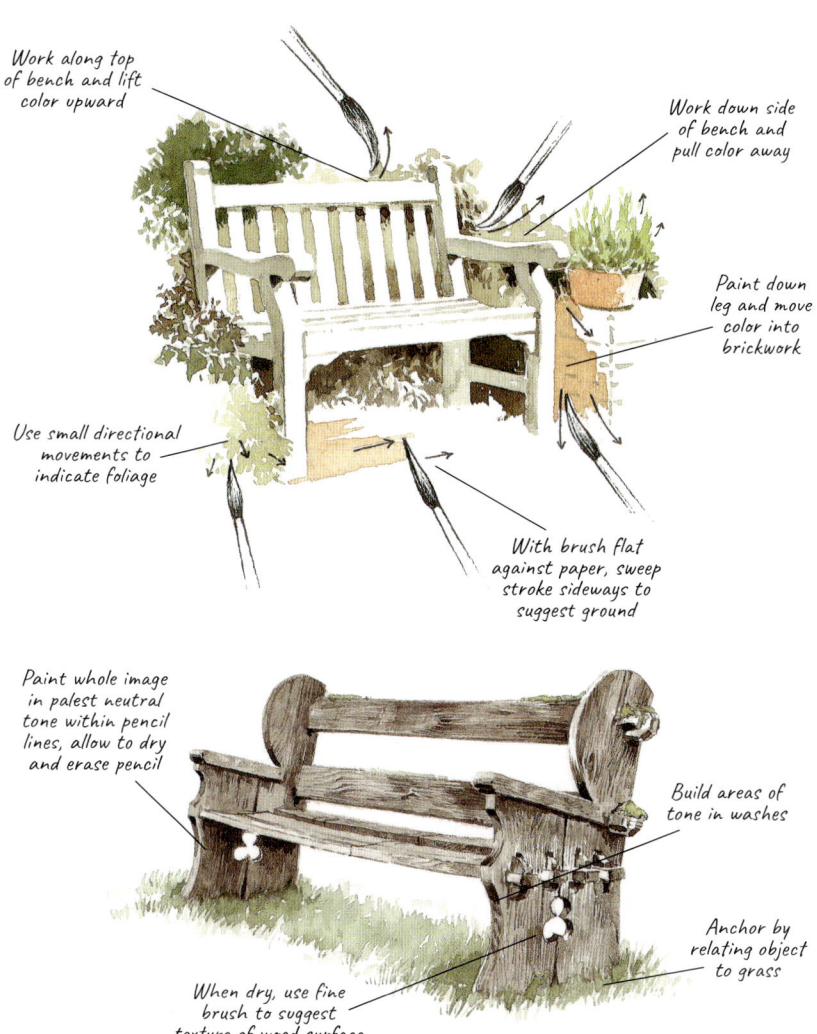

Work along top of bench and lift color upward

Work down side of bench and pull color away

Paint down leg and move color into brickwork

Use small directional movements to indicate foliage

With brush flat against paper, sweep stroke sideways to suggest ground

Paint whole image in palest neutral tone within pencil lines, allow to dry and erase pencil

Build areas of tone in washes

Anchor by relating object to grass

When dry, use fine brush to suggest texture of wood surface

Half-Hidden Objects

A lack of understanding and knowledge regarding the use of negative shapes can lead to a flat and patterned effect rather than the desired three-dimensional impression.

Typical problems

This painting suffers from the typical beginner's difficulty of knowing how to mix colors effectively, leading to the unnatural hues on display.

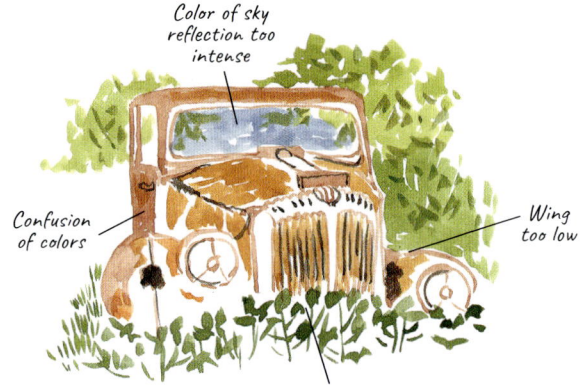

Color of sky reflection too intense

Confusion of colors

Wing too low

Foliage painted dark on light, although seen as light in front of dark background

Using a drawing to help find shapes

Alternate between holding your pencil vertically and horizontally, and look along the edge to find the most helpful positions for drawing guidelines.

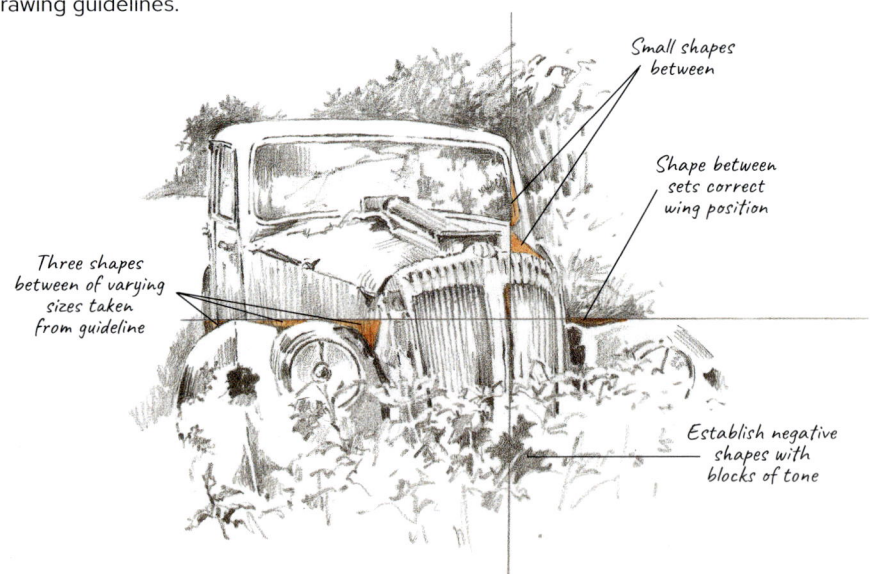

Small shapes between

Shape between sets correct wing position

Three shapes between of varying sizes taken from guideline

Establish negative shapes with blocks of tone

Solutions

Using a few colors effectively

It's a challenge to work with a limited palette of three colors (here, Indian red, raw sienna and cerulean blue) that may not be a natural choice for the subject, as it encourages you to consider the proportions of pigment in your color mixes. In addition, in order to use dark negative shapes to full advantage (to provide rich contrasts to light areas) you need to experiment with color intensity. The nature of the pigments here means that you are likely to discover some separation of color in your mixes, which can create some exciting effects.

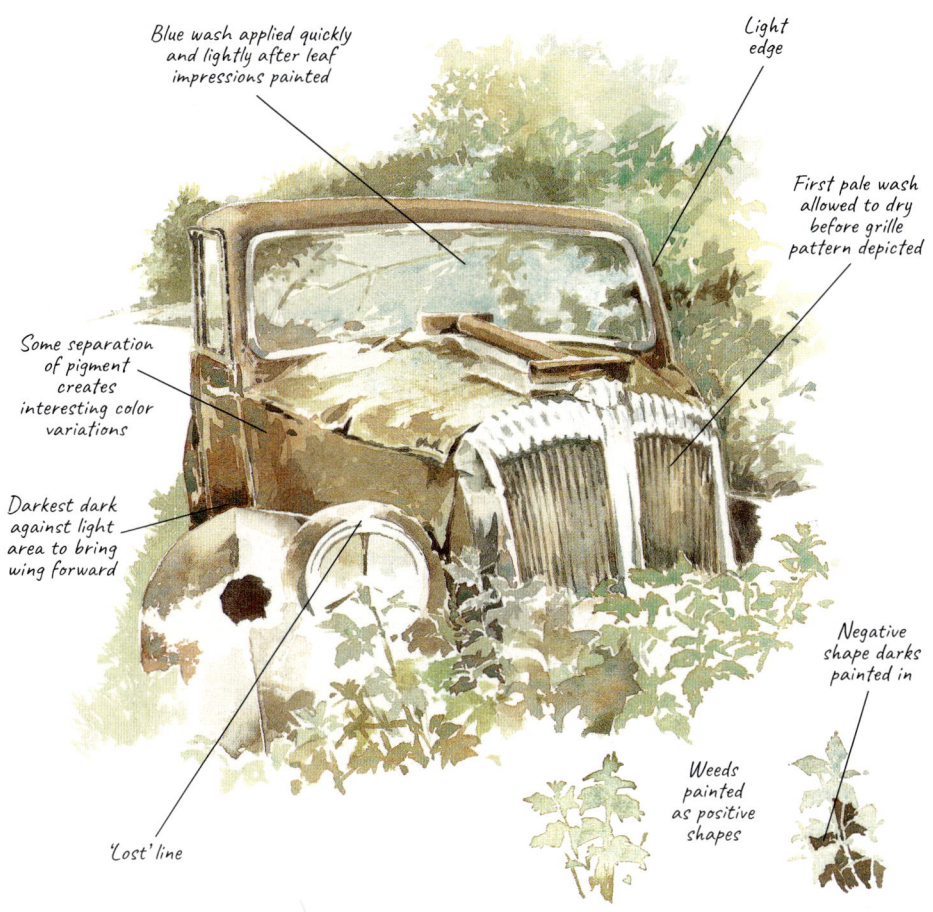

Blue wash applied quickly and lightly after leaf impressions painted

Light edge

First pale wash allowed to dry before grille pattern depicted

Some separation of pigment creates interesting color variations

Darkest dark against light area to bring wing forward

'Lost' line

Weeds painted as positive shapes

Negative shape darks painted in

Vehicles with Rounded Shapes

An old farm machine such as a tractor abandoned in a field can provide the artist with interesting subject matter, as it offers a variety of color (against the greens), the texture of damaged metal, tonal contrasts (engine in shadow) and various curves and contours.

Typical problems

Beginners who are unaware of a guideline method of drawing may experience problems with perspective as well as their interpretation of the subject in paint.

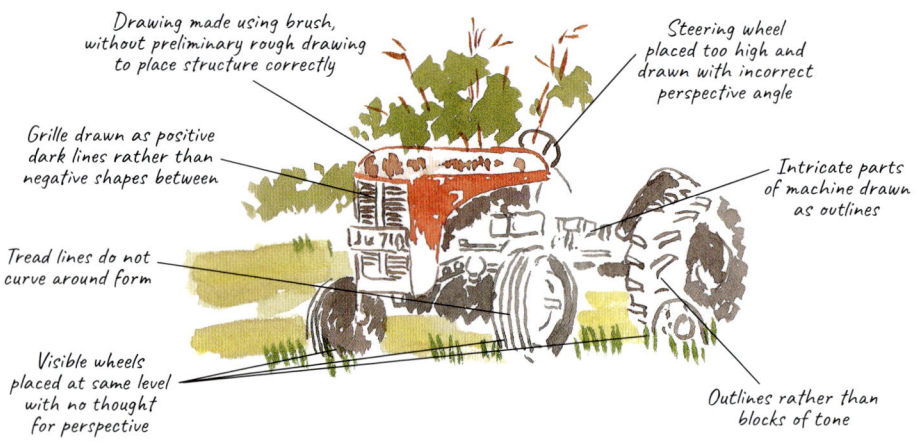

Drawing made using brush, without preliminary rough drawing to place structure correctly

Steering wheel placed too high and drawn with incorrect perspective angle

Grille drawn as positive dark lines rather than negative shapes between

Intricate parts of machine drawn as outlines

Tread lines do not curve around form

Visible wheels placed at same level with no thought for perspective

Outlines rather than blocks of tone

Drawing correct contours

There are many curves to be found in this subject – the steering wheel and below the bonnet and wheel arch, as well as the tyres, where the front wheels are angled slightly. Practice finding these contours on a preliminary reference drawing.

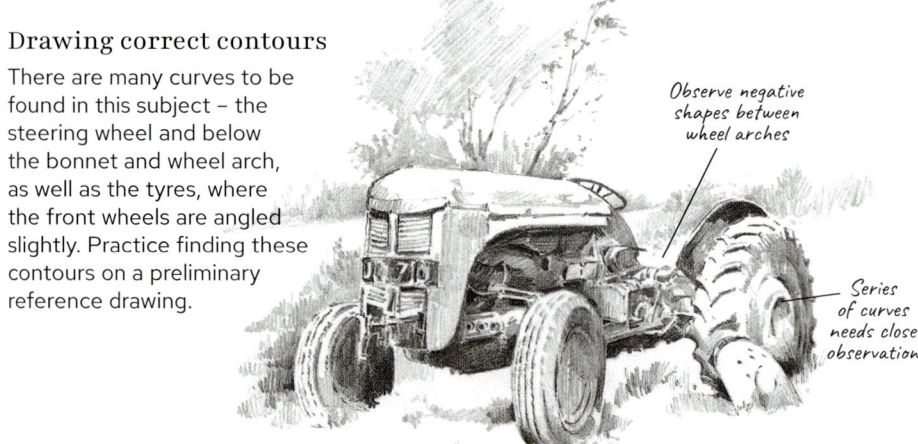

Observe negative shapes between wheel arches

Series of curves needs close observation

Solutions

Building washes

Although strong contrasts are an important part of this study, they are not painted dark initially. Instead, pale colors are applied to the lightly drawn pencil work and are allowed to dry before the pencil is erased and a gradual building of washes is undertaken.

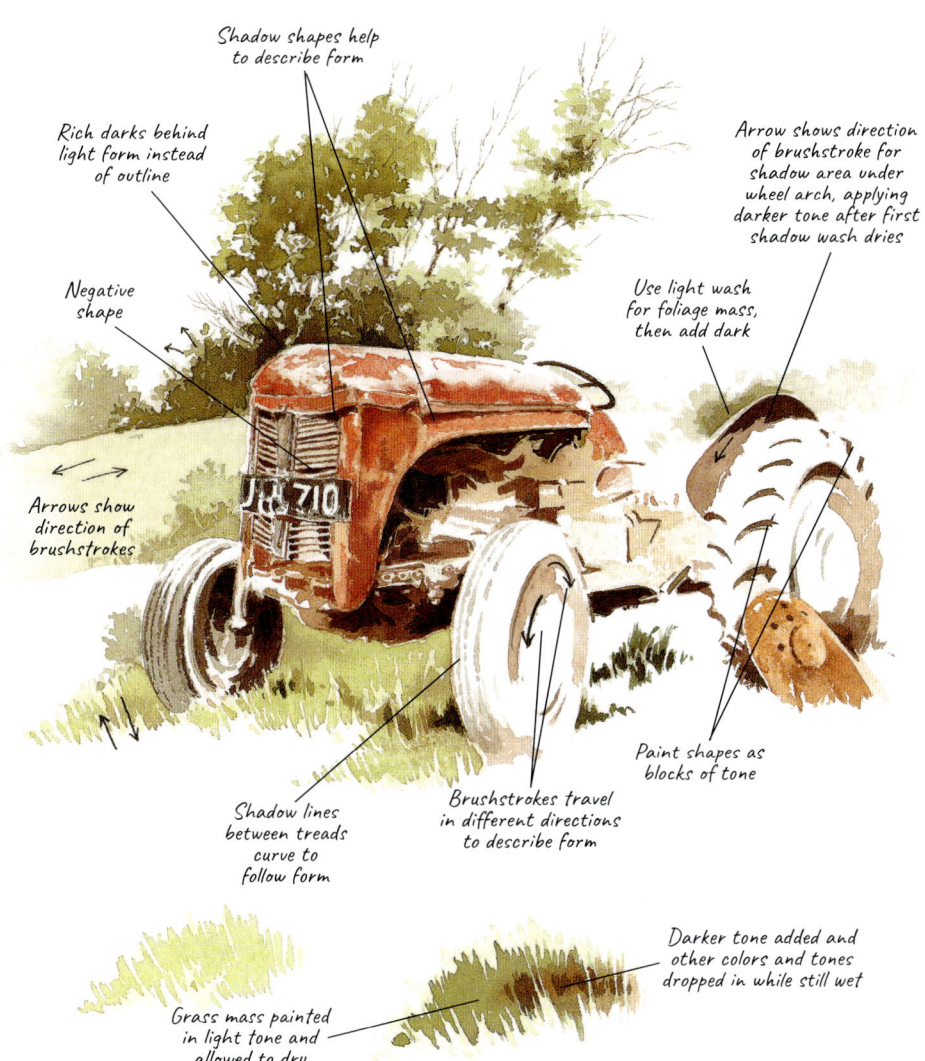

Shadow shapes help to describe form

Rich darks behind light form instead of outline

Negative shape

Arrows show direction of brushstrokes

Arrow shows direction of brushstroke for shadow area under wheel arch, applying darker tone after first shadow wash dries

Use light wash for foliage mass, then add dark

Paint shapes as blocks of tone

Shadow lines between treads curve to follow form

Brushstrokes travel in different directions to describe form

Darker tone added and other colors and tones dropped in while still wet

Grass mass painted in light tone and allowed to dry

Straight-Sided Vehicle

An old trailer tilted at an angle in a field offers the opportunity to make a perspective study using guidelines to establish the correct angle. In the painting below, problems arose with the treatment of side panels and tyres as well as with the perspective and the angles in the composition. It may be that the subject itself is complex and could be simplified (without losing its identity).

Typical problems

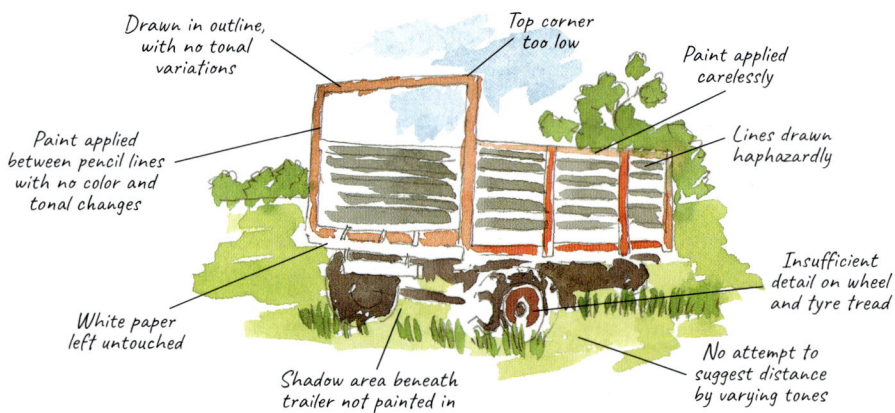

Drawn in outline, with no tonal variations

Top corner too low

Paint applied carelessly

Paint applied between pencil lines with no color and tonal changes

Lines drawn haphazardly

White paper left untouched

Insufficient detail on wheel and tyre tread

Shadow area beneath trailer not painted in

No attempt to suggest distance by varying tones

Drawing what you see

This drawing shows exactly how the trailer appeared – with corrugated sides and heavy tyre treads. A sense of recession is suggested by the angles of the top and base lines.

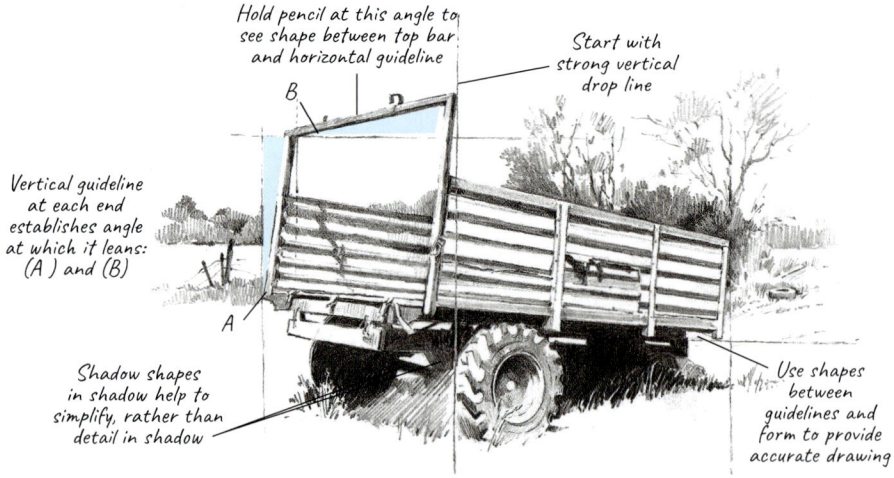

Hold pencil at this angle to see shape between top bar and horizontal guideline

Start with strong vertical drop line

Vertical guideline at each end establishes angle at which it leans: (A) and (B)

Shadow shapes in shadow help to simplify, rather than detail in shadow

Use shapes between guidelines and form to provide accurate drawing

Solutions

Finding the basic shape

A flat surface has been substituted for the corrugated sides, and the tyres are now smooth. A couple of sacks were added to provide interest within the interior.

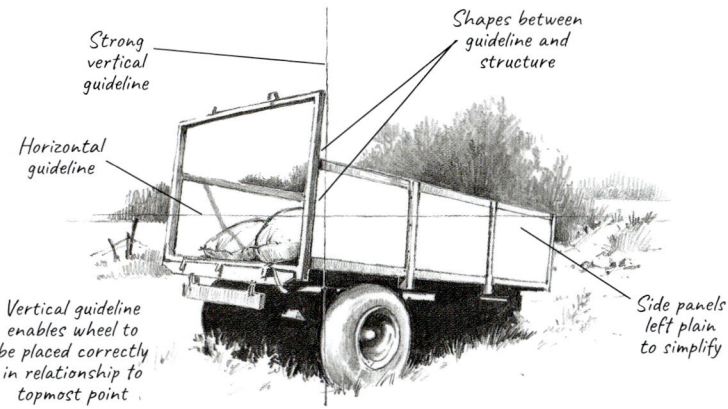

Strong vertical guideline

Shapes between guideline and structure

Horizontal guideline

Vertical guideline enables wheel to be placed correctly in relationship to topmost point

Side panels left plain to simplify

Painting simple shapes

For some simple shapes, it is useful to practice swift brushstrokes. For others, such as the tyres, just suggest the tread rather than going into detail. To create a little incidental texture on the plain panels, Saunders Waterford 300gsm (140lb) Rough paper was used.

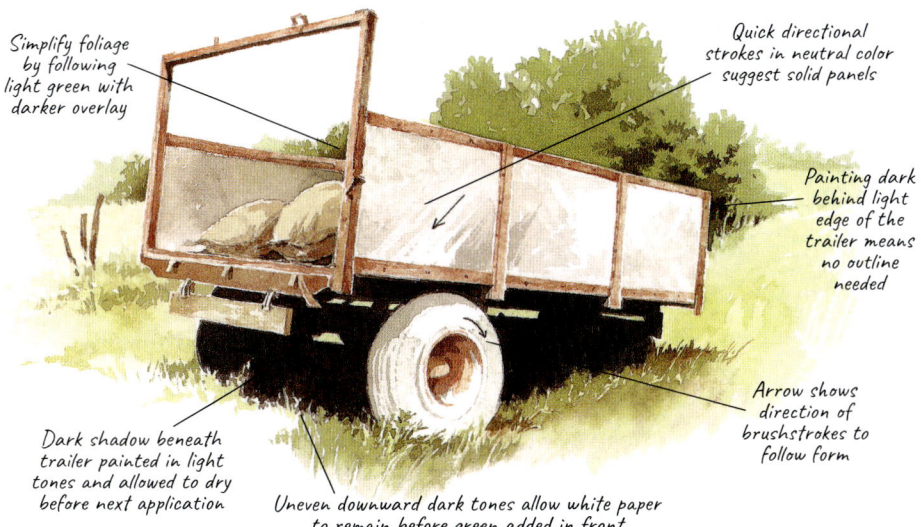

Simplify foliage by following light green with darker overlay

Quick directional strokes in neutral color suggest solid panels

Painting dark behind light edge of the trailer means no outline needed

Dark shadow beneath trailer painted in light tones and allowed to dry before next application

Uneven downward dark tones allow white paper to remain before green added in front

Arrow shows direction of brushstrokes to follow form

Boats on Sand

When the background is stronger than the objects it surrounds,
beginners sometimes treat it in a way that overpowers foreground.
A simple solution is to choose a tinted paper to unify the study.

Typical problems

The band of dark concrete behind these boats, plus a tree-covered bank
above, vie for attention with the boats in the foreground.

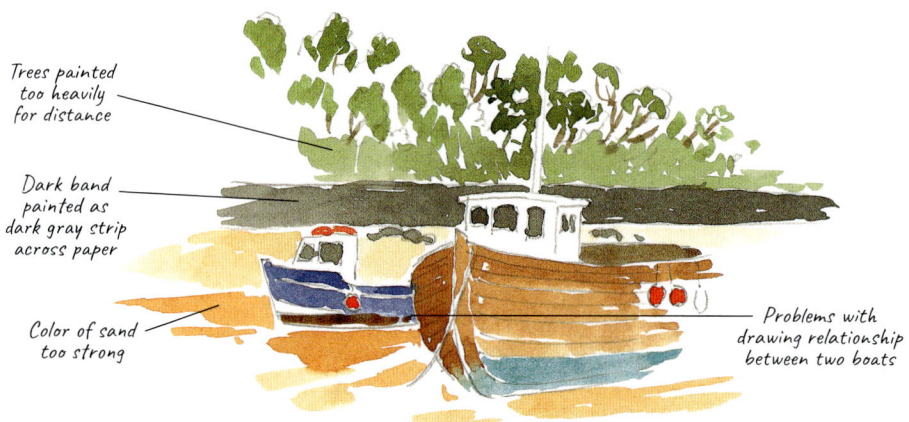

Trees painted
too heavily
for distance

Dark band
painted as
dark gray strip
across paper

Color of sand
too strong

Problems with
drawing relationship
between two boats

Establishing a relationship between the main subjects

Use a drawing to make sure that the subjects in your composition relate
convincingly both to each other and to the surroundings.

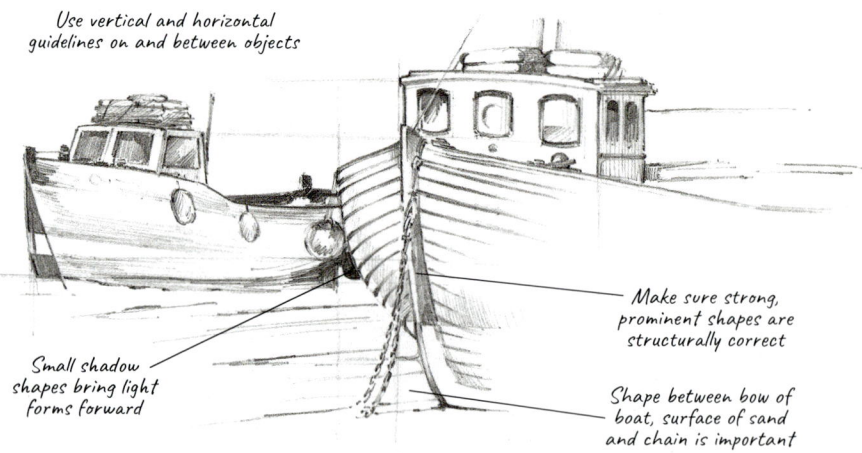

Use vertical and horizontal
guidelines on and between objects

Small shadow
shapes bring light
forms forward

Make sure strong,
prominent shapes are
structurally correct

Shape between bow of
boat, surface of sand
and chain is important

Solutions

Blending on tinted paper

Cream-tinted Bockingford 300gsm (140lb) watercolor paper was chosen for this study, where the predominating color is that of sand. The tint works well under a blended green to suggest a tree-clad hillside in the background, and allows a little Chinese white to be added to the painted surfaces of the boats in order to lift these areas out of the middle ground.

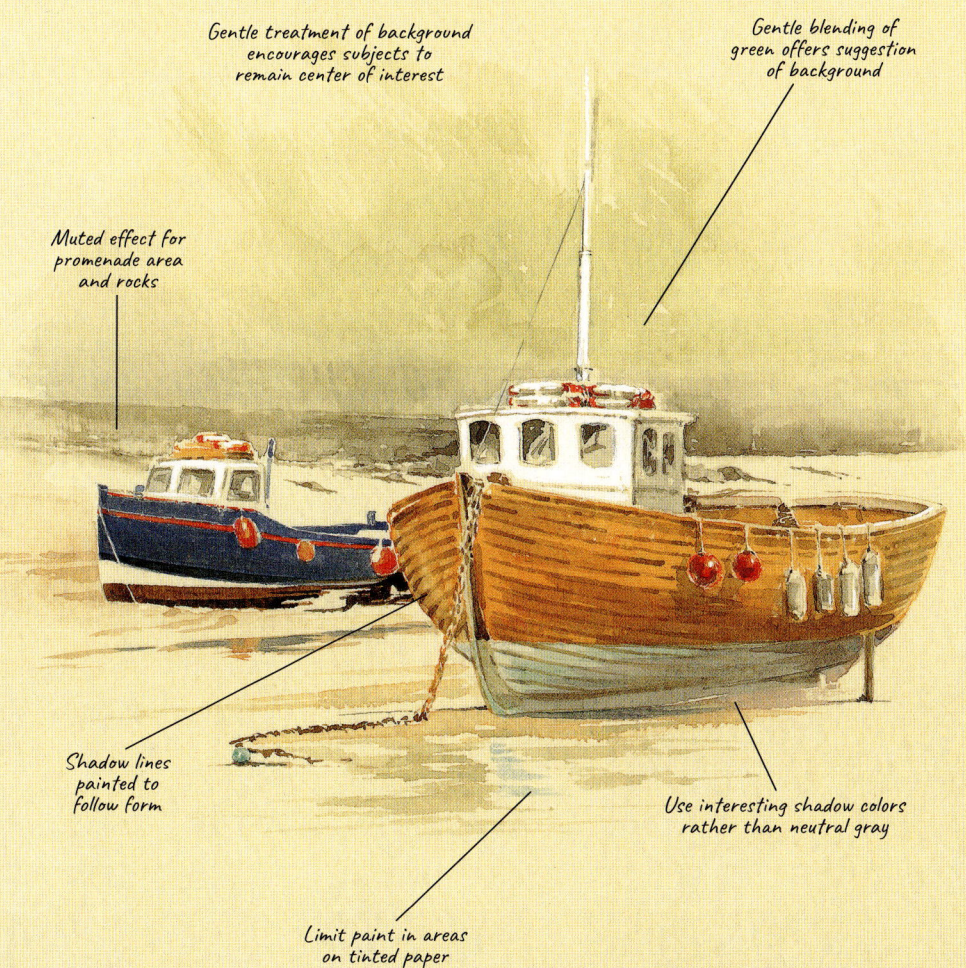

Gentle treatment of background encourages subjects to remain center of interest

Gentle blending of green offers suggestion of background

Muted effect for promenade area and rocks

Shadow lines painted to follow form

Use interesting shadow colors rather than neutral gray

Limit paint in areas on tinted paper

STILL-LIFE MATERIALS
Basic Brushstrokes

These exercises are designed to help you understand how to depict highlights on smooth surfaces such as copper, porcelain and glass, and to realistically paint folds within fabric, often used as a background in still-life paintings. The basic brushstrokes are shown below, while on the opposite page they are incorporated within some of the still-life objects that are covered in this theme.

Fine lines for crisp edges

A natural painting/writing position was used for these exercises. These lines are basic on/off pressure strokes, as explored in the basic brushstrokes exercises in many of the other themed chapters.

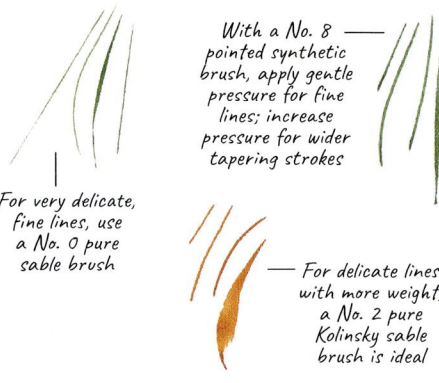

With a No. 8 pointed synthetic brush, apply gentle pressure for fine lines; increase pressure for wider tapering strokes

For very delicate, fine lines, use a No. 0 pure sable brush

For delicate lines with more weight, a No. 2 pure Kolinsky sable brush is ideal

Curves and squiggles

Mirrored images, especially those found on curved or uneven surfaces such as copper containers, require a feeling of movement in the brushstrokes.

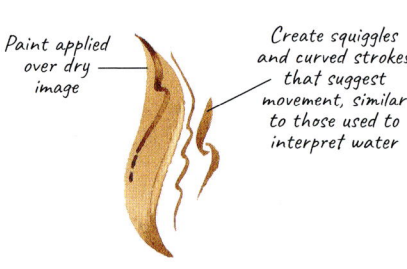

Paint applied over dry image

Create squiggles and curved strokes that suggest movement, similar to those used to interpret water

Cutting in and contours

Curve the edges of tonal blocks and incorporate fine lines – either as dark lines on light paper or as a white line created by toning either side.

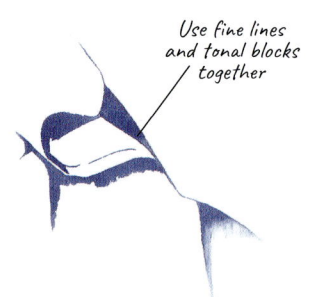

Use fine lines and tonal blocks together

Developing Brushstrokes

Incorporate crisp edges (as seen on glass, copper and mirrored images in other smooth surfaces), strong contrasts (useful in all subjects), and gentle blending (shown to advantage in fabric folds and highlights). By practicing these exercises you will learn how to retain white paper when indicating highlights by painting around these areas, and how to subsequently blend away from the highlighted areas and dark contrasted shadow shapes.

Bottles and other glass object

This is an extension of the fine lines for crisp edges exercises. These two exercises show how to work around the area to be highlighted, using rich color.

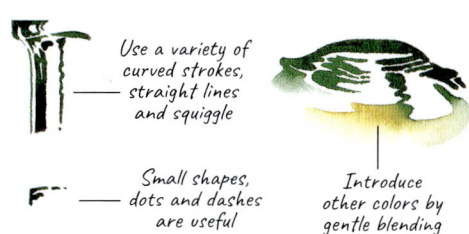

Use a variety of curved strokes, straight lines and squiggle

Small shapes, dots and dashes are useful

Introduce other colors by gentle blending

Mirrored images on copper

This is an extension of the curves and squiggles exercise. First, paint the shapes of the reflections you see within the surface, allow them to dry, then swiftly sweep a yellow glaze (I used Winsor & Newton quinacridone for mine) over the area where no white paper is to remain.

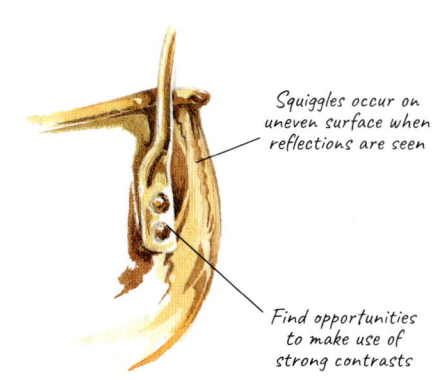

Squiggles occur on uneven surface when reflections are seen

Find opportunities to make use of strong contrasts

Fabric folds

This is an extension of the cutting in and contours exercise. Note the crisp light edges brought forward by the dark tones that suggest areas of recess.

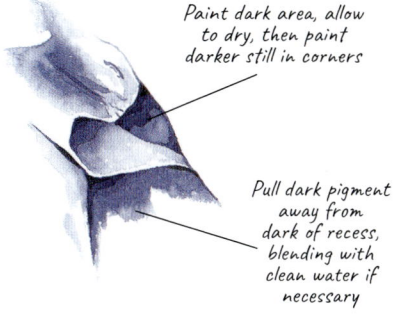

Paint dark area, allow to dry, then paint darker still in corners

Pull dark pigment away from dark of recess, blending with clean water if necessary

Glass

Although glass objects may be uniform in color, remember that because of the way light shines through them, the density of color will vary. Highlights where the light bounces off the surface are also critical for a three-dimensional form. Objects reflected in glass are distorted in shape, and clear, colorless, glass often picks up colors from objects nearby. Precise observation is key in order to position the reflections accurately, especially when another object is placed alongside.

Typical problems

In the study to the right there is no beneficial relationship between bottle and glass. The bottle is not translucent because too much strong color has been used in a careless manner, and as a flat wash over a pale wash. There is only one highlight area, when many more could have been observed.

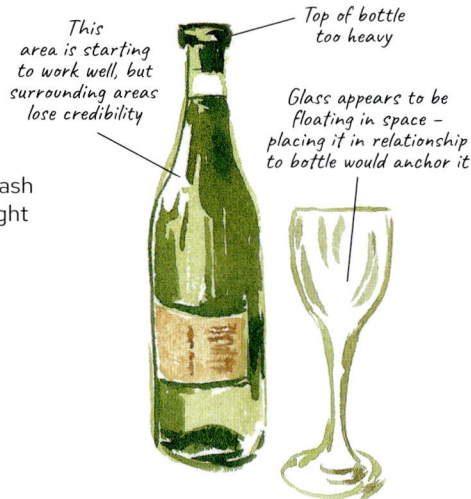

Top of bottle too heavy

This area is starting to work well, but surrounding areas lose credibility

Glass appears to be floating in space – placing it in relationship to bottle would anchor it

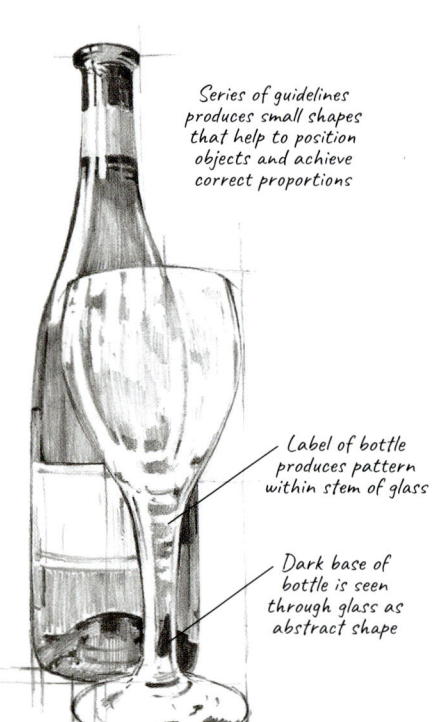

Series of guidelines produces small shapes that help to position objects and achieve correct proportions

Label of bottle produces pattern within stem of glass

Dark base of bottle is seen through glass as abstract shape

Drawing subjects closer

Use guidelines to achieve correct proportions. Place the glass in front of the bottle and see how perspective affects scale. The top of the glass and bottle are slightly above eye level and curve in the opposite direction to their bases.

Solutions

Separating objects to show distortions

If you pull the glass a little away from the bottle, you can
see how the distortions become more apparent – as if the
colorless glass is absorbing color to enhance its own image.

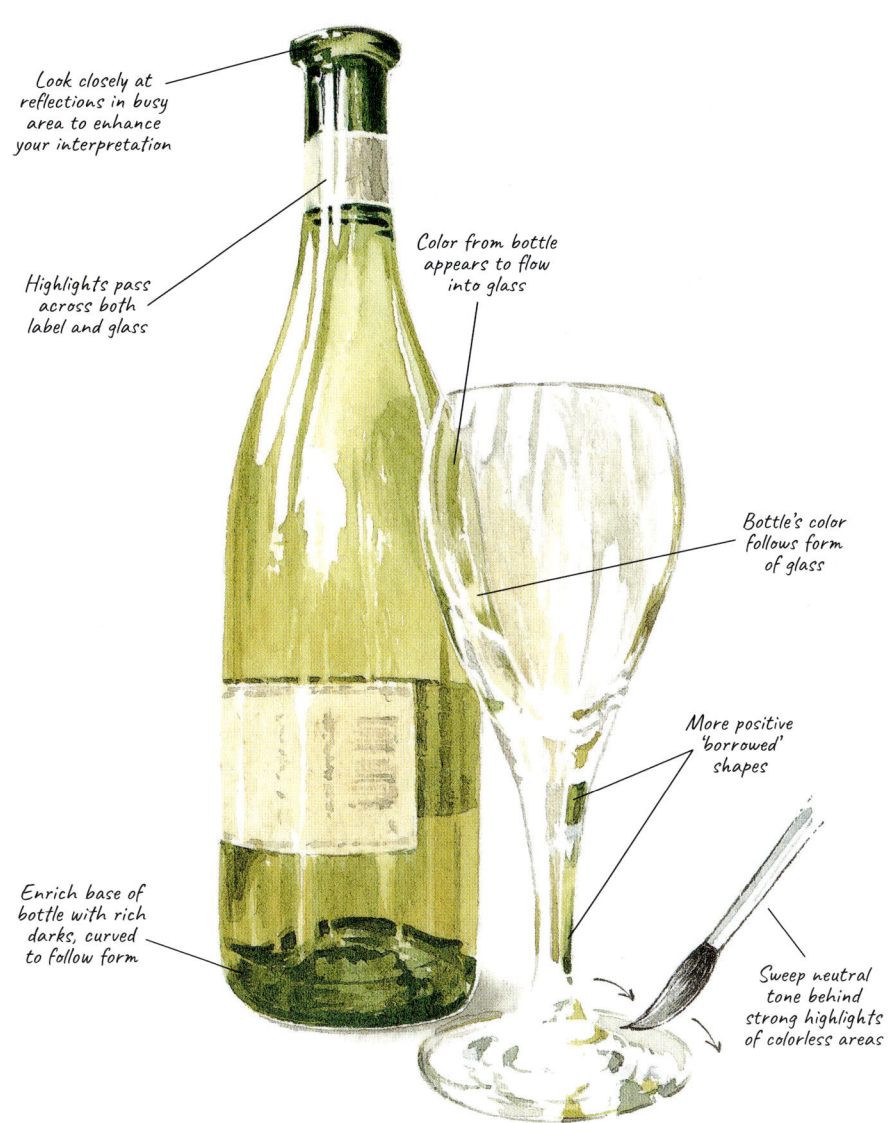

Look closely at
reflections in busy
area to enhance
your interpretation

Highlights pass
across both
label and glass

Color from bottle
appears to flow
into glass

Bottle's color
follows form
of glass

More positive
'borrowed'
shapes

Enrich base of
bottle with rich
darks, curved
to follow form

Sweep neutral
tone behind
strong highlights
of colorless areas

Ceramics

Objects made of fine china lend themselves to being painted in a very delicate style, especially if the porcelain is white. In this case the existence of a pattern on the surface adds interest, and because it follows the form of the surface, it can help to achieve a three-dimensional impression.

Typical problems

In the study below right the artist has painted the pattern to follow the form of the vase, but in the left-hand painting it appears flat and disjointed.

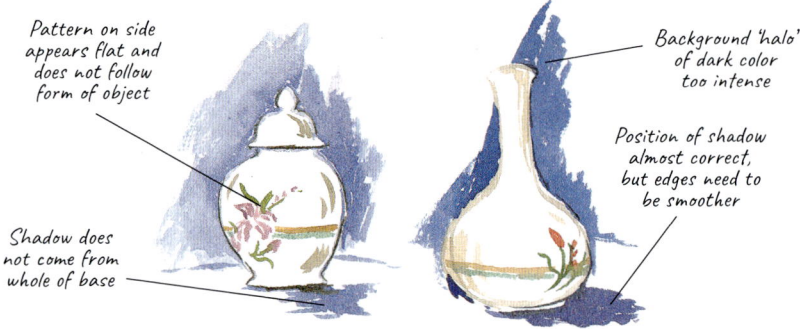

Pattern on side appears flat and does not follow form of object

Shadow does not come from whole of base

Background 'halo' of dark color too intense

Position of shadow almost correct, but edges need to be smoother

Drawing upon knowledge

Even if you eventually want to paint each object individually, placing them as a group in relation to each other helps you gain knowledge of their shape and form. Look at the objects from a different angle, and separate the object itself if possible (in this case a lid was removed) in order to draw and understand ellipses.

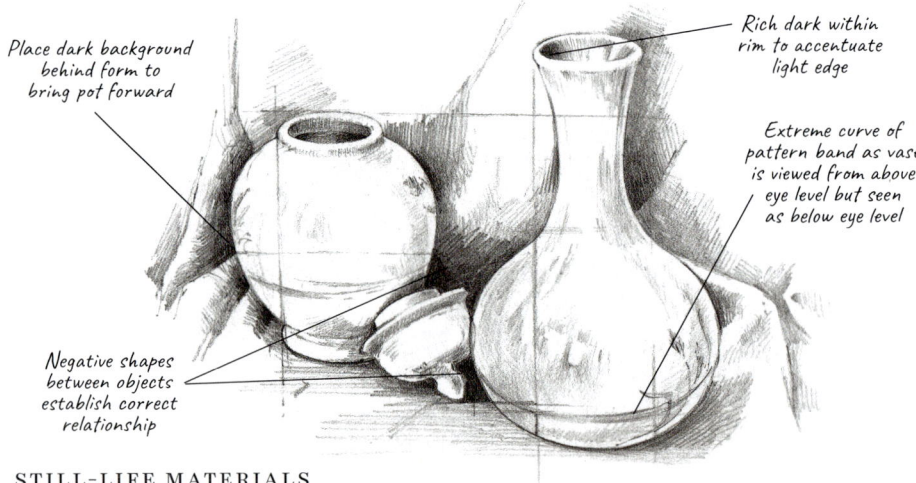

Place dark background behind form to bring pot forward

Rich dark within rim to accentuate light edge

Extreme curve of pattern band as vase is viewed from above eye level but seen as below eye level

Negative shapes between objects establish correct relationship

Solutions

Depicting white

Most depictions of porcelain rely on the use of white paper as the objects themselves are white. With a shadow side, a neutral color is used, both to work around the areas to be left white and to accentuate any highlights on the surface of the porcelain.

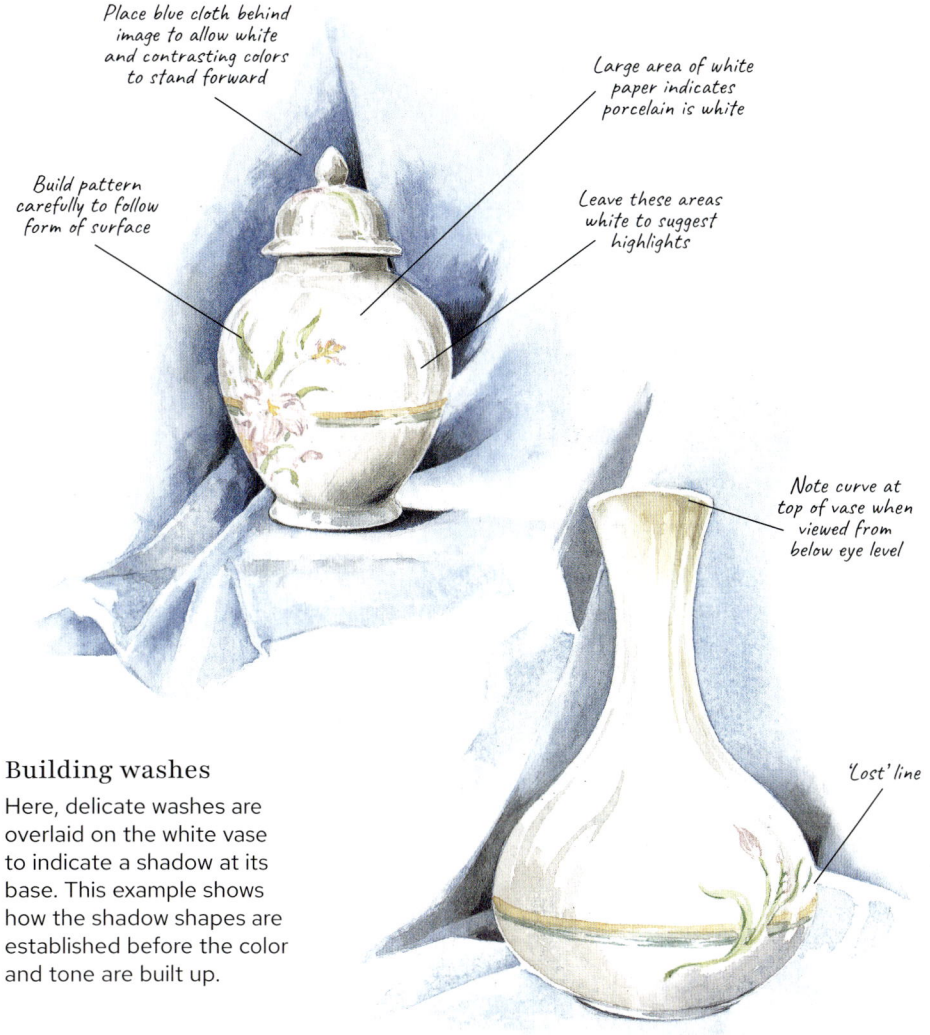

Place blue cloth behind image to allow white and contrasting colors to stand forward

Build pattern carefully to follow form of surface

Large area of white paper indicates porcelain is white

Leave these areas white to suggest highlights

Note curve at top of vase when viewed from below eye level

'Lost' line

Building washes

Here, delicate washes are overlaid on the white vase to indicate a shadow at its base. This example shows how the shadow shapes are established before the color and tone are built up.

Metals

Some metals reflect their surroundings in the same way as water. A curved copper surface, for example, reflects and distorts the contents of a room. It can, therefore, appear to be a very busy image, showing the colors of surrounding objects to a limited extent, which are always influenced by the copper color.

Typical problems

In the painting below you can see some typical drawing problems regarding scale, proportion and perspective, as well as the problem of how to deal with distorted mirror images.

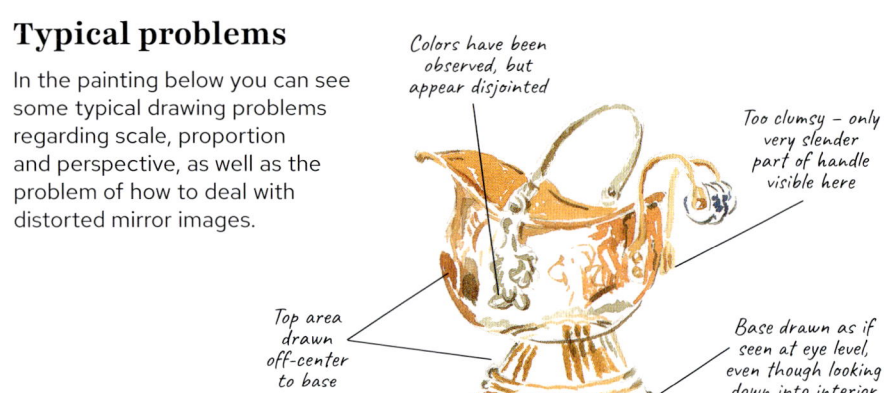

Colors have been observed, but appear disjointed

Too clumsy – only very slender part of handle visible here

Top area drawn off-center to base

Base drawn as if seen at eye level, even though looking down into interior

Drawing from a different viewpoint

To help you become familiar with this, or any other subject, draw it from a different angle. Note the ellipse that appears as you look down into the receptacle, and also at the base.

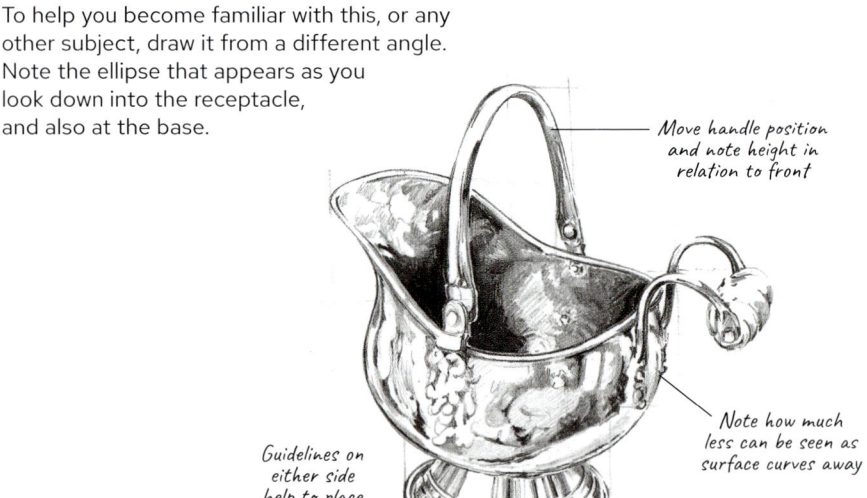

Move handle position and note height in relation to front

Note how much less can be seen as surface curves away

Guidelines on either side help to place centrally

Solutions

Colors and contours

Before you start painting, select a limited range of colors to suit the subject – in this case copper. Remember the importance of leaving white paper for highlights, and practice making sweeping, curved strokes with your brush.

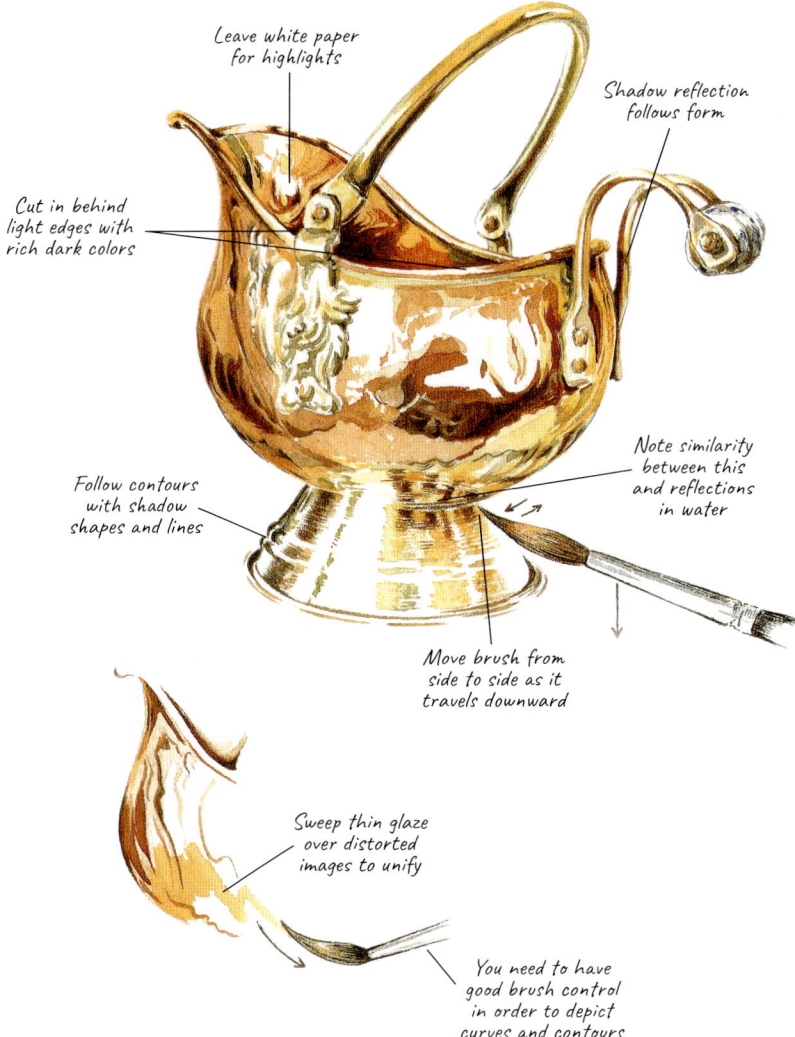

Leave white paper for highlights

Shadow reflection follows form

Cut in behind light edges with rich dark colors

Note similarity between this and reflections in water

Follow contours with shadow shapes and lines

Move brush from side to side as it travels downward

Sweep thin glaze over distorted images to unify

You need to have good brush control in order to depict curves and contours

Fabric

*Fabric is often used as a background for still-life groups, as
the folds help you to form a relationship between the objects.
Used as a cover, fabric follows the form of the object beneath, for
example a cushion cover or an item of clothing being worn.*

Typical problems

A hung or draped shirt or blouse
provides you with an interesting
array of folds, as well as other
related components like pockets,
buttons and the attached sleeves.
For many beginners it is these folds
that cause problems, as seen here.

Drawing to describe folds

Using a very sharp pencil, gently
tone layer upon layer to build the
darks. Follow the form, curving
around contours and cutting in
behind light areas to suggest
undulations of folded material.
Leave the white paper for
highlights.

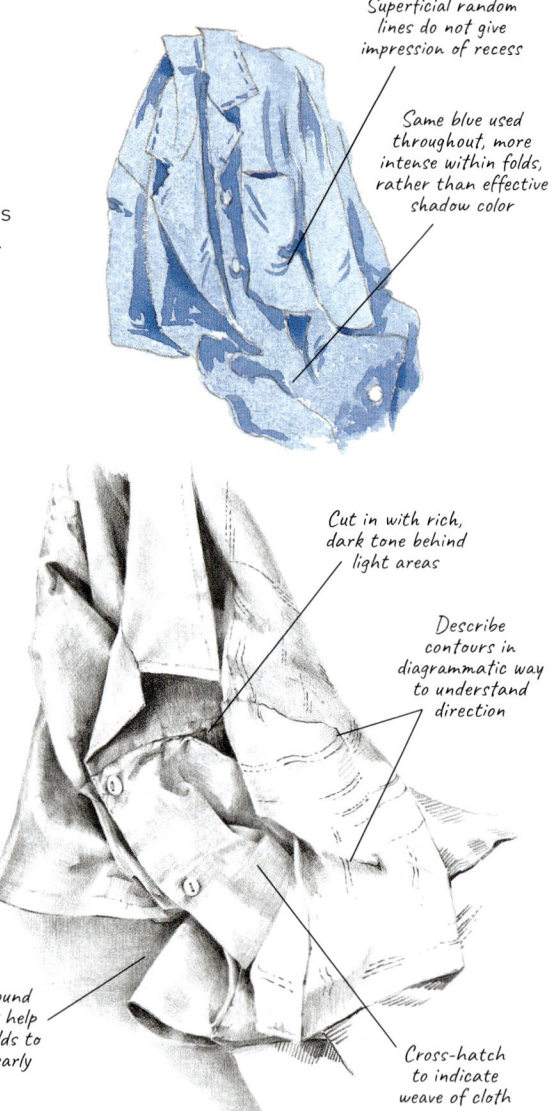

*Superficial random
lines do not give
impression of recess*

*Same blue used
throughout, more
intense within folds,
rather than effective
shadow color*

*Cut in with rich,
dark tone behind
light areas*

*Describe
contours in
diagrammatic way
to understand
direction*

*Tone background
in areas that help
highlighted folds to
stand out clearly*

*Cross-hatch
to indicate
weave of cloth*

Solutions

The 'ins and outs' of folded material

For this exercise, imagine an insect wandering in and out of the folds of a garment – when the insect is at the highest level, it is probably standing on a highlighted area. Leave these highest areas as white paper and apply your tones, in varying degrees, behind it, working from the lightest to the very darkest tones.

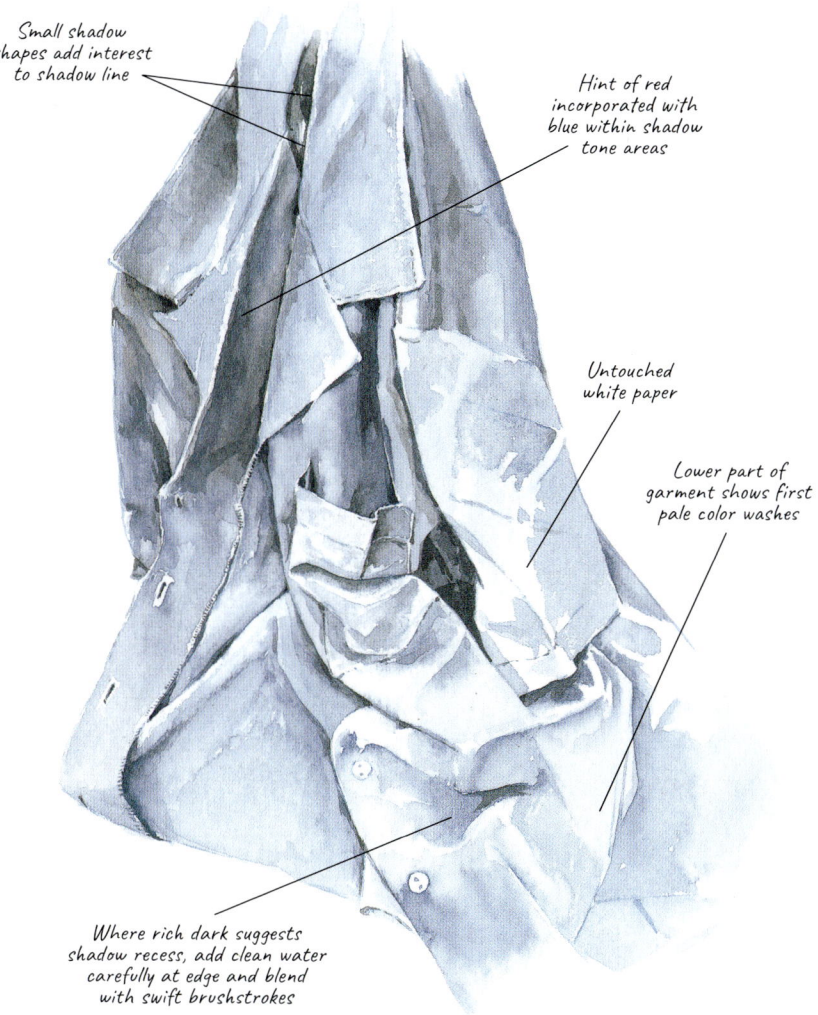

Small shadow shapes add interest to shadow line

Hint of red incorporated with blue within shadow tone areas

Untouched white paper

Lower part of garment shows first pale color washes

Where rich dark suggests shadow recess, add clean water carefully at edge and blend with swift brushstrokes

BUILDINGS
Basic Brushstrokes

These exercises are designed to help you become aware of the importance of the varied and directional brushstrokes required to depict the textured effects used when painting buildings. I mixed burnt umber and French ultramarine to produce a brown hue, and blended with water for pale tones.

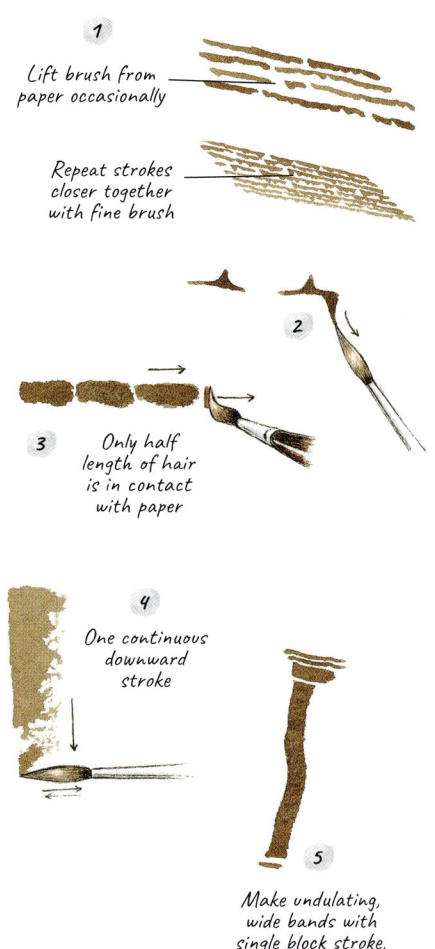

Angled, varied pressure strokes *(1)*

Use the normal painting position for these strokes. Note the effect that can be achieved by just varying the pressure on rough-textured paper.

Wide shape, narrow shape *(2)*

Use the normal painting position for the first part of the stroke, angled toward the paper to complete the stroke as you pull down or along. Use the tip of the brush.

Block and lift stroke *(3)*

Hold the brush a little more vertically for this solid one-stroke impression. Place another stroke immediately alongside.

Partial drybrush effect *(4)*

This is suitable as a base texture for many surfaces. Hold the brush horizontal to the paper, letting the whole length of hairs remain in contact throughout the stroke. Note how the rough surface of the paper robs the brush swiftly of its pigment.

Narrow lines, wide bands *(5)*

Use the normal painting position for this variety of stroke, where the aim is to depict gentle undulations.

Lift brush from paper occasionally

Repeat strokes closer together with fine brush

Only half length of hair is in contact with paper

One continuous downward stroke

Make undulating, wide bands with single block stroke, or paint in with smaller strokes

Developing Brushstrokes

These five exercises are developments of the basic brushstrokes.
Rough-textured Saunders Waterford paper was chosen to
enhance the effects of four of these. Explore how paper choice
affects the impressions you create by experimenting first.

Varied pressure strokes *(1)*

This extension of the basic brushstrokes exercise is designed to suggest a tiled roof.

Wide shape, narrow line stroke *(2)*

An extension of the wide shape, narrow shape exercise in basic brushstrokes, this shows how two may be joined. Use this stroke to depict smooth stone walls – remember to enhance the negative 'shapes between' with a rich, dark hue to suggest recesses.

One-block stroke *(3)*

An extension of the block and lift stroke, this exercise shows you how blotting-off (see Materials and Techniques: Blotting Off) works on a brick or stone image.

Drybrush overlay *(4)*

To depict textured surfaces of walls or timber, apply a further stroke of the brush over the initial partial drybrush effect exercise seen in basic brushstrokes.

Narrow lines and wide bands *(5)*

This exercise shows you how the basic brushstroke can be used for a mirrored image on glass-fronted buildings. This image is best suited to a smooth-surfaced paper, but, as you can see here, it can also be painted onto rough texture and still achieve a smooth effect.

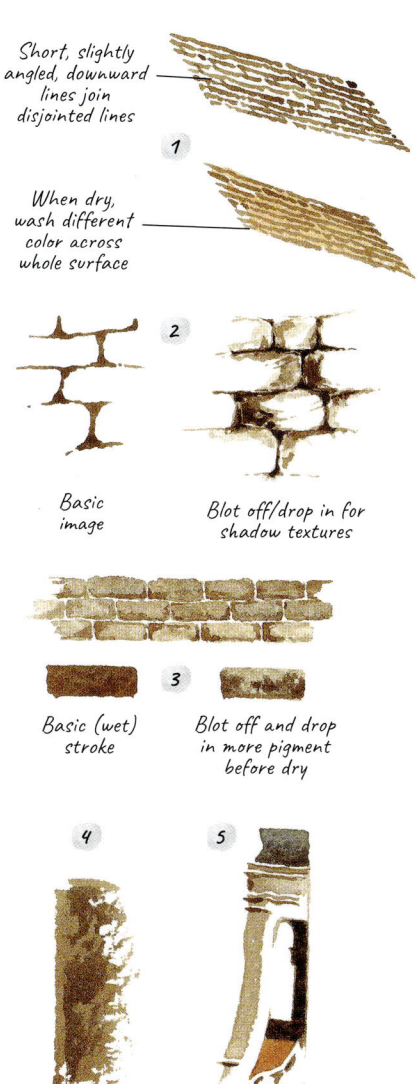

Short, slightly angled, downward lines join disjointed lines

1

When dry, wash different color across whole surface

2

Basic image

Blot off/drop in for shadow textures

3

Basic (wet) stroke

Blot off and drop in more pigment before dry

4

5

Timber

A timber building in a neutral hue can offer a pleasing contrast to its surroundings. However, many beginners, in their quest for color, fail to take advantage of the subtle neutrals and paint a variety of browns, as seen in the picture below.

Typical problems

This painting has lost harmony, and the numerous lines, drawn without regard for tone and texture, are overpowering. Do not be afraid to take advantage of a monochrome effect for certain subjects – the background greens can almost be a monochrome study in themselves – as there are occasions when understatement has its own charm.

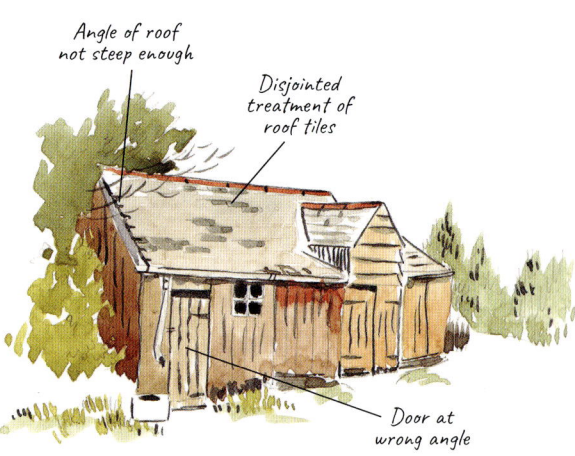

Angle of roof not steep enough

Disjointed treatment of roof tiles

Door at wrong angle

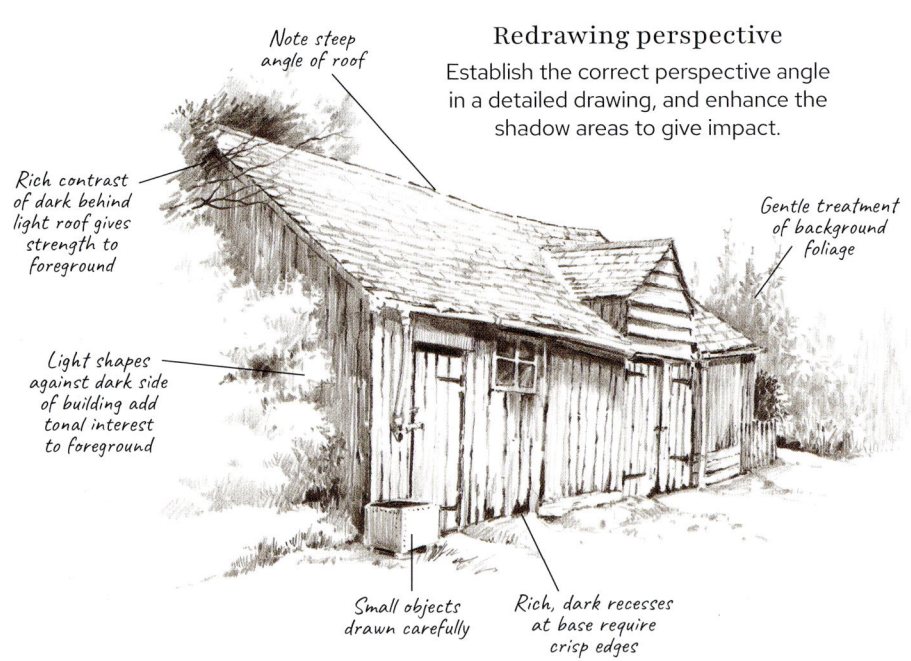

Note steep angle of roof

Redrawing perspective

Establish the correct perspective angle in a detailed drawing, and enhance the shadow areas to give impact.

Rich contrast of dark behind light roof gives strength to foreground

Gentle treatment of background foliage

Light shapes against dark side of building add tonal interest to foreground

Small objects drawn carefully

Rich, dark recesses at base require crisp edges

Solutions

Working in monochrome

This painting is limited to the neutrals of the timber building and the greens of the foreground and background foliage. The only additional color is in the blue sky. A monochromatic approach focuses on tonal contrasts rather than hue.

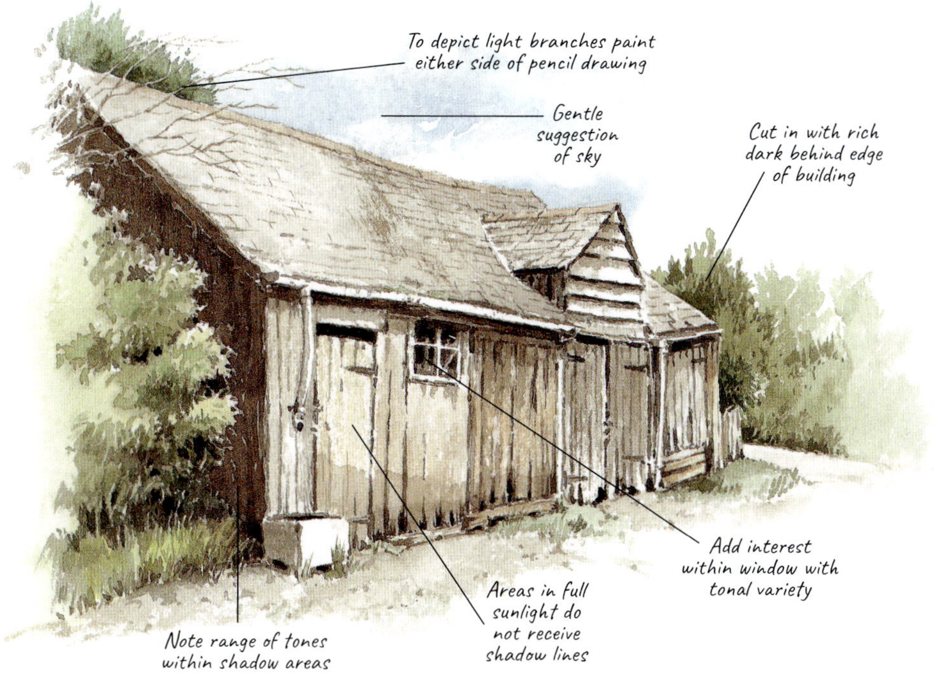

To depict light branches paint either side of pencil drawing

Gentle suggestion of sky

Cut in with rich dark behind edge of building

Add interest within window with tonal variety

Areas in full sunlight do not receive shadow lines

Note range of tones within shadow areas

Ways to create textures on timber

Here are a couple of exercises to help you discover ways of creating a textured surface effect: (1) rough texture with drybrush; (2) creating darks.

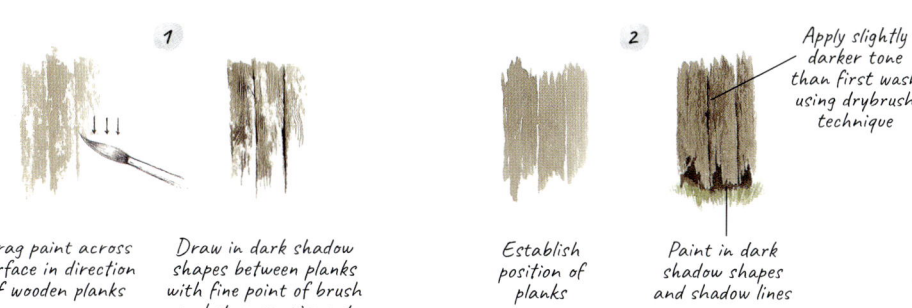

1

Drag paint across surface in direction of wooden planks

Draw in dark shadow shapes between planks with fine point of brush and stronger pigment

2

Establish position of planks

Apply slightly darker tone than first wash using drybrush technique

Paint in dark shadow shapes and shadow lines

Corrugated Iron and Stone

Old or derelict buildings may be made up of many different materials.
With so much to observe, it is not surprising that some beginners
simplify everything to such an extent that the essence of the building
and its setting are lost in a mass of conflicting colors and patterns.

Typical problems

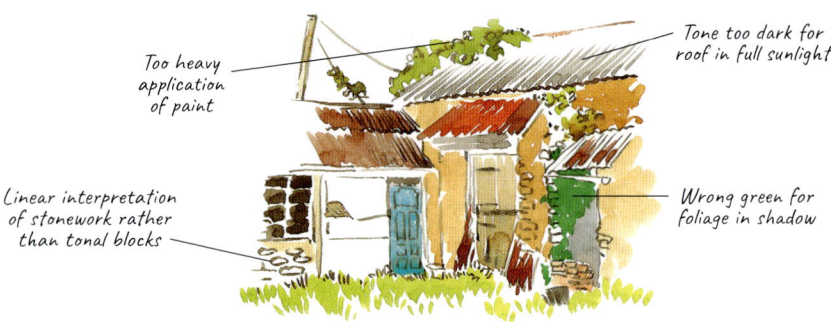

Too heavy
application
of paint

Tone too dark for
roof in full sunlight

Linear interpretation
of stonework rather
than tonal blocks

Wrong green for
foliage in shadow

Correcting perspective

The (A) and (B) 'shapes' are below the
guideline, and (C) and (D) are positioned
above the guideline. In this way the correct
perspective angles of roofs can be established.

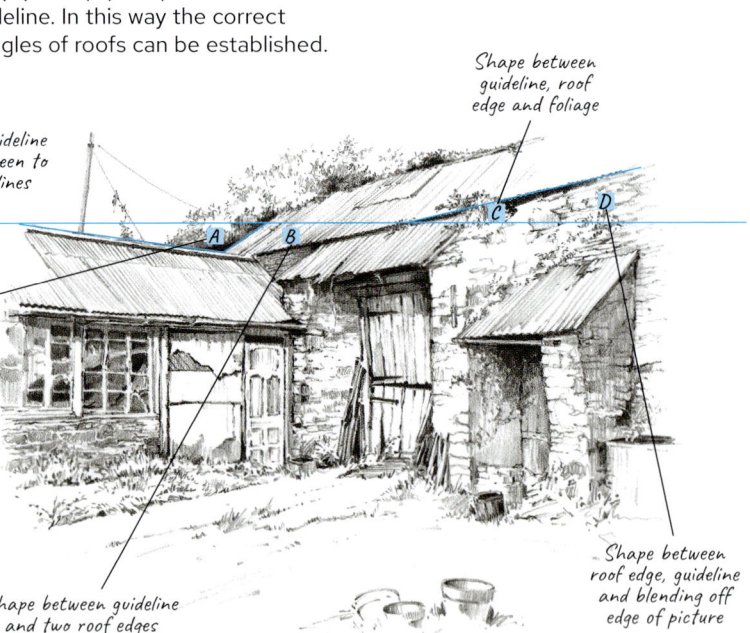

Shape between
guideline, roof
edge and foliage

One horizontal guideline
gives shapes between to
help place roof lines

Shape between
guideline and
two roof edges

Shape between guideline
and two roof edges

Shape between
roof edge, guideline
and blending off
edge of picture

Solutions

Tackling textures

This study required many brush angles and pressures to achieve the effects of a variety of textured surfaces. It shows the various stages of underpainting used, and also how the subsequent washes were built up gradually until the right color and depth were achieved.

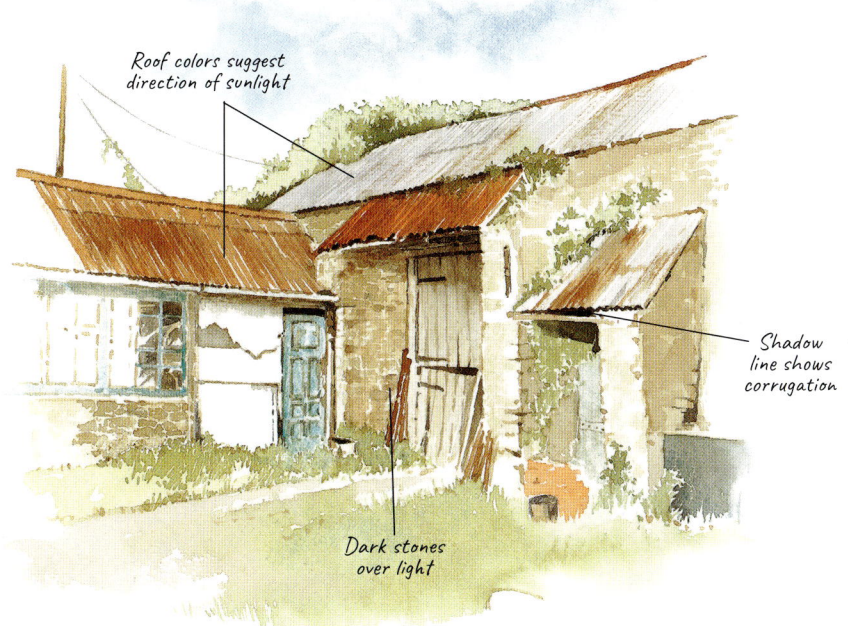

Roof colors suggest direction of sunlight

Shadow line shows corrugation

Dark stones over light

Depicting details

Practice details (1), (2) and (3) before incorporating the techniques into the painting.

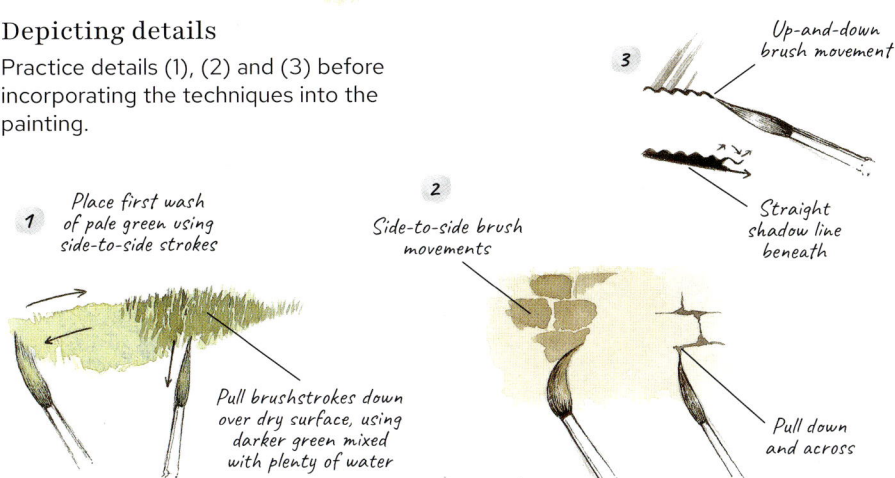

3 — *Up-and-down brush movement*

Straight shadow line beneath

1 — *Place first wash of pale green using side-to-side strokes*

2 — *Side-to-side brush movements*

Pull brushstrokes down over dry surface, using darker green mixed with plenty of water

Pull down and across

Street Scenes

A variety of buildings within a street setting will be viewed at different angles. Perspective problems may be overcome using the 'guidelines' method – aligning parts of one building with another. Any awareness of scale can be helped by the inclusion of a figure, but this needs to be treated with care. It is far better to draw/paint a figure slightly too small than too large.

Typical problems

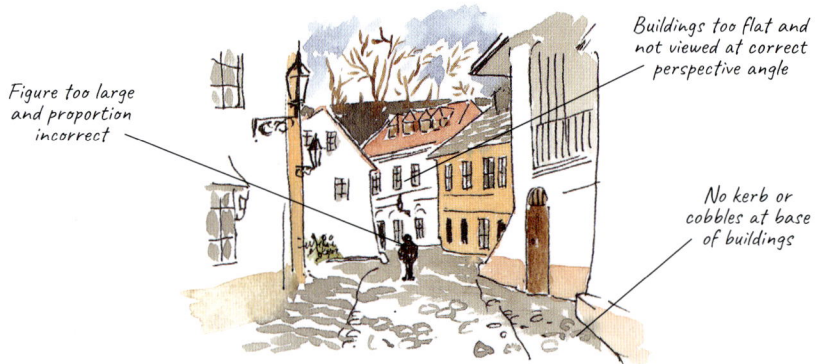

Buildings too flat and not viewed at correct perspective angle

Figure too large and proportion incorrect

No kerb or cobbles at base of buildings

Quick sketchbook impression

Here, a fine-nibbed pen was drawn over the surface of textured paper to establish a wide view of the scene, before moving in close to the center of interest.

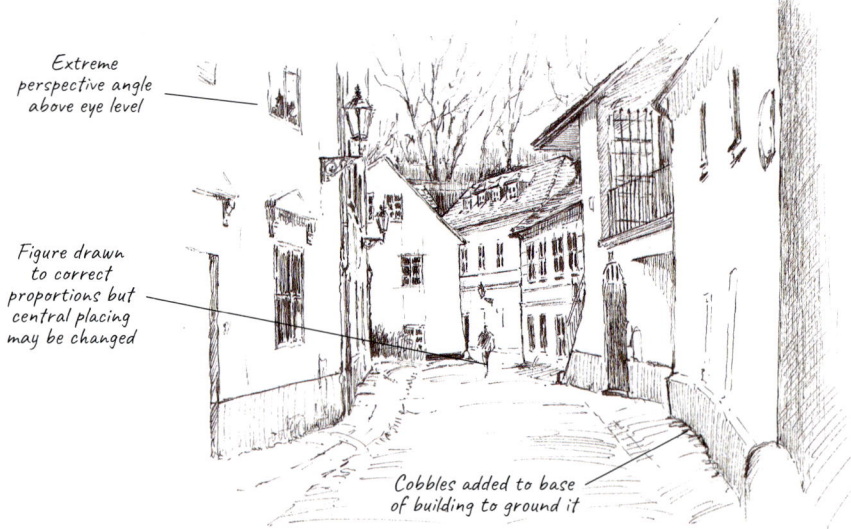

Extreme perspective angle above eye level

Figure drawn to correct proportions but central placing may be changed

Cobbles added to base of building to ground it

Solutions

Drawing and tinting

For this exercise, draw the entire scene in pen and ink on textured watercolor paper, using a thick-nibbed pen for the wider lines. Vary the pressure on the pen to encourage it to create interesting lines, then work with the texture of the paper to enhance these effects.

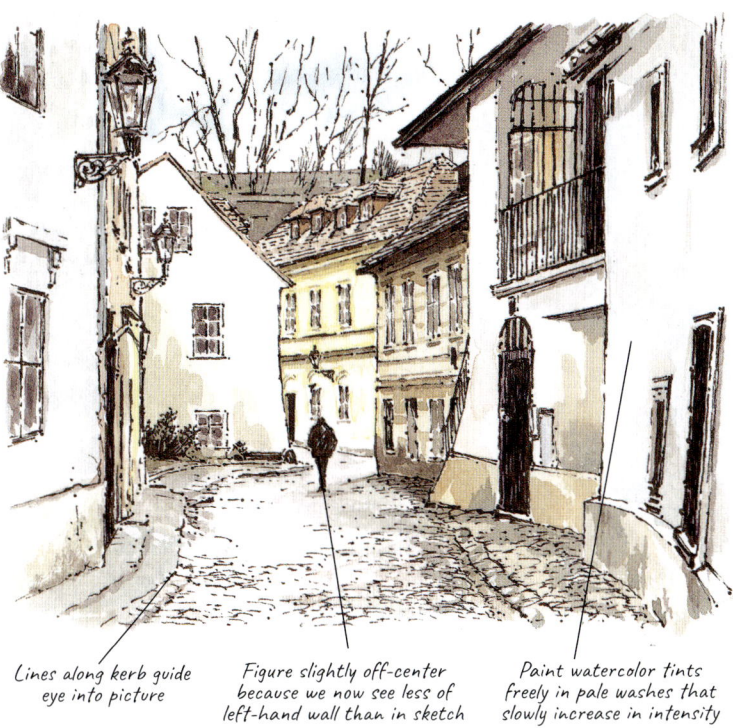

Lines along kerb guide eye into picture

Figure slightly off-center because we now see less of left-hand wall than in sketch

Paint watercolor tints freely in pale washes that slowly increase in intensity

Penwork details

Practice your penwork with warm-up exercises (1), (2), (3) and (4) before starting the final drawing.

1 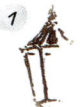 *Squiggles and lines of varied pressure plus tonal blocks give effect of quick impression*

Draw right angle first, then curves and pattern shapes **2**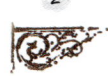

3 *Vary pressure on lines that differentiate buildings*

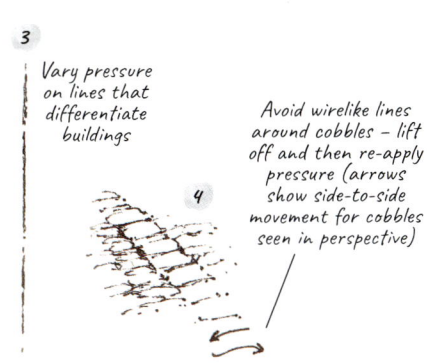

Avoid wirelike lines around cobbles – lift off and then re-apply pressure (arrows show side-to-side movement for cobbles seen in perspective)

4

Glass-Fronted Buildings

*Glass-fronted buildings that reflect their surroundings
produce images reminiscent of surrealist paintings.*

Typical problems

As an artist you may feel that the
interest lies not in the overall shape of
the building, but in the reflected images
distorted by slight undulations of flat
glass panels – but the maze of vertical,
horizontal and distorted lines are difficult
for a beginner to view, let alone draw and
paint with accuracy.

Drawing distortion

Close observation of the scale and
perspective in the scene are the primary
considerations. Once these are noted
you can consider how they have been
altered through distortion. Here, there is
a helpful grid of vertical and horizontal
bars, so that you can concentrate on one
section at a time.

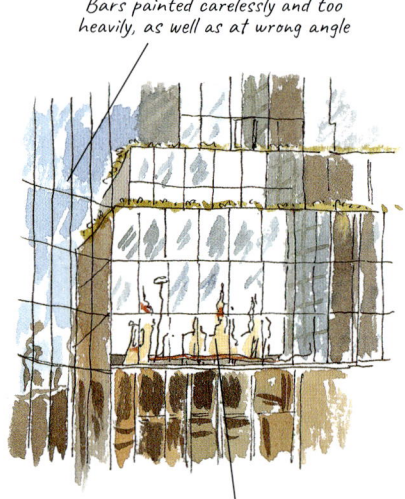

*Bars painted carelessly and too
heavily, as well as at wrong angle*

*Loose 'squiggles' with same
color in each one do not give
impression of range of buildings*

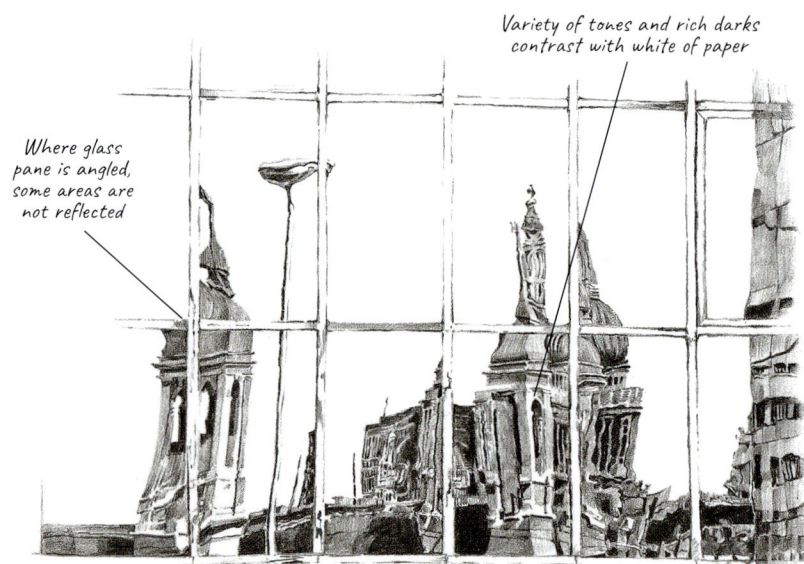

*Variety of tones and rich darks
contrast with white of paper*

*Where glass
pane is angled,
some areas are
not reflected*

Solutions

Quick impression

The quick sketchbook impression to the right establishes the building as a whole before selecting an area for detailed interpretation. Drawing on-site, where you can establish basic proportions and perspective angles, can be regarded as a warm-up exercise. There is no need to draw precise details if it is the preliminary to a more detailed drawing and painting of a small area.

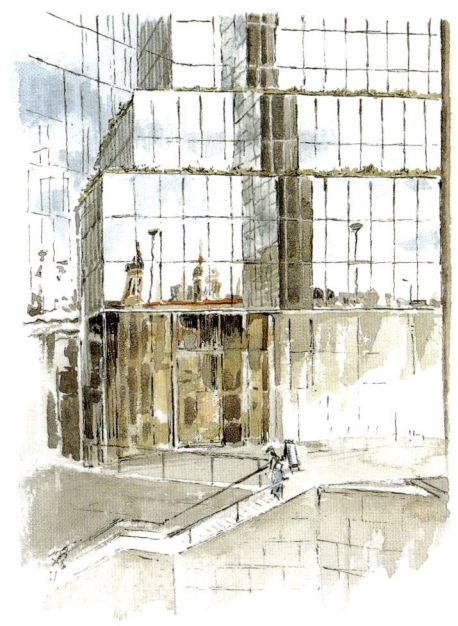

Building a mirrored image

Place the grid and consider the content of each section in its own right, as well as regarding the picture as a whole. Show some of the external glass side-panelled wall of the building in order to retain identity. Then start by painting everything as an undercoat of pale washes.

Retain identity of building by portraying part of one side

Paint reflects blue sky to enhance white (paper) images of glazing bars

Undercoat of pale washes

Enrich dark areas in final washes

Note undulations of reflected shadow lines

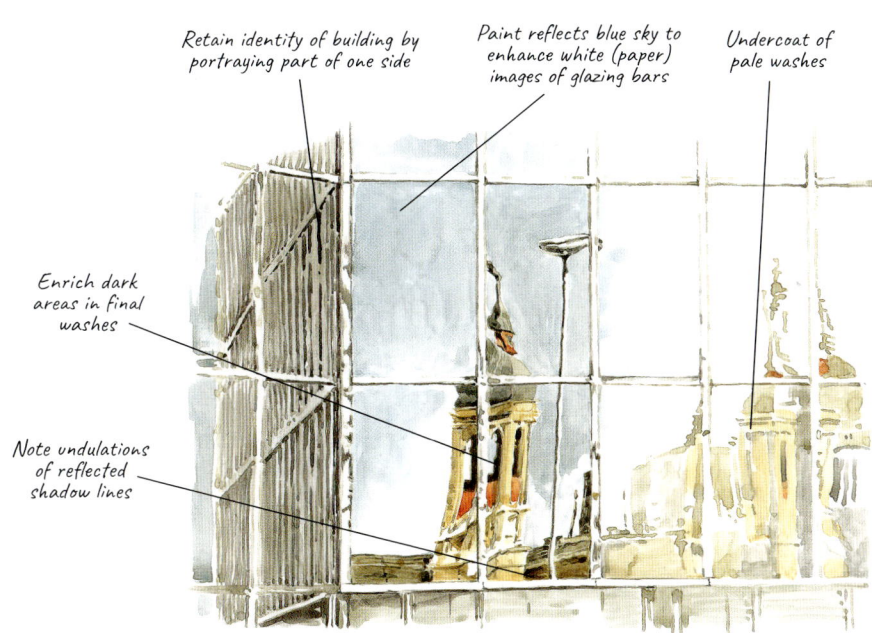

INDEX

ISBN-13: 9781446315354 paperback
ISBN-13: 9781446316436 EPUB

This book has been printed on paper from approved suppliers and made from pulp from sustainable sources.

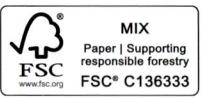

MIX
Paper | Supporting responsible forestry
FSC® C136333
www.fsc.org

Printed in China through Asia Pacific Offset for: David and Charles, Ltd, Suite A, Tourism House, Pynes Hill, Exeter, EX2 5WS

10 9 8 7 6 5 4 3 2 1

Publishing Director: Ame Verso
Senior Commissioning Editor: Nigel Browning
Publishing Manager: Jeni Chown
Copy Editor: Cheryl Brown
Lead Designer: Sam Staddon
Designer: Anna Wade
Pre-press Designer: Susan Reansbury
Production Manager: Beverley Richardson

David and Charles publishes high-quality books on a wide range of subjects. For more information visit www.davidandcharles.com.

Share your art with us on social media using #dandcbooks and follow us on Facebook and Instagram by searching for @dandcbooks.

Layout of the digital edition of this book may vary depending on reader hardware and display settings.

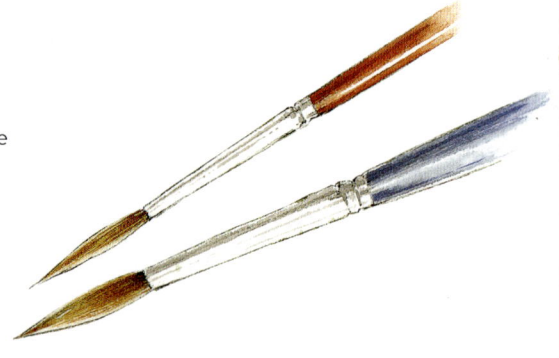